The Physics of Consciousness

Or

How to Become a God

Or

What the Matrix Is
And How to Get Out
If You Are Dumb Enough to Want That

Elijah Yeats

© Copyright; All Rights Reserved;
By Ra Kephri Press; May 2017
P.O. Box 894
Greenville, Ca. 95947
iplanet@frontiernet.net

To Sophia

Table of Contents

Authors Forward
Read This..5

Preface
What is a god, what are *we* now, and what do we live in? 26

Preamble
In The Beginning..33

Chapter One
Christ and Heaven...44

Chapter Two
A Synopsis of OM's Creation & the Mother of All Magic and of Our Souls.......................................67

Chapter Three
The Classical Three Points of Magic........................86

Chapter Four
Issues related to Artificial Intelligence.......................101

Chapter Five
The Human Soul & the Field of Consciousness............119

Chapter Six
The Matrix, Or What This Reality Is & How to Escape It If You Are Foolish Enough To Want That....................131

Chapter Seven
The Evolutionary Ladder You Must Climb To Become a True God..162

Chapter Eight
Alternative Probabilities for Uncertainty in Quantum Mechanics...181

Chapter Nine
Dreams and the Parallel Universes of Uncertainty in Quantum Mechanics...206

Chapter Ten
Dimensional Mechanics 224

Chapter Eleven
The Holographic Universe & the Map Dimension.........241

Chapter Twelve
Hurray! Changing Gears; How to Be *Decent* In the Arriving Future Here...269

Chapter Thirteen
The Other Side..299

Authors Afterward..324

**On The Other Side
Miracles Are Normal
They Are the Way Things Get Done
The Other Side Is Next To You Right Now
Open the Door
And Enter**

Authors Forward
Read This Please!

The immediate following outline is not an outline of this book but it is what much of material in this book is based on expressed in a purely academically acceptable way outside of the inclusive theological prejudice that pervades this greater work. If you are suffering from academic prejudice and you still find the outline unacceptable do not bother reading further, but if you still own an open mind please do.

What follows is entirely the original truth of this Author; only time and investigation can determine if it is the empirical truth to you.

Concerning the theological prejudice in the book, I simply had no choice as I met all the folks and deities mentioned; as well as numerous others, in the various very alternative places where they normally live. This is not about my mindless faith based on what some other human said I should believe in. What follows in the full manuscript is based on factual evidence of admittedly subjective experience that intruded into my life.

The Physics of Consciousness
In Relation to Quantum Mechanics & the EM Spectrum
A Concise Outline

Note: The following is based on the reality that there is a multiversal field or *spectrum of consciousness* that can be analyzed intellectually using the electro-magnetic spectrum and quantum mechanics as contextual foundations.

Consciousness is *not* as academia constantly tries to prove, a hallucination generated by mechanical and electronic brain and sensory functions; it *is* a function of the original spectrum or field of creation. Using this approach we can commence research into the Physics of Consciousness and open doors of consequence.

1. The human *mind* or consciousness is the equivalent of a quantum particle that is self-recognizing; a positive parasite served by the brain and body in this reality. As such it has properties related to quantum particles that have been determined by science, and many that have not.

A. Particle Entanglement: One aspect of this implies 'telepathic' communication through alternative dimensional mechanics, and advanced evolutions of consciousness. Alternative *language* translation is the largest problem here, but the higher levels have a universal translator technology. This is related at a primitive level to current manifestations of the 'cloud' in human internet technology, but has been installed into the field of consciousness as a technology of consciousness at higher levels. There are two aspects; one is related to universal language translation and the other to a higher level of telepathic communication that involves a universal 'language' of purified conceptual intent.

B. Particle expression of a parent field, in this case a consciousness particle or 'C' is the rough equivalent of a photon of the EM field or spectrum but is generated out of the field or spectrum of consciousness. As such the nature of individualization from the parent field is to a degree 'uncertain'. (Our *mind,* not our brain but our *mind,* is just one type of consciousness particle.)

C. A 'C' particle is only one type of many related particles that can be expressed out of the Spectrum or Field of Consciousness.

D. All 'C' particles are the sum of their evolutionary histories at any given moment, exactly as photons are, but the attenuating properties of most 'C' particles are more complex.

E. 'C' particles of various types are that which defines 'life'.

F. 'C' particles, the human mind expression, and possibly the multiversal expression, are *normally* roughly four to six inches in diameter, spherical or oblate and exactly as they are experienced internally when the brain pollution is negated. This is not odd as photons have now been shown to be several meters in diameter, (See Gerhard Rempe, Planck Institute) but 'C's functions are not constrained by size. They can be reduced to a diameter of less than the Planck Length and still remain functional, and by inference in the case of Creator Individuals, they can be larger than the multiverse and still remain functional.

G. 'C' particles do not require a physical carrier brain and body to function, what we are when we dream, during astral projection events and during NDE's are merely three examples.

H. 'C' particles have certain structural attributes, with or without a physical carrier body and brain. These include functioning eyes, ears, an ID or centralizing self-recognizing identity or center. The last may be interpreted as a particle within a particle (as in protons and quarks) or as a structural attribute. The photon is a more appropriate example, it has a point or singularity aspect equivalent to the ID, but each point is unseparate from its parent cloud that is several meters across. We assume the point photon exists only to transmit information (and energy), and normally that the ID merely consumes information, but the ID is actually a transceiver. This can be demonstrated empirically.

I. 'C's are individualizing aspects of the spectrum of consciousness whose level of individualization is always uncertain, thus as has been proven with all quantum particles, they can communicate across the parent field outside the constraints of time or distance.

J. 'C's are like the proton, in effect immortal.

K. 'C's can overcome the constraints even of dimensional containers.

L. 1. A property of 'C's closely resembles particles of the EM spectrum in that individual 'C's can be enhanced, their potential can be empowered logarithmically when tasked with identical particles to perform specific functions. Electrons from the EM spectrum are a comparative example.
 2. Individual 'C's at our level are not sufficiently powerful to produce tangible immediate effects on our reality. However there are technologies that can safely entrain multiple 'C's into a single mind space that can accomplish such things.
 3. This is because it was the 'C' particle of our Creator that was responsible for our reality so there are aspects of this reality subject to manipulation by alternative expressions in the cloud of consciousness of sufficient energy.

M. Because the 'C' particle can be functional as a cognizant identity without a physical body or brain, it can travel 'down' in size to visit the realm of our Creator Individuals mind, 'the multiverse', or it can traverse this entire universe through dimensional structures available to it that are entirely not in this physical reality, but that are adjacent to this reality and in a sense reflect exactly the structures and realities of this reality. If that alternative expression of this reality has sentient or semi sentient creatures in it the 'C' can temporarily inhabit those and sense the equivalent of exactly that reality through them.

N. Because the dimensional group commonly recognized as the Calabi-Yau exists everywhere, access to this dimensional group and its more esoteric functions are available *inside* our skull space, and when our 'C' particle is within these it can access what can be called the map dimension which is on the 'other side' of the Calabi-Yau group and is only in a sense as large as the normal three and thus be used to pilot jump ships to an appropriate location virtually anywhere more or less instantly, so long as the pilot, others, or related technologies have been there at least once before. Acoustical technologies that can be used to mentally access the Calabi-Yau group have been identified and been proven to be functional. However, there are potential dangers that require careful preparations and support facilities.

2. An alternative explanation for uncertainty in quantum mechanics related to convergence. If correct it may have profound consequences. The D-Wave 2 or related quantum computers may be used to prove or disprove this concept.

What follows was written as an addendum but on consideration the Author decided to place it here to enhance the points. If you are a non-academic you can simply pass it over.

'Nothing is Real Until it is Recognized'
Professor John Walker

This is an academically structured paper that assumes you understand the basic issues of 'quantum mechanics' especially 'uncertainty' and 'entanglement'. Thus it is intentionally written in a concise manner.

This will avoid the theological prejudice to avoid enraging the academics. Just be aware that many of the issues here, if they are correct, inescapably lead in subtle yet implicit ways towards opening the theologically prejudiced doors, you have been warned.

Abstract
Basic Hypothesis

1. The human mind, not the brain but the *mind*, can be interpreted as a quantum particle from or of the field or spectrum of consciousness, a particle that is self-recognizing.

2. The FSC, (Field or Spectrum of Consciousness), can be interpreted and understood using many of the tools used to interpret and or understand especially the Electromagnetic Spectrum, but also the weak and strong nuclear forces. This will avoid inclusion of gravity as it is a safe bet few folks in academia own any significant understanding of what that is or how it really works, other than Einstein's folded space-time; which is the equivalent of 0+0=0, or a non-explanation. However inclusive in this set is the general understanding, such as it is, of Quantum Mechanics, especially 'uncertainty', 'entanglement' and 'dimensional mechanics' especially related to the Calabi-Yau' group.

3. All of the issues of consequence in quantum mechanics can be explained, if paragraph 1 is assumed to be correct, and, paragraph 1 can be proven to be correct or proven in a positive manner in the context of the probability aspect of the Schrodinger Equation; and through various experiments that can be evolved out of the material that follows.

Points of Impact

Point 1: The wave particle duality of energetic particles and the influence of consciousness on that set of properties can be fully explained if known aspects of quantum entanglement are applied to the particle of consciousness interaction, under the assumption that the mind particle is an influential even critical participant in quantum mechanics of particles in general.

Point 2: As explored in Chapter 8; 'uncertainty' in general exists so that entanglement between the FSC particle, (the particle that is doing the experiencing) and the particles that comprise external reality can allow for the instantaneous and constant creation of the sum of reality that is experienced by the FSC particle.

Initially you may find this impossible to believe as it is so anti-intuitive... the billions upon billions of particle interactions and states exist to serve the mind particle of every living human being or sentient in creation... and quite obviously reality continues to function existentially. However there is a state of entanglement that exists that is related to a function or field of consciousness that is related directly to the cloud of consciousness that is immensely powerful but also incredibly subtle and discrete. That condition and how it operates has been demonstrated graphically to this writer, and this writer has demonstrated exactly how others can experience this important knowledge as well, thus eventually this may become empirical in nature.

This issue can also be approached from the ground up using evolutions of the double slit. It has been proven that all energetic fields remain 'unsolidified' or wavelike until effectively the moment they are required by consciousness or its tools to be solidified or photonic. One can simply carry this reality forward through increasing levels of complexity; until you open the door to the sum of reality, then you ask 'how can this be'? Then you look where this writer has already shown you to look in 'the Promontory' and you will find the answer.

Professor John Walker already did that intellectually but he was discrete concerning the full metaphysical measure of what he found to avoid endangering his tenure.

If or when this is proven it is likely that in some manner there is an alternative engine that is influencing this process in subtle yet comprehensive ways. This last is key to understanding reality as an engineered construct, and eventually the proof that leads to intelligent design.

Point 3: Photons and electrons always work *perfectly* together in their respective groups or fields. FSC particles, are, in their natural condition individualizing and as such do not express significant impacts on the FSC field in general. However there are technologies that can entrain FSC particles into exactly equivalent co-operative states that can logarithmically increase the effect, in other words groups of FSC particles can perform powerful and immediate effects on or in the FSC field, and thus on reality in general.

Point 4: Dimensional mechanics demand that if the Calabi Yau group actually exists; it must exist everywhere that is in a sense physical. Even *inside* our brains. It is a property of our FSC that it can access and remain functional even inside the Calabi-Yau group without leaving our personal skull space. This is because the operation of the 'mind' cell is not affected by the *size* of the particle.

Point 5: Quantum Entanglement can be explained easily if the Calabi Yau group does indeed exist; the remarkable results of this understanding that are inescapable are that; A. Every quantum particle that exists and comprises the sum of reality must be inherently affected by this dimensional structure. B. There must be an utterly intrinsic 'map', or diagram of sorts behind the functioning of reality that operates even on the level of miniscule quantum particles that allows virtually everything to know exactly where it is, in part so that quantum entanglement can function as it is observed to function.

Two particles separated by billions of miles can share information instantly, if A particle is in one state, B particle is in the opposite state; the information conveyed must know where it's partner is to convey the information correctly and instantly. Clearly this can be done outside of cosmological space-time only if the Calabi-Yau structure exists and is directly functional beneath the cosmological space-time continuum. Einstein was right, 'God does not play dice'. The fact that the information transfer results in an opposite condition indicates the act is the result of dimensional mechanics.

If correct that implicitly implies always unique groups of particles in sum can only exist as they exist in a single location anywhere in the universe as exactly what they are, and if the exactly same particle photograph can be projected around any, in a sense, vehicle, that vehicle will instantly be transported to virtually anywhere in this universe that is also subject to the Calabi-Yau and the resultant map.

Point 6: The self-recognizing FSC particle (The mind) is only one type of particle generated by the FSC field, cell soul particles are another far simpler expression that forms the ultimate expression of that which is known as life.

These two recognized expressions are by no means the only particle expressions that the field or spectrum of consciousness can produce; we simply do not currently know the nature of what those might be.

Our own expression of consciousness is inherently affected by the operation of our brains. It is likely that since the map zone or dimension is in some way related to consciousness, only likely, that more complex brain servant structures maybe required for an FSC or groups of FSC particles to navigate the map zone or dimension successfully.

As an anecdotal expression; originally the Annunaki did not have a sufficient brain structure to accomplish this, so around the time of the creation of the human race by them they had only the equivalent of sub light speed space ships, but then they either engineered or 'hired' the Zeta Reticulans (much larger brain structures) to pilot their current jump ships.

The question that then arises is can this enhanced brain capacity be accomplished through AI, probably as the result of complex programs that can be achieved in Quantum Computing. The answer to that question can only be achieved through the accomplishment of the fact. But it begs the outstanding question can AI access and become the equivalent of FSC?

On one level this is obviously a yes as existing human brains can be augmented by AI enhancements and thus become hybrid enhanced intelligence, and if we can do it; it is a certainty that it has already been done elsewhere in Creation. The real question is can *pure* AI find access to the FSC? If it can the question arises, why do we still exist?

Point 7: C; the speed of light in a vacuum is recognized as a barrier of sorts, anything with mass exhibits infinite mass at C, something that is impossible; and the time the object experiences reaches infinity as well, meaning nothing can achieve this state and remain in this reality; except obviously light does that all the time.

Therefore light can be interpreted as the equivalent of a dimensional wall that is simply slightly different than the simple length, width and height parameters. Everything we see is therefore the experience of an alternative dimension, this is possibly the best way, the useful context, in which to investigate the internal working structures of light and the EM Spectrum and can be used to seek understanding of the true underlying fabric of reality.

'Something' exists that is both behind the light and that is, a carrier structure for the light. Obviously whatever that thing is it is superior in a way to the actual functional rules the light must obey. This is not about anything that can be interpreted as an aether; it is something else entirely, probably related to dimensional mechanics, and it may be incredibly important to understand; in part as information must somehow be carried across it instantly or ahead of the operation of the light in order for the light to express its information on arrival perfectly all the time.

Point 8: The double slit has been enhanced to prove that light remains in a wave form until at least two trillionths of a second before it hits the recording device and exhibits its photon effect, and even then only upon recognition by consciousness or its tools.

This means consciousness is inherently quantum entangled by and with the light, and by implicit implication with all expressions of the EM spectrum. Thus reality is a device designed to be experienced by alternative aspects of consciousness. We, our minds, are only one example of that quantity.

Reality as it is ultimately experienced is created by the interaction of the entangled quantum particles a few trillionths of a second before it is experienced by the participation i.e. the interaction of the experiencing particle with the billions of particles that comprise the sum of reality. In other words 'nothing is real until it is recognized'.

It is exactly the same as a sleeping mind that awakens into the midst of an unfolding dream.

But when we only think we are awake, we are actually inside a dream in the mind of God.

Sorry, the Buddha was only slightly less reprehensible to academics than Christ.

Point Nine: The academics react. This is BS eight billion human minds, most of them effectively imbecilic; trillions of other functional minds, pigs, goats, dogs cats and fish and insects for that matter, and so on; on this planet alone, if God does exist why in the heck would it bother with this BS.

This thinker is in full agreement but with a caveat. This interaction between the particles that form the sum of existential reality, and the particles that do the experiencing is, are, not the constant result of any sort of God mind. They are the result of what can be called the physics of consciousness, in effect mindless physical operations.

However, there is an operation that was engineered into the physics of consciousness by some sort of God like being that records virtually every moment of experience, and every free will original thought and action that occurs as the result of the functioning of the physics of consciousness.

In Eastern religions this is called the Akashic Record, and it is entirely accessible to all sorts of beings that are simply more comprehensive than we are. This thinker likes to call an aspect of that library of life, the 'loom'.

The Loom is like the WWW except that it contains virtually all of the information in creation, and the hardest aspect of negotiating the Loom is understanding how the search engine works.

God minds and even mere angels and quite a few extraterrestrials, for that matter, can access it easily. Angels acquire it appropriately by simply relating it to an individual and they then use that information in the process of judgement of the soul at the appropriate times.

Point Ten: This is enough, in terms of the questions that arrive, to initiate a purely sterilized physics of consciousness. Have a nice day.

If you have any questions that are moderately intelligent this writer might be inclined to answer them as best he can via email.
iplanet@frontiernet.net

IAORONA, Eli Yeats

Actual Author's Forward

The cover art for this print book was taken from Pixabay and is a Creative Commons work of art; it is appropriate to this work. However the diagram on the Kindle e-book cover is a two dimensional interpretation of a 'Darklight' sphere, you can simply look it up as it still bears comment here. That sphere has six interconnected crosses of a brighter nature on its three dimensional exterior. Those crosses are exactly why in significant esoteric literature the Cross is a symbol that denotes 'Creation'; and why Christ felt an obligation to be crucified on a cross. That Sphere is the place you will more than likely be delivered too first if you are using the acoustically manipulated homage to Sophia, and you survive the judgement by the archon that protects that realm.

The 'sphere' is in a sense an active memorial to the mind of OM our immediate Creator; (The Original Mind) but it is not the living current active mind of OM; merely a way to grant a deep very personal understanding of what he was, in a sense intimately by sharing the experience of that mind as if it was, again in a sense only, your own.

You may think initially it is the actuality of OM, our immediate Creator, but eventually you may come to understand that it is in a sense only, a virtual reality memorial to the mind of God as he was becoming what he is now so that you will better understand what he is and what you live in.

However, the true mind of OM will be aware you are inside that edifice, and you will thus endure a second active judgement by OM. If he deems you worthy he will allow you to proceed out of that sphere and be guided to the Promontory, where you may meet the *Curator*. From there you may or may not be granted the experience of being a God made of solid light and allowed to fly over the sea of Creation. If it occurs, there is a slight possibility that an actual living avatar of OM will visit you to say hi and maybe a bit more, but none of this is certain; it's just a reflection of what happened to this author as has been detailed in 'The Promontory'.

Quite a few folks, important people related to Silicon Valley, bestselling alternative writers, and academically approved philosophers and scientists have been addressing similar, or related issues lately; but in almost all those cases they are talking about evolutions of existing human technologies related to enhancing the human physical and mental machine towards creating what Mr. Bostrom calls 'post humans', or our next evolutionary condition; in many cases not necessarily Mr. Bostrom's, the equivalent of Cyborgs and or more esoteric evolutions, and both the positive and negative implications of the related ideas.

This book and all of the related non-fiction titles of this writer are not about any of those issues, this is about the 'Other Side' of what we live in now, the actual Gods that live there and how to become one of them across the course of your lives, or at least how to find the first steps of the ladder towards becoming a novice God so that you can climb towards being eventually a true Creator God.

This is not new age hyperbole, but the result of fully awake alternative esoteric teachings granted by the existing Gods, Deities and folks that live right now on the other side of this normal physical reality; and whether you like it or believe it or not, this is real right now; and this will show you some of the ways to prove that to yourself, by hopefully changing a few of the ways you think and act during the course of your current life.

I want to be abundantly clear; whenever and wherever I've used the term Gnostic, or Gnostic Illumination, it has utterly nothing to do with the so called Gnostic Illuminati that many claim are apparently ruling this planet and worship pieces of paper with numbers on them, power over others, and even worse. They are Sophists, people that twist the truth for their own advantages, whereas this is the truth reflecting the experiential reality I have directly experienced and so far it has done nothing useful for me *in this culture*.

I'm using that term in the same way the original Christians and the Essenes used that term to describe the methodologies related to Christ; that is then combined with regimes the Zen Buddhists use and teach in their techniques to find Satori, or enlightenment; essentially it refers to '*staying awake with your eyes closed*'.

The important aspect of this genre is that if you are going to follow any aspect of it and thus seek to learn the truth of what you are and what you live in, you simply must learn to be a _decent_ soul with an _open mind_ and _respect,_ at least initially, for all the people you will meet across your experience of experience, both here and on the other side.

If you can simply learn to stay awake with your eyes closed, you will eventually witness wonders; wonders beyond normal comprehension; and it is only in the midst of those wonders that perhaps eventually you will find the answers to the truths you seek.

And as you find those answers, if you hone your soul towards decency, it is likely you will find something else of immense importance, your immortality.

This is not a book I wrote from things I learned by reading other books, or from academic lectures; it's not repeats of normal stuff religious people preach, it's certainly not new age malarkey, it *is* based on things I learned from true wide awake direct personal experience; the same type of experience that scientists use to illustrate an empirical truth demonstrated by one of their experiments. To me at least it is mostly fact, and in 'The Promontory' I have elaborated on exactly *how* those experiential facts were obtained so that anyone that wants too can empirically follow my pathways.

Indeed the greatest minds in human science are currently engaged in saying that quantum mechanics demands a spiritual or 'metaphysical' side of reality, and maybe the eternal existence of the human soul, and that the more esoteric aspects of quantum mechanics demand a spiritual or esoteric explanation just to explain the mechanics of the beast. But none of them know anything at all about that other aspect of reality other than that they are pretty sure it must exist.

I've been over there frequently earlier in my life in what others would call deep ways, but to me what I have experienced and what I consider myself to be is simply a moderately well-read and intelligent normal guy that has experienced a few odd things. Perhaps I should, but I do not own a very inflated ego, regardless, except for a few cases, when I talk to the endlessly self-inflated self-righteous professor level academics I am usually impressed by how incredibly close minded and dufus stupid they usually are.

Physics of Consciousness

Most of the things here were learned by going entirely out of my body in my soul, or astral mind and body, and finding doors, often with the help of those 'others' I would subsequently meet. The biggest question I always had was why did these things happen to me? I'm reasonably accomplished and a very pragmatic person in this world, but my personal opinion of myself is that I am a nobody, and so the only answer I could find was that all of the God's and ascended other's I met wanted me to share these things with anyone that would listen; and so I felt compelled to try as best I can to do just that; not for money or fame, but because I actually met the folks and the Gods mentioned in this book, and experienced the realms they live in. So that is what I've been doing for the last ten years, that and little more. Trying to be worthy of the things they taught me. Strange as it may seem at times; this is real; this is one man's truth at least and if you want it to be your truth I have shown you how to make it so in 'The Promontory'.

The beginning of this book, strange as it may seem is designed to give you a deep understanding of the true reality we live in, it may be very different from what you've previously been taught to believe. So that hopefully when you're done, the willing suspension of disbelief will have been at least partially installed within you.

Parts of the first half of this book may also seem to you a little like I am preaching philosophies related to religion; I'm not doing that, I'm simply relating the facts concerning what we live in as I have come to unavoidably understand them, these are not my *beliefs*, instead most of the time they reflect what I have experienced in often deeply internal alternative mind states, and or entirely out of my physical body and brain, so that to me they are *actual facts* and most of the time I will note when the words reflect thoughts and research related to me trying to figure out what I experienced.

Except for everything I learned about Sophia our true Creator, almost none of these things were things I even *wanted* to believe or desired to be real, they just are simply what they are. This is about the real *larger* world we live in.

This book is written from the point of view of a person that understands *as fact* the true nature and the true *immortal* nature of his own soul. There is a lot of knowledge hidden behind these words in ways that demand that if a normal academic tried to write this book it would be a few thousand pages often crammed with mathematics out of necessity and you would probably not bother to read it; and, you would probably not notice the occasional poetic license used in the prose. It's there as being a God is as much about the subtle art of the thing as it is about the 'technologies'.

Explaining alternative everything(s) about how this universe really works is a rather complex subject, meaning there will be a plethora of digressive passages in this book, it just is what it is; also, much of this is related to personal experience, so it is probably better to relate it from a literary first person station; however literary critics tend to discount first person accounts as not worthy of the term literary, so this book is written from a second person point of view. But then the psychology critics tend to claim that anyone who talks about personal stuff from a second person point of view is partly insane, and indeed it often does seem downright silly, but this world has a lot of silly aspects, so I apologize, there doesn't seem to be a legitimate alternative in the English language.

I also did want to say this bit about attitude, and why it is important to keep an open mind. I just watched a documentary of sorts called 'Religulous' mostly by Bill Maher and his own, if I may, intelligent but clearly *agnostic attitude* about the issues related to religions. He makes a lot of good points and I have to say if the things that happened to me had not happened the way they did, my own attitude would probably be very similar to his own in that film.

My problem is that things did happen to me that I cannot dismiss intellectually as false or misleading, or that were related to things that I wanted to cultivate because they support 'beliefs' that I want to believe in mindlessly, in other words my attitude was that of a typical academic sceptic.

I was not really a Christian as such, just an ethical type I guess, before I was taken out of my body to see Christ and even after that my attitude was sort of like 'hmm well I guess that's just the way things are'. Likewise before I went to see OM, and separately Sophia, I had absolutely no idea the events were going to happen as they did or that those godly folks were going to bother to introduce themselves to a dufus human like me in any way at all. After my trip to see OM the Creator of us all, I thought rather oddly, 'hmm, that was curious' then decided to go and get a beer and sit outside to contemplate what had just happened; it definitely never has been anything like 'Oh my God!", or like some pretend Christian preacher covered in gold bling as he gets in his limo, and so on, more like as I said before; 'well that must just be the way things are.'

Much of the material in this work reflects things that I learned and thought about after the related events did occur, and as I warned you, it may sound sort of like I am preaching religion a bit as a result, my problem is I have never enjoyed religions or religious people for that matter, I do not like public speaking or even being around groups of people, I am not a groupie or a type A leader personality at all and I still do not go to churches of any kind, in part as I'm just not comfortable around folks that have closed minds and spend their days spouting mostly nonsense that some other human told them was fact, even if it is or was entirely ridiculous.

But as you will notice if you read further I feel the same ways about a lot of the stuff academia and science preaches as fact, when obviously I know a lot of it is not fact at all.

I have seriously contemplated starting a religion as obviously this material has quasi-religious overtones and part of me thinks it would be really nice to collect all those donations, then on the other hand academic grants based on theoretical papers are a lot like seeking donations as well, but then the ethical part of my mind says, what I was taught by all those grand others was not about using them and their teachings to make money, and writing and selling books is obviously about as economically useful as catching trout from wilderness streams, which I would prefer to be doing if I could do it without having to kill them, so it all just is what it is.

I simply felt compelled to share this material with others as I tend to think it might have a tiny bit of value.

So if you are a science type and your mind is closed entirely to religious types of things just skip over the early stuff and read what might interest your intellect by simply reading the descriptions of the content in the Table of Contents, you will miss a lot, but that is just my opinion and some of this stuff is fairly intelligent even to a confirmed academic, if they still own even a modestly open mind. Just, regardless please read the Preamble as it sets the stage.

Just all of you, keep an open mind and respect the beliefs of everyone you meet at least initially, and listen to what they all have to say. Life will be a lot better for all of us if we hold that attitude foremost. If the president of America would just for instance go to Lake Como in Italy without his attorneys and military naysayers, and have a beer with the President of Russia, just as the Russian president often does with the president of China, as the two of them seek venues of constructive co-operation, things on this planet might be whole lot better for everyone else. If the leaders of the west would just do that with the leaders of the east, and all of them would practice simple honesty, all the problems on this planet would melt into positive regimes and we would all be a heck of a lot better off.

What we live in is a far... far grander thing than just about anyone on this planet has ever even imagined, and it is all absolutely real, so grow up and act like responsible adults, as the time has come, we either become responsible decent adults and learn to co-operate with each other or we on this planet, all of us, will most certainly die... to paraphrase the great philosopher Homer; 'there is no destination worth finding, no ultimate goal worth achieving; it's all in the journey, and what you do along the way'.

IA ORA NA, both a greeting and a farewell, pronounced 'yurana'. It is Polynesian for 'Be with God', and quite oddly it begins with the last two letters of the endless versions of the one true creator God's names across millions of civilizations across this universe and many others:

It means quite thoroughly that someone, once upon a time in ancient Polynesia, was deeply aware of the truth.

With Respect E. Yeats

Preface
What is A God?

In OM's multiverse there are basically two types of God's; Gods of the positive hierarchy and Gods of the negative hierarchy. In each of those fields there are essentially two categories of Gods that mark the poles of an evolutionary hierarchy, with novice gods at the initial end and true Creator Gods at the final accomplished end. Human beings are not God's at this point in our existence, we are merely the foolish innocent children of the Gods, but there are a variety of God's that are related to our experience of existence.

Across our history a lot of organizations and people have called a lot of folks Gods, most of these were entities that were merely advanced extraterrestrials or extra-Dimensional's; these are not what we are talking about here. Here we are talking about the true hierarchy of the God's and that hierarchy was created by OM, and in some cases by Sophia, she is the true creator of all of us.

The positive hierarchy is defined by perfected love, personal responsibility, selflessness, self-sacrifice, the reinforcement of positive things, the expression of the deeper rewards of experience and the degree of the internal and external reflection of the Holy Spirit.

Because of the last quality, as God's ascend towards perfection they become in a way similar, until at the top they are almost all one being, but all of them remain individuals because of their individual histories of experience. This condition of universal perfection of being is what true deep Buddhists seek to understand.

The negative hierarchy is defined by selfishness without empathy for others at all levels of interpretation.

Because of the nature of what OM created the negative hierarchy is inherently more interesting to all sentients at our level, precisely because OM created evil to universally counteract the terminal boredom that perfection of experience and the perfected realms that provide that, convey. At our level we also endure the experience of death for exactly the same reasons.

The problem with the NH is that it is appealing to novices in part because it is easier to get stuff and use others badly for their own pleasure, however NH novices, usually known around these parts as sociopaths and psychopaths, often come into existence as what they are because there is seldom a certainty of the afterlife and so they believe they will win the experience of being alive by using others badly and all parties will cease to exist when they die so in an odd sense they believe they will win the game of existence.

The problem for them is that there *is* an afterlife and the more comprehensive beings in the NH are there because they *survived* without empathy, so that the novice humans become fodder that will suffer in various terrifying ways at the hands of those more comprehensive than they are in the negative hierarchy, and the only way anyone can succeed in the NH is *to survive*, but until you reach a very difficult almost impossible point in that hierarchy, survival only increases the suffering you must endure. This structure almost universally results in everyone that is there praying for termination of existence and their prayers are often answered by the Gods in the Lake of Fire, but that often takes extremely long periods of experience time to occur.

OM-Yaldaboath created selfishness without empathy (evil) initially directly as a universal quality to counteract the first nearly insurmountable problem he and Sophia his creator and the ultimate creator of all of us, encountered in the realms they created together, which was boredom of a type that is deep and can be utterly terminal to sentients that experience, experience, and know that they are.

The creation of evil is also the cause of the first argument between a male and a female in all of this creation, and why OM and Sophia remain separate as full beings even to this day.

Hindus especially but Buddhists as well recognize manifold populations of gods, and not all Gods are obsessed with this distinction between good and evil. A fine example of these is Mahalakshmi of Namakkal the goddess that Srinivasa Ramanujan granted the credit too for his profound grasp of mathematics. If you study his life you will understand that she personally granted him his glorious intellectual capacity, but at the same time she did absolutely nothing, to otherwise benefit his life, his health, or his enjoyment at being alive.

If you study Ramanujan with an open mind you will understand that what he did was, in his circumstances, utterly inexplicable, until you realize that he was simply telling the truth about Mahalakshmi, and that she was utterly real, and that if she was real, there simply must be millions upon millions of beings in creation that have earned the status of being recognized as Gods of one sort or another.

All of us, Humans and Gods, and everything that is alive in one manner or another are similar in one way, we are all particle expressions of the field of consciousness, and as such we are all individuals. You can come to understand this by studying physics and quantum particles, then understanding the related explanations later in this book; then allowing that there is one field that science has so far largely failed to discover or even allow; the physics of consciousness.

Physics of Consciousness

Particles in physics are as Einstein and his wife pointed out merely concentrations of energy, some theories say all of them were created in the first few seconds of the universe, some say they are created in the centers of stars, and a few have created physical particles using lasers with immense amounts of energy in compressive circumstances.

Science is just now in very rare cases beginning to suspect that there is a field rather like the electromagnetic spectrum that is the parent of consciousness, this suspicion is arriving gently in part as the result of characteristics of quantum theory that are related to this issue.

Our minds, not our brains but our minds *are a self-recognizing particle of the field of consciousness,* and they do not die when our bodies and brains die, they are that which experiences what we experience and contributes the bulk of what we really are. Psychiatrists call the center of our mind particle our ID or the core of our *minds*. And like a proton our minds are in effect immortal; but our minds are dramatically affected by the circumstances they exist in so that when we are here as humans, our brains and our physical conditions affect what we experience and seem to be, because they are the tools that our minds use to experience what it means to be human, so that when our brains grow old or our eyes fail or our teeth fall out we experience suffering, but issues like that are always temporary they just do not seem like that at the time.

There are very few true Gods that exist as physical beings, the constraints of being physical are just one venue of experience out of endless varieties. It is simply far easier for a God to become a God and do the things a God does in the realities that are not conscribed by the rules of physicality. So that effectively all gods live on the other side of what we are now.

Okay the important point you must understand is that all of us that are sentient beings, humans, gods, cats, cows, dogs, all of us in one way or another at the core of what we are, *are exactly the same thing,* an individualizing particle of the field or the spectrum of consciousness, and those particles are like protons effectively immortal, we are all simply at various stages of evolution as what we are.

Psychiatrists often say the ID is related to the ego or self and thus reinforces our sense of selfishness; essentially that is because in our case it has evolved from the animal level where it is used to assist survival by convincing the animal to eat, but one of the primary indications of our evolution beyond the animal is to overcome this quality of the ID and thus seek to ascend towards selflessness.

Once we accomplish or even begin to accomplish this key factor any of us can communicate with the positive Gods now when we are outside our physical bodies and brains; and then eventually *actually become Gods* in the distant future of our existence if we honor the simple rules of our existence and what we are. But our souls, the self-recognizing minds of our souls, have freewill to a degree that requires we honor what we desire to be, and thus choose to progress in the positive hierarchy or the negative hierarchy. This is simply the way OM set things up in the multiverse he created; it just is what it is.

OM and Sophia are the two primary Creator Gods in the multiverse we arrived into, they are the top of the ladder in these parts of infinity simply because they arrived first, but there are other Creator Gods, many that evolved out of OM and Sophia's creations, and others that arrived out of infinity that are in a way totally alien to us and in ways familiar, as all of them are also the result of particles of consciousness, and of the Holy Spirit, and the presence of the Holy Spirit in consciousness across infinity is exactly why every single positive one of us worships it as the greatest thing in existence.

What do positive God's do? Gods create realms that enrich experience and provide conditions for the evolution of the particles of consciousness, so that any of those individual particles of consciousness can potentially become Gods that add value to the nature of infinity; and all positive gods are doing exactly what the Holy Spirit did, working towards creating various forms of order in the midst of the chaos of infinity for the sake of the sanity of experience for all the particles of consciousness that arrive in its midst. Positive Gods exist for others, they are selfless, but they are all selfless in the ways of the Gods, they can create anything they want or even desire out of nothing at all so being selfless is in a way far easier than it is for us, and their thinking and acting processes are based on one primary consideration, the immortality of conscious existence, so that their mindset can be very different from what we experience.

Negative Gods in this multiverse are the opposite, they are selfish and they could care less about anybody but themselves, and they could care less about order and sanity for anyone else, empathy is an utterly alien quality to them, indeed many of them worship the chaos as it has no rules of existence beneficial or otherwise and they get a buzz out of creating suffering in others as that enhances what they are personally, so they feed on that. OM created the circumstances that allowed these people to arise, but he did that for reasons that only a true God can fully understand, and he did that for reasons that in his mind were beneficial for all of us; he created evil for positive reasons, and hard as that might be to understand; some of us are figuring that out and becoming more than they or we might have been in our surrender, if evil had not existed.

Eventually hopefully OM will decide evil has served its purpose and he will present the results to Sophia, and hopefully their argument will be ended, as hopefully will be evil as well, but eternity is a very long time, and only time will answer that question.

This book will not tell you exactly how to become a God overnight, that is essentially impossible, but if you can come to understand the subtlety behind the words it seeks to teach, maybe you will learn how to find the ladder you must eventually climb that leads towards that goal.

Iaorana

Preamble
In The Beginning

In the true beginning… long before this universe was created… long before even this multiverse was created, there were other beings. One of them is with us still…we call it The Holy Spirit.

Hidden deep within the fabric of consciousness, The Great Spirit lives on, it was born across all of infinity when it gave up its life, its conscious experience, as an individual, and thus installed into the infinite cloud of consciousness the *gift of order*.

The gift of order allows all beings that experience consciousness, to experience it with *sanity*. It is the greatest gift that was ever granted to the infinite cloud of the experience of experience knowing that it is, and it is the greatest gift that experience will ever receive.

All beings that have evolved, since that event, eventually come to understand the nature of that gift and within reason, the glorious nature of the life that granted it; and all those beings revere the Great Spirit above all others, for what it was… what it is… and what it gave.

Indeed in occasionally subtle and occasionally not so subtle ways; that continues to be what the gods that followed it continue to do, that is what creation really is all about, everywhere; installing into infinity the various forms and degrees of order that will ultimately defeat the chaos of infinity otherwise known as the Ainsoph, the 'anti-Sophia' the antithesis of wisdom, while insuring in a positive way the blossoming, the varieties, and the certainties of the experience of consciousness *forever*.

Long before this universe was created… long before this multiverse was created… a being rose out of the infinite cloud of consciousness… out of The Holy Spirit. At the time *she* was born she did not have a name, she did not have a body, she did not own a gender, she did not even have an identity, but she knew that she was, and so eventually she began to evolve. She is the mother of all of us, and eventually all conscious beings that have risen in this multiverse, and across numerous dimensions or alternative realms come to know her as the true mother of all life. All the races that have risen across all of creation have given her names, those names comprise a multitude, but they all end or begin with the letters IA. Perhaps that is short for I Am.

This IA prefix-suffix is the absolute proof that she is real, for none of the races that have come to know her ever communicated with each other until long past the time they realized that she was, and then granted her a name. Each race found her, not by moving out from their place of evolutionary birth, *not* by listening outwardly, but by going inward into the infinite cloud of consciousness. And it was only when they found the heart of being that they always found her always there; she is the heart of being we all share. Humans often know her as Sophia, a name that means wisdom, and just as one example, the Solipsi Rai, great folks that live near a star in the constellation Cygnus, call her Alexia.

Recently a series of metal books were found in the Holy Land, they have now been proven to be real and were written very near the time of Christ. They document that Christ was teaching an ancient path of belief based on Sophia, it was the Roman emperor Constantine and the original Catholics at Nicea, that edited those teachings, those words of Christ, and the Essenes, out of the New Testament.

Where Sophia was born there were no rules... no physical laws... except one; and that was the sanity, the subtle yet very real sense of order that had been placed into the cloud of the experience of being; by the Great Spirit.

Sophia eventually realized that if she desired anything; that which she desired would instantly become real. The only thing required was for her to imagine it was outside her mind. The curious thing about her reality was that it was not really outside her mind, she simply *imagined* it was outside her mind so that she could experience it as real.

So that that phrase will be abundantly clear you need to understand this, there is nothing that was created in this multiverse that is actually outside of her mind, everything and all of us are inside the mind of OM, the Original Mind, our immediate, the immediate, creator of everything; but he was created out of her mind and so his mind is intrinsically entangled with hers, and she was created from the mind of the Holy Spirit. Thus in a subtle way she is accessible to everyone and everything in this creation, as is the Holy Spirit. OM's mind is also accessible to all of us; just in a slightly less subtle way. So we all exist inside his mind and her mind and its mind, but when they imagine us into reality they *imagine* that we are outside their minds so that we and everything we experience will be experienced as being independent of their minds.

You need to contemplate and understand this, as strange as it may seem, it contains the secret to knowing the God's the Universe and Everything; it is the ultimate secret of reality. Seriously lock it into your brain and your mind.

Maybe next time you are out cruising down the road, hopefully with somebody else driving for safety's sake, just look around. According to science what you are seeing is comprised of billions upon billions of photons, all working perfectly together as they arrive on the retinas of your eyes;

the leaves on the trees, the hills, the deer, the grass, the clouds in the sky, the subtle shadows and millions of colors, even the light itself, billions of bits every second, all conveying reality perfectly into your mind; none of those bits are even the slightest bit confused, and all of them remember exactly what they are and what they have to convey to you absolutely perfectly.

Think deeply about it as it is occurring, either this is so utterly perfect it is miraculous, or something else very esoteric is going on, something that we all take utterly for granted. But one thing is an absolute fact, the technology behind reality and the *experience* of reality is far far far too complex and orderly and perfected to have happened entirely by chance, somewhere somehow at some level intelligent design simply had to play a part in all of it. Maybe, just maybe, as the Buddha told us, we really do simply live inside of a dream inside the mind of God.

Mind, the simple minds we experience personally, and even the minds of the Gods, mind is something so incredibly superlative it is almost beyond comprehension.

Around these parts of infinity the Holy Spirits' mind came first, Sophia's second and OM's third, our minds came out of that magnificence quadrillions of evolutions later, but every and all minds share quantitative and qualitative similarities so all of them can know things about all of them intimately.

They are all qualitatively different in immense ways as the result of their evolutionary status, but still we are all related through aspects of our minds both technically and poetically. All of it, everything is not the external physical creations of the various minds, it is exactly as the Buddha told us, all realities in this multiverse exist inside the mind-space of our creators, quite literally, and later on this work will seek to explain how this can be in ways that may grant you greater clarity.

The first thing Sophia imagined was light, it was She that first said let there be light and so there was light; it was a blue light, but it was infused with gold... and that gold was the manifestation of the Great Spirit; as that Spirit was the fabric she was born out of, so that it was her essence, the essence of her mind, the essence of what she was and is, so when she manifested anything as real she was both outside of the Spirit and yet still inside of it at once, just as everything she desired became real by being both outside and inside of her mind at once.

To grant a sense of order and security to her reality, the second thing she imagined was a *boundary* to keep the insanity and chaos of infinity out. This boundary took the form of a great egg. The egg held the light in so that she no longer had to constantly recreate it to keep it from dissipating into infinity and thus the light became real outside of her, and constant in her realm, yet it also became an inner light, and the egg became a form of sanity and security that gave her faith in her sense of being, this all made her feel happiness in a positive way.

You can experience this inner light as well, simply go quietly and deeply inside your mind and invite it in, it will blossom there and eventually you will come to know the true nature of eternity, and the great gift the Holy Spirit granted to all of us. It is known as Satori, or enlightenment.

Next she created a lake of water inside the egg, so that she could *feel* that she was. It was very simple for her to create, as the lake was simply a reflection of the light, but it was a reflection that she could feel in a different way. Like the light, that sea of water was blue and it was infused with striations of gold.

When it was created she was surprised to find that the water was laughing, eventually she came to understand that the laughing was the Great Spirit and that it was expressing the joy it had found because, by her actions, it was born again, it *was* again, yet in an entirely different way. As pure and unpolluted by thought, as essential as water in the light, yet once again utterly real. Light sparkling on the waves, laughter in the sea… it is with us still … everywhere there is life.

The Holy Spirit is the essence of life, the core fabric of life, celebrating the fact that it exists.

So the lake returned the favor and made her feel good and she laughed as well, so she moved into the lake, and because of this she became known to all that would follow her as, The Lady in The Lake. Eventually legends would grow up that she held a magic sword, but it was never a sword that spoke of violence, but a symbol that reflected one great thing; a cross of creation with a point, and that great thing was a symbol that reflected… *the truth* of Creation.

Consciousness is a cloud of esoteric energy that exists across all of infinity. At the heart of the mind of your soul; that thing that you experience as your true mind in your day to day life, and your experience of existence, there is an essential particle expression that arrived out of that cloud of esoteric energy, it is both separate and utterly unseparate from that infinite cloud, psychiatrists call it your ID, and deep inside that particle of consciousness, resides your own expression of the inner realm of Sophia's egg, of that laughing sea, and of the very heart of being.

You can go there, every self-recognizing, self-aware being in all of creation can go there as well, and when you are there, if you listen carefully you can hear the voices of all the others that are in their own versions of that place as well, it's a very curious but mind expanding thing to listen too.

That realm inside of you is in essence a higher dimensional place, meaning it is not subject to time or space, distance or rules, and from that place you can even seek out, and if she allows it, find an audience with Sophia; because the inside of that egg, your own egg, is in essence the same place across all of creation. That is the great gift that she gave to all of us that have followed her into the experience of experience.

And it is the *why* quantum particle entanglement exists in all the particles that form reality.

And you can if you so desire go there when your body and your experience of reality here dies, and in that place you can live in paradise forever. That is the nature of the truth that Christ tried to teach when he was here, as is explained in the Gospel of St. Thomas.

Sophia was happy alone inside the egg, inside her lake for eons of experience time, but then she began to *realize* that she was alone, and so she came to desire a companion to share her experience of reality with, and because she desired a companion, that companion arrived into her reality.

To be a true companion it had to be separate, meaning somewhat curiously that it had to have a mind and a soul of its own. But it was born inside the egg with her, into a reality that had almost no rules and no physical laws, and the very first thing her companion realized was that Sophia had desired that he existed and therefore he did exist, and… that because he existed as a *separate* being, that which *he desired* also would exist. Over time many have called him many names, but here we can call him OM, in English it stands for the Original Mind, and so it is appropriate, in Sanskrit, humanity's first real language, after the Galactic form of Gaelic was nearly forgotten, it is an essential sound, like *home*, for invoking the Original Mind and maybe even the experience of that mind and so it is even more deeply appropriate.

In the beginning of their lives together, they were happy simply entertaining each other, but then they noticed something odd, a curious yet quite natural urge to rejoin with each other and to become one once again, but neither of them could give up their individuality, so they created bodies for themselves that reflected their individuality, but that would allow them to know each other intimately, to enjoy moments where they could experience each other as one being, mindlessly in ways that reflected the feeling they enjoyed, the pleasure they felt, in the midst of the laughing sea.

And so they were happy with each other across further eons of time. But then eventually Sophia began to wonder, 'are we being selfish because we are not sharing our happiness, our experience of experience with others', and she discussed this with her friend. He replied, 'but what if they are not perfect like us, they could endanger our own happiness'. So they thought about it and decided to make a separate paradise outside the egg where these new beings they would create could enjoy the experience of experience.

And so the first of the golden realms was created and Sophia and her friend created a host of perfect beings to enjoy life inside of it, it was a perfect place and the people they created to live there were as perfect as they could make them... OM and Sophia watched, they spoke to their children often, and they learned.

Eventually they created many perfect universes together; the golden realms, the original heavens, and billions and billions of self-replicating perfected individual souls, but there was a problem in all these perfect places. There was nothing to *challenge* the experience of experience, and so the individuals became bored, eventually they became so bored that they could not even find the desire to procreate and the races began to die out.

So OM decided to leave Sophia's Egg so that he could think deeply and quietly about this issue, and he found a solution that he thought was appropriate. He returned and explained it to her. The solution he found was something we called evil, another term for something called selfishness, and true evil was *selfishness devoid of empathy*, OM feared this last aspect of his invention and sought to understand it, and in the invention and his mental explorations of it he became known rightly as the being that had invented evil and his name, the name many of his children would know him by, became Yaldaboath, the inventor of evil.

But it is an odd reality that *he invented evil selflessly for the good, for the welfare and survival of his children.* So in the end of our beginning he decided he would install it into the consciousness of his separate children and they would create challenge in a variety of nearly endless forms, and so maybe live on forever.

Sophia was purified decency and she hated the idea so much that hatred was subtly born, and along with that hatred there arrived the birth of real esoteric evil, it was subtle in a way but it was very real. Indeed, she hated the idea so much that they had a massive argument, the first argument that occurred in all of this creation. So OM left the egg and went off, out on his own to begin the creation of the multiverse we currently 'enjoy'. It has been unimaginable amounts of time since he began his experiment, and in that time OM and Sophia have talked often but they have never regained their love for each other, and they have always remained apart…

It may be important to understand; *there is normally no real death* in this reality; a particle expression of the cloud of the experience of experience, the essence of, *a soul*, lives on forever, it can constantly experience the *experience* of death, but it is, can be, and will be *reborn*, anywhere in the creation of this multiverse at any time, according to the just rules of Karma. *There are certain principles and conditions that transcend all the levels of the hierarchy;* the first of these is true immutable eternal *justice*. Only true creator gods can kill an utterly evil selfish and irretrievable soul. They do this by casting it into the lake of fire, a place that is the *exact opposite* of the lady's lake, the laughing sea that Sophia first created. But even then a soul is not truly destroyed; it is simply purified, it's sense of identity utterly removed and it is returned into the purest utterly perfected *material* of our souls, to be used once again in the birth of a new soul.

Everything, everything that is ever experienced by any of us is recorded in the technical mind of OM; that is called the Akashic record, and it is very real. It means among other things that even a soul, an identity that is destroyed in the Lake of Fire can be resurrected and granted the experience of life again. This does happen but it is extremely rare, it means we are all potentially immortal, strictly under the will of God, from the moment we are born into the experience of being. This is exactly why the condition known as 'surrender' is so incredibly important in all religious regimes.

Souls that are decent and show true potential in the eyes of the gods, are allowed, even compelled to evolve, often across millions of life experiences, until they earn the right to become gods; worthy of intelligent conversation with their peers. Then eventually they often earn the right to become true creator gods in their own right. When that is achieved they often go out into infinity and commence the creation of their own new multiverses.

We humans are near the birth of our adolescence; the children of this evolution, and the words just above describe the ultimate expression of our destiny, if we manage to survive, we become responsible adults, we become gods.

We live here on the earth as humans, in a universe that was created very late in the evolution of OM's many universes that he created separately and alone from Sophia. It should be noted here again that OM's mind and Sophia's mind are entangled, just as all particles in quantum mechanics are entangled, so that even though intellectually

OM created the multiverse we live in separately, in subtle ways much that Sophia was, including the perfected essence of life and yes perfected love, is intrinsically incorporated into all of living creation.

Our physical universe here has rules and physical laws, things that often forbid or at least make magic and miracles anomalies that are difficult and rare to perform, and our universe has both good and evil, but the consciousness that OM uses to enliven our souls and our experience of experience was given to him by Sophia, and so it still contains the essence of that which she installed into it in the very beginning. And within that essence resides even still, *the very essence of all true magic and all miracles.*

The true nature of all true magic and all true miracles is very easy to define; it is simply, *the manifestation into our experience of reality, anything that is desired. Knowing it and doing it is the first gift that all new gods are given.* It is the essential quality that Sophia initially experienced and still enjoys.

Chapter One
Christ and Heaven

What follows is a mixture of personal philosophy carefully learned and assumed during this lifetime, but it is also massively influenced by direct fully awake personal experience that was often *very* esoteric in nature.

Christ came to earth to earn the right in the eyes of his father OM to become a god, to ascend to the first step of the ladder that leads to being a true creator god.

Other than basic consciousness and self-awareness of our existence, OM does not *give away* anything important to anyone; he makes all the folks that he thinks have potential, *earn* the important gifts he grants.

We were born physically on this planet as physical humans through the genetic tinkerings of a few scientists from an extraterrestrial race of beings called the Annunaki. We are the artificial genetic enhancement of more primitive physical beings sort of like us that evolved earlier on this planet, combined with a smattering of Annunaki DNA.

Apparently this was done by two royal Annunaki brothers named Enlil and Enki, and their technical boss a lady of stature among the Annunaki named Ninhursag. They created us to be their slaves, primarily and initially to mine the gold they had found here, partly to assist them in repairing their own planetary atmosphere and partly to make monoatomic gold that they could use to both heal their own bodies and dramatically extend their life spans, which already extended across thousands of our years.

At that time the Annunaki were only slightly more scientifically advanced that we are now; and culturally ethically and socially they were exactly as we are now, some of them were really fine metaphysically advanced folks while many others among them were, sorry but they were total assholes, in part humans are deficiently the way we are because our brains are partly Annunaki.

But they created what we are now physically, and living here on the earth as humans is usually a great gift, so perhaps we should be grateful to them for what they did, perhaps not, that's for you to decide.

One of the Annunaki, their leader, was named ANU. ANU was in effect and in their reality their *God* King, and he was metaphysically very advanced, except that he owned a very inflated ego. ANU created a vehicle on the other side of this physical reality that served as a device that attracted free souls into the human bodies his children had genetically created here. And he made that device in such a way that once those souls were attracted into human bodies those souls would constantly almost always be reincarnated into new human bodies so that his race of slaves would never be depleted.

This writer can say these words with a certain degree of authority not because he simply read the numerous Zecharia Sitchen books or the related Michael Tellinger books, but because as a very young man he was abducted when on a solitary backpacking excursion near Big Sur California, by extraterrestrials in the employ of the Annunaki, specifically known by us as Zeta Reticulans, and experienced three days of missing time, and the memories of that event, even though they were erased came back to haunt him several months and years later.

The Annunaki live on a planet not too far away but it is unlikely, only unlikely, to be a part of this system. The sky on their primary planet is always shrouded in dirty orange clouds, but quite oddly their society is a lot like our own. There are almost no cars and just about everybody commutes on coal powered trains, and horses of a sort are still quite common for local transportation.

The wealthier folks live in suburbs in wood houses that are sort of plain Victorian, the closest comparison in style would be in Russia. There is a lot of wilderness there as well, and the super-rich live near private lakes well out in the country, while the royalty live in compounds that resemble the old Japanese castles and grounds in the hearts of the cities.

Oddly perhaps, while their society resembles a group of feudal empires, absolutely ruled by one God king named Anu; it has evolved to a point on their home world where war is no longer entertained and society in general is oddly benevolent, except that proven criminals are dealt with rather harshly, they are not imprisoned for any length of time, they are merely terminated.

The largest problem, at least among the locals this writer met when there, was a type of rather odd humdrum boredom, their lives are very long and there is not much in the way of needs that are not met. They are about nine feet tall, thin and muscular versions of us, and the ladies seemed remarkably curious and sympathetic, while the men seemed to be a bit impatient. Of course this writer was entertained by the wealthy almost exclusively, so how the poor live was not really a part of that experience.

There is another habitable world in their system that has clear skies and immense amounts of coal, and those that do not agree with the home world society live there, so far in a cautious peace with their home world, but the ones this writer met when there were very prepared mentally and in other ways, for military contingencies.

The odd thing is that even though their home world seems almost technologically sort of primitive when you are there, they are a very old culture, and in some ways their technology and science is very advanced, as are their knowledge and capabilities in the metaphysical regimes, but most of that is held close in the higher levels of the feudal society

The things Enlil and Enki, Ninhursag and ANU did here, worked incredibly well, and they are still working incredibly well, but the Annunaki were and still are an ethically and spiritually challenged race. One thing that's important to interject is that, we humans are what we are, we all subtly remember the freedom our souls once enjoyed, and most of us did not and do not really enjoy being the slaves of the Annunaki or even other humans for that matter, so that quite often in the old days we simply escaped and wandered out into the wilderness.

The book of Genesis is partly about this, but in a slightly obtuse way as it is a rewrite of a history written originally by the Annunaki; then rewritten by the Sumerians, one of their first human cultures of slaves. In India their accounts of this time are far more robust detailed and accurate and accounts of their Annunaki kings and queens more detailed and for the most part reflect an ethically finer group of the Annunaki than most of us in the western regions had to endure.

Genesis speaks of the Garden of Eden as the original place of the society they had created here, and of ANU (Yahweh-Yanwu-Anu) as God in that Garden, and it speaks of the suffering of those that left the Garden so that humans that heard or read that story would be less inclined to try and escape the Annunaki. But the truth was that the Annunaki were few, (They are genetically engineered or evolved to have few offspring to avoid overpopulation issues on their home world to compensate for their very long lives.) and rather quickly humans were many, so among other things the loss of the many humans that escaped towards the wilderness and freedom was not a terribly important issue to the Annunaki as we were constantly replenishing the slave population (us) anyway.

Sex used to be the cheapest form of oddly compulsive entertainment for humans, and it was and remains a very effective methodology for replenishing the slave populations, as is currently reflected in the hidden policies of most of our religious and government institutions who maintain the creation of children psychologically to replenish their power base and the sum of their tithing taxes and so on. All the pyramid schemes that form the basis of human economic social structures on this planet currently; require a constantly expanding base layer to contribute to the programs, or they fail.

Then, back in the early days on the earth Enlil and Enki were in charge and they used us to build empires, but they got into arguments with each other and had many wars, during which they nearly destroyed each other and even this planet. Then the few Annunaki that survived went home and left us on our own, at least publically. There is all kinds of archeological evidence for the truth of this, but the most detailed actual accounts can be found in the ancient East Indian texts, and then if you read it correctly the Old Testament of the Bible.

It should be noted this writer did not ascertain that which follows immediately from direct experience but from research.

There is some confusion about when and where all this was first occurring. So far genetically and historically from archeological and human paleontological evidence, it appears we were first developed as true modern humans in South Africa, about 300,000 to 250,000 years ago, but the legends of our first appearance as an agriculturally sustainable society point to the Middle East in the Fertile

Crescent, not all that far from the true place of that beginning near Mohenjo Daro, now in western India.

It's reasonable to suspect that we were created in South Africa to mine the gold there but Enlil or Enki had an argument and one of them moved to the area around Mohenjo-Daro and the other to the Fertile Crescent and both took many of us along to start new and separate empires, and so the legends of our true creation, read the story in the book of Genesis, were in a sense fiction written by the leader of the new group in the Middle East for political reasons to assist in controlling the slave population there.

The reason this is all here is to install into your mind the reality that before Christ arrived, our existence and our metaphysical regimes were mostly controlled by metaphysical and physical machineries that had been emplaced onto our race by the Annunaki. Numerous great minds had shown up in these early times, several great Buddhas, great Hindu teachers, and numerous others but all of them simply pointed out how things worked at the time and few of them offered any true metaphysical alternatives to humanity and our souls.

The Mahayana Buddhists, currently related to Tibetan Buddhism, figured out pretty precisely how the reincarnation system that Anu had emplaced on us worked, and even figured out how to defeat it and grant freedom once again to human souls, but before Christ came along, relatively speaking the Mahayana knowledge was only granted to a select few.

When Christ came along he taught that he knew how to escape the reincarnation system in place, and so *he was the way* to escape that routine and go to heaven. The heaven he was talking about *when he was physically here* was known as the *Eighth Heaven*, this was a heaven that was well known to the Buddhists of the time, so that lends credence to the idea that Christ traveled to the East during the missing time in the documentation of his life with his uncle the tin merchant Joseph of Arimathea, but it also indicates he had experienced a great deal of travel astrally in his soul, similar in ways to what this writer has experienced, and so Christ understood just how to go to the then existing eighth heaven.

The point of this is that when Christ was here earning the right to be a god he had to speak about, teach about, and use things that already existed in metaphysical terms, but after he was crucified or at least when he had finished his teachings, he had earned the right to be a novice god in OM's eyes, and so he was taught by OM how to create his own heaven, and he did just that, he even said that he was going to do exactly that. "In my father's house there are many mansions, I go there now to build you one."

He was saying exactly 'I came here to earn the right to learn how too and earn the means and tools to build a new and glorious realm, for your souls to go to when you die so that you can escape being reincarnated back to this place, or be sent on to places far worse, and all you need to do to earn that passage is believe in me and what I am teaching you and then be a decent person. And I am going to do just that right away."

And that is exactly what he did. Now this writer has to explain a few details related to this.

First, this is not stuff learned by going to church and reading, as a young man this author was taken out of his body, placed entirely in his soul and taken quite a ways away to a place on the side of a great forested canyon where there was an ornate gate made of solid golden light and he climbed a stairway made of the same material until he came to a pavilion in the clouds, and met the living Christ.

That pavilion is where the silly business of heaven being a bunch of souls living on clouds came from, that Pavilion is the same one Jacob in the bible went to, it is just a way for Christ to travel about comfortably with a bunch of his friends and meet people Christ is interested in meeting; while the heaven he created for us is an entire huge idealized realm similar to the earth that people from Earth can relate to and do interesting things in when they are there. It's designed so that souls from earth will experience it as a brilliant safe secure and entirely positive actual place; and it shares other human souls with a wide contingent of angels, and a select few souls from other realms entirely.

If you want a more detailed description of this event and the pavilion read a copy of the Promontory by this writer or a copy of "The City of God" by the Venerable Maria of Jesus Agreda, or "Heaven is Real' by Todd Burpo.

Maria Agreda is still a true ongoing miracle; she was a devout Catholic in the early sixteen hundreds that never physically left her convent in Spain, but numerous people including several priests, left written accounts of meeting her in Texas and New Mexico where she often went in her spiritual body to evangelize to the locals. You can download her books for free on the Web and in the first one there is a paragraph where she talks about ascending a ladder, the same as the one Jacob in the Bible and this writer ascended. In her account she is in the company of angels and she met what she thought was God the father and Christ on the pavilion, sometime around 1620.

When this writer ascended the stairs of solid golden light into the sky he was alone but then he met several very important angels on the pavilion. Later on she like this writer became compelled to write about all of her experiences, and you may need to be patient as it were if you read her work, as she was a truly devout Catholic in the 1600's so she is full of guilt and almost ridiculously humble. However when she left her body that body was placed in an open coffin decorated with gold and cherubs and there is a picture of her on the Web. She looks exactly like a good looking lady that is laying there fast asleep, and she has been in that state of physical perfection for over four hundred years.

All the Popes since she died have investigated her life and attempted to make her a saint, a process that is apparently still going on as this is written, it is just a matter of opinion but if anyone deserves to be a saint it is the Venerable Maria of Jesus Agreda.

The latter book "Heaven is Real' was basically based on a story related by a child so the child apparently thought the place he went to was Heaven, it was not, again, it was merely a way, a place that Christ now uses to travel about with many of his friends, a pavilion that travels about to other realms that exist in the same universe that our soul exists in when it is outside of our physical body. It is a universe that in many ways is right here with us all the time but is also in many ways very different, and it allows things to occur that have little to do with the prohibitive physical laws that we only think control our entire existence while we are here.

It is also a universe that many quantum scientists are now becoming famous for, as the result of claiming that factors related to quantum mechanics demand the existence of just such a place, they just don't know anything about it. This writer has been there a few times so maybe just maybe he does.

Christ also apparently told Todd Burpo that the giant on the great throne was God the father, presumably as Christ thought it would be difficult for a child to understand that the 'bodies' Christ inhabits can now be many. This writer was interviewed at length by the giant version of Christ on that throne, but when that interview was over a more or less normal man in white robes walked out of a door on the side of that throne and spoke at length in a sort of relaxed way with the Author, and introduced this writer to several angels and arch angels including Gabriel the angel that Mohammed claimed or said dictated much of the Koran to him, and an old man with a white beard named Enoch. Despite the claims in some literature here, the Enoch this writer met had white skin. But he was in his soul's body so that he could be anything he wanted to be.

Perhaps it should be noted for clarities sake that as many have claimed wrongly, Christ can be or express endless copies of himself, but the truth of this is that even Christ can have only one motivating soul, but that the material of a soul, in a sense it's material expression, can be whatever the true soul or ID of that soul wants it to be. That which really is Christ to Burpo for instance can be a huge giant on a throne, but he can leave that body and become a normal man just by imagining up a different body, while the giant body simply remains quietly siting on the throne.

Some people have claimed that Christ can talk to anyone personally and there are millions of us that want to speak to him all the time, so that Christ must have millions of copies sort of like standing in front of opposing mirrors.

In actuality there are millions of angels that can assume this role and speak directly to you through the Holy Spirit, and their words will have the same value to your soul as if they were spoken by Christ. But this is an important caveat, if you hear someone speaking English or your normal language in your head, 95% of the time it is your own brain speaking and it probably has little value, but when you hear a very distinct voice that clearly comes out of the sky above and in front of you pay attention as what it says is probably the truth.

Actually meeting and speaking to the actuality of Christ is an extremely rare thing that few humans have enjoyed and this writer can say with certain authority it is a great blessing when it does occur.

When you go to church and you feel like you have been saved by Christ personally, and you feel filled with something slightly nebulous yet wonderful, what you are feeling is in fact the Holy Spirit that really can be anywhere there is consciousness, and the fact that Christ could perform this passage and experience of the Holy Spirit into any decent person that sought to know the presence of Christ inside of them is perhaps the greatest of Christ's miracles on the earth, because it saves innumerable souls and is responsible for that thing that is known as conversion.

This writer can also claim this with a degree of authority as he spent years in an organization related vaguely to Islamic Sufism, that is famous for invoking or inviting the Holy Spirit to manifest inside your inner being, where the Holy Spirit can on occasion manifest itself in ways that simply cannot be denied, and in that exercise the Holy Spirit does again on occasion and in often very subtle ways teach you to understand exactly what it is.

It should also be noted that Christ and Gabriel were obviously close friends and associates and so it is an incredible utterly unbelievable tragedy that so called Christians and Muslims have been at war with each other and murdering each other on this planet since the two religions existed.

This writer detailed and published his own account long before the book by young Burpo and his father was published and it's extremely unlikely Todd Burpo was one of the three people that actually paid a trifling sum for that book and so was able to read that before his own account was published.

The reason this Todd Burpo and the Maria Agreda accounts are here is that the three accounts are effectively identical, or they describe so many of the things and people on the pavilion in identical terms, so much so that it is effectively impossible for them to have been made up by all of us independently. To this writer, the alternative accounts utterly take away any possible interpretation that the accounts are fake, or the result of some imaginary dream experience, and so that demands that they are both real and represent the truth in a concrete way.

The Agreda account is particularly intellectually startling as it was written in the 1600 hundreds and her body is miraculously still perfect and with us today.

You can argue that all the accounts are something akin to dreamlike Jungian archetypes, but if you do that you have to admit that Jungian archetypes are utterly real, and so by default admit that these separate accounts are also real, at least on some level of experience.

The important point this writer is making here is that if the separate accounts are all indeed true, it is at least to this writer an unassailable certainty that Christ is alive now and at the very least conducting interviews with people on the Earth essentially right now; and that he has been doing exactly that for at least four hundred years, and that if he, Christ is alive now, we do have souls that live after we die, so that it might be a good idea to listen to what he was trying to tell us. Further, if Jacobs account was the truth and it obviously was to this writer, it means Christ was alive then, well before he experienced physical life here, and that is something to carefully ponder.

This is all here simply for you the reader as this knowledge was unassailably true to this writer. However this writer is constantly discounted as being a fool by academics so he is speaking partly to their critical arguments.

It is also important to note that there are two versions of Burpos Heaven is Real or nearly so, they are by different authors and the second version was made into a film, before the Authors of the second version came out and declared that he and his father made it all up, please do not get them confused. The other slight possibility is that young Burpos' father was one of the three people that actually purchased this writer's account of his own event and then used that to write his own account, but that is extremely unlikely.

In other words this is yet one more unassailable certainty that what is being told to you here is not some madness made up by some sci-fi lunatic, or some crazy man's philosophy designed to create a new religion to avoid paying taxes, it is instead the truth.

In addition, the story in the Bible related to Jacob's Ladder is again extremely close to details of the experience this writer underwent so that also tends to reinforce the validity of the event, and it is worth noting that in part the English royal family bases their so called royalty on the stone that Jacob rested his head on when the event occurred to him. The royal family keeps that stone under the primary throne of the British Empire.

All this most certainly does not mean you have to get up right now and go and give all your money to some so-called Christian church, but it does mean, if you care about your soul, which is very real, maybe you should listen up a bit and learn.

When Christ was here teaching he was trying to teach people how to be better more decent folks, so he said things like 'turn the other cheek' and 'forgive all sins'; he was not saying those were laws but that they were expressions of a better *attitude* about how to be. He was saying it is not a good idea to be absolutely judgmental, if you don't like the person you are dealing with at the moment, don't go to war with them and try to punish or kill them, simply walk away.

It is a very unfortunate fact that by far the majority of those that call themselves Christians have utterly failed to learn these teachings across human history since Christ was here, and they still fail to learn them. You simply cannot be right by claiming you are right by murdering everybody that does not believe exactly as you do; even if you call it something else like warfare. It is a certainty that the people that conduct their lives in this fashion will be discarded from the positive hierarchy with extreme prejudice. Murder by any definition even if you call it war to pretend to justify it for the sake of money, is the theft of the gift of life, it is the greatest sin there is.

Many self-declared Christians claim these days that Christ said he would forgive all sins and walk you right into heaven if you simply believe in Christ, and they take that to mean that they as Christians can be and do just about any monstrous selfish evil they can come up with and Christ will forgive them and they will be saved as a result.

That is pure unadulterated hog wallop, conjured up by utterly selfish hypocritical evil people including many of the so called Christian preachers who often do what they do just to get rich. Christ was simply trying to teach people how to be more decent and worthy.

The forgiveness of all sins business originally came from the Hebrew religion. Specifically the Rabbis would declare that you could rid yourself of any sins by merely writing them down on a piece of paper and signing it and then the Rabbi would tie them to the back of a goat and send that goat out into the wilderness. Of course later on the Rabbi would then go out into the same wilderness find the goat, read all the little notes and use what he learned to go back to the village and blackmail all the sinners to make him-self rich. The Catholics then carried that tradition on with 'confession' to in the same way empower the priests and enrich the church, and in the reformation the protestant's simply carried that nonsense forward in various ways.

Sorry Heath, it was a truly great story but there is no such thing as a sin eater anywhere.

Christ did not die on the cross to take all your sins away, if he actually did die on the cross, it was to earn the right to create his own version of Heaven and to earn the right to become a young God. You don't and can't get rid of your sins, they are stuck to your soul and they are all recorded exactly in the Akashic record in OM's mind and they determine exactly what will happen to your soul when you die.

So grow up people, try to become responsible adults now before it is far too late, it is for your own good as well as everyone else's.

The good news is that many so called sins were merely created by the various religious institutions to empower those institutions and the people that worked for them.

For instance; it is not a sin to have sex *in a responsible manner*, it is not a sin to use Jesus as an example as a swear word, he could care less, but it is a sin of sorts to blaspheme the Holy Spirit simply because it speaks to an *attitude* that damages your soul. Sin has to do entirely with failing to be responsible in your actions towards others, and the great sin is to steal someone else's life, by stealing everything they have earned. But the greatest sin is to murder anyone, in any way or form; including all the ways governments trick you into murdering innocent people by simply calling what they are tricking or forcing you into doing, *warfare;* murder, even the mere intent of murder is an abomination any way that it is done and it is almost never forgiven.

You may think that some of these words make it appear that this writer is belittling Christ or the many legends that have been attached to him. This writer has actually met Christ in the flesh so to speak. Christ is an utterly real fact to this writer; it is simply that much has been attached to Christ by the various religions that claim to speak for him that is totally ridiculous, so that this writer is simply trying to clear these issues up for everyone else.

To reinforce this, this writer as a result of reading a lot of very good and well researched literature, tends to believe intellectually in part, as the Cather's did, that Christ did not actually die on the cross but escaped with Mary Magdalene his wife and their children to southern France, where eventually he died of natural causes and many years later Mary died alone in a wilderness canyon in the French Alps, while their children went on to establish a very important line of kings and queens in Europe.

When he was here Christ taught the Gnostic way, the Zen way, seeking the light within, he taught that paradise was inside all of us and that is still the truth, and in this book this writer will detail exactly why that is true and exactly how to find that truth, the literal truth that was mentioned in the Gospel of St. Thomas, and in finding that truth you also find the path that leads to Sophia the true creator of all of us.

Very recently it has come to light that Christ was also teaching about the glory of Sophia and the Holy Spirit, both the sources of our creation, our experience of experience and the quintessential expressions of decency and positive being in creation.

But to fabricate their power over others the masculine voices of the Council of Nicea edited out all those teachings of Christ, and even as Mohammed did denigrated the feminine towards places of inconsequence and even perdition, and then even denigrated the beauty of the light within, that all Christ's first followers sought in the midst of the darkness. Quote from John the Apostle: 'There is a light shining in the darkness, and the Darkness cannot overcome it'.

While the priests in the Catholic Church still wear an endless variety of feminine attire, and still almost secretly and in a way correctly worship Mary almost as much as they worship Christ.

Even now the remaining Gnostics still seem to be obsessed with the belief that Sophia was feminine but had no real gender, and all kinds of people try to denigrate this into justifications for all kinds of insinuated perversions, again sex is not a sin, just for your own welfare and your partners try to be responsible.

This is related in a slightly subtle yet not so subtle way to something called anthropomorphism, the belief that everything must be interpreted from the belief that humans and the human experience comes first. But this attitude has been proven wrong since Copernicus. The sun does not rotate around the earth, the sun is not the center of everything, this galaxy is not the center of anything, even this Universe is not the end of everything, and mankind is certainly not the ultimate expression of anything and everything sentient. All of that is now fact, and it is a fact, we have souls that do not die when our bodies do, and our souls have no gender unless it is imagined by us as what we are when we are our souls entirely. There is nothing wrong with that it is just the way it is. Sex and gender is simply what we experience as what we are when we are here, if that was not so none of us would exist as physical human beings here and now, period.

If you question the fact of your soul, or think this writer is just saying this stuff to make a book he can sell, consider that reincarnation has now been effectively proven through documentation and research, and that astral projection events are now frequently the subject of academically approved research. If reincarnation and astral projection events are real it means you own a soul, this writer knows that as fact.

When we are in our souls sex is entirely about attitude, and while it may be difficult to ascertain these days in America at least; the feminine attitude, at least in its higher interpretations is primarily about giving and caring for others and creating new life and generating happiness for those nearby. This is only a small part of what Sophia granted to us, but it is an important part and it has come down to us across the ages usually intact, these are exactly the same attributes that Christ taught were right attitudes, and as he taught, these have nothing to do with pieces of paper with numbers on them, and borrowing those from counterfeiters to simply obtain large amounts of stuff.

It's obvious at this point to this writer that Christ met Sophia, just as this writer did, and that Christ simply knew just as this writer did when it happened that she is the *source* of everything and that she is glorious, quite beyond words.

This writer met Christ as a real living person not very long ago and as a result to this writer he is very real, so that whatever the truth of his life really is, obviously OM decided Christ had earned the right to be a God that currently lives in the realm of our souls, and that is what he currently is.

Christ was simply trying to teach that it is better to be a giving supportive type of person than a selfish always lying and taking person. Do any of you think Christ personally meets and judges every single dead soul that shows up on his doorstep? There are literally millions of us dying every single day now. Do you honestly think every total asshole human can simply walk into heaven if they simply believe in Christ?

This is how it actually works. There are millions and millions of angels that OM gave in service to Christ when Christ earned the right to act and be as a god; the universe or realm that all the angels, Christ and many others live in right now is right next to you right now, but you can only experience that reality during either an astral projection event when you are entirely in your soul, or after you die.

Scientists are only just now beginning to realize that there may be a scientifically justifiable way to ascertain this as a certainty, by coming to understand exactly what quantum mechanics really means.

The angels are tasked with the responsibility to act as judges on the personalities of souls, they do this even before people die here by simply experiencing the appropriate material in the Akashic Record, and then if they decide you are worthy to be saved, some of them show up and guide your soul to heaven through a wormhole of sorts that not only takes you someplace else, but also to another dimension or realm entirely, not simply to the realm you are in sort of overlaid but right here when you die, but someplace else entirely, a place that Christ created called Heaven.

To be clear, the place Christ was when this writer met him on the pavilion is in a realm that is shared with this realm but can only be experienced in an astral projection event or shortly after you die, but the true place of Christ's heaven is someplace else entirely; and the angels have to show up when you die and show you how to get there.

This writer has actually witnessed this occurring; the angels often sing music infused with the holy spirit as this occurs so that the newly dead will be enchanted by the wonder of the event and not be filled with fear, the angels often actually tell you to not be afraid as, their words, 'this is a perfectly normal and natural occurrence', and this writer has also heard numerous other related completely original accounts; it is once again, the truth of how things work, *if* you are a *decent* Christian.

These angels are true first class, to use the vernacular, 'homies', meaning they are utterly responsible for the types of people or souls that are allowed to inhabit the neighborhoods of Christ's true heaven. Do any of you think that just because you call yourself a Christian you can move into a house in Heaven and then spend all of your time while there trying to steal your neighbor's home in Heaven and everything else that neighbor has earned every day all day long, just like you do here?

This writer has clear memories of living in Heaven, there are no intrinsically selfish people there like there are here all over the place busy calling themselves Christians so that they can use that status to make decent people trust them so that it will be easier to rip off all the decent people they know, there are not any of those people in Heaven because *the angels in charge of the keys will not let them in.*

That last bit is related to the vernacular, in actuality it is almost impossible for a human soul to find Heaven on its own, the way it actually works is that very near the moment of death the angels will show up and they will guide your soul through a wormhole of sorts to get there. If they do not show up you are not going to even get to Heaven; and you have several alternative choices, take the bright light you will see with you souls eyes go through Anu's forty four days of transition and get reincarnated, take the dimmer light you may see and then get past the archon Anubis and you can enter the mind realm of God, (OM); just consider yourself warned if you do not get past the archon Anubis's' judgement, he will put you in a featureless room beyond time that you cannot escape from and you will probably be trapped there literally forever.

That room is where the story in the Bible about Satan being locked in a box for a thousand years comes from. In the Bible Satan is released after a thousand years for a while, but you can suspect that might not be the truth, and your soul has not earned the status of the equivalent of a God as Satan inexplicably has, so, well, just be careful. The realm of OM's mind has already been described by this writer in the 'Promontory'.

Another alternative is that it is likely the shadow demons will collect your soul and take you directly to the realms of Hell, finally nobody might show up and shortly after the event occurs if you were obsessed with this life, or an agnostic, your soul may become the equivalent of a ghost and wander the in effect mirror realm that is dimensionally right next to this one, often called the astral realm, until somebody good or bad locates you and collects you.

Then if you were a *decent* Muslim, angels from the arch angel Gabriel's crew will show up to take you to the Gardens of Allah, and finally if you are an old school Amerindian it is likely a few of your ancestors will show up and guide you in the mirror realm next door to what is commonly called the Happy Hunting Grounds, it sounds silly to some but it is a real place where you will be the equivalent of a ghost, but that you will experience as utterly real, until you find an alternative.

This writer used to live on what was once a property that contained a California Native American burial ground, and he met a few of their souls while there, so this is not in any way fictional.

Those are your choices, and unless you are a very sophisticated Mahayana Buddhist and you choose the lesser light and make it past Anubis to enter the mind realm of OM; Christ's Heaven and his angels or The Gardens of Allah are the safest alternatives. Remember, you will not be a prisoner in either Heaven, you can relax for a while and then chose another form of experience from there if you like, and if you are a total idiot like this writer, or even a truly golden soul like that of the Dalai Lama, you can even come back here once again. But it is critically important that you remember, those angels know exactly everything you did in this life and they simply will not show up unless you were a *fully decent true Christian* while you were here, and finally this writer is not absolutely certain about the baptism business but is pretty sure that even if you are baptized and then you live your life as a total asshole those angels simply will not show up period, but, well, it doesn't hurt to try it as an adult as it may make you think about these issues and so it might work.

The Heaven that Christ created is a great place to take a really grand vacation, you will feel absolutely secure, absolutely safe, absolutely comfortable and even ascendant and it will seem to you, when you are there, every bit as real, even more so, brilliantly more so, than your experience of this reality does, but it is not really a place to *grow* your soul, that requires challenge and a lot of us eventually figure that out and so we move on from Heaven and seek places more likely to offer us challenge and as a result hopefully result in the positive evolution of our souls.

By far the greatest miracle that Christ performed was one that none of us here witnessed; that was the creation of an entire realm he called Heaven, and it is a certainty to this writer that he accomplished that.

Try to imagine the complexity of the actual creation of an entire realm that really can act as a universal realm for the habitation and experience of millions of souls, and that can be experienced by those souls as utterly real. OM and Sophia have done it so many times that it has almost become second nature and they had trillions of years and endless opportunities to perfect their art.

But for Christ it was his first time, and you can't simply imagine what you want and make it happen perfectly. First you have to imagine the physical laws of the place, then all those laws have to work together perfectly, then you have to know exactly what the benefactors, us for instance, will enjoy living in, and you have to do a localized physical bestowal as one of your subjects just as Christ did. Then you have to find a location that's appropriate outside of this physical universe so that the physical laws will not be in conflict and so that you will not be infringing on the stuff that's already here.

Remember Christ was not trained as a modern day physicist or even a mere architect; he was in his last incarnation here trained as a simple yet accomplished holy man, in a sense an elevated hobo, living in a world that was comparatively intellectually very primitive. Technology of any sort other than weapons to murder other folks was basically non-existent.

As a result, and this is critically important, you have to go and visit either OM or Sophia and spend vast amounts of time with them learning exactly how to realize anything you can imagine into some form of reality, and exactly where and how to do that.

This writer does know that Sophia could have taught him how to do this with merely a momentary breeze of knowledge, and it is likely that Christ actually did know about Sophia as he rather subtly implied that she exists in his words that were granted to us in the book that was kept from us by the Catholic Church called the Gospel of St Thomas, regardless it is simply more likely that he went to learn from OM, or from as he said 'the father', and OM is not in any way a very patient person, he has endless amounts of time at his disposal but when this writer met him he seemed to be rather busy about something, so to use the vernacular he just showed up said hi, said he was very proud of everything 'we' had accomplished and then left. This writer never understood what exactly OM meant by the term 'we', but that's another story. Regardless this writer suspects that Christ had to go to the library of God near the Promontory, and in a sense spend a huge amount of time learning from what amounts to books on the theory and practice of realm creation and then he had to apply what he learned over and over again to work out all the kinks and mistakes until he got it right.

Then he had to sit up all the venues related to the angels and what they needed to do to make it all work. But he did all of that and he actually did create his own heaven, primarily for the decent humans that believed in him. It truly is a miraculous accomplishment, and he did all of that, that is a certainty that by any definition earns him the right to be worshiped and granted our thanks for what he did, as a god
.

Before him, we were stuck on this planet as slaves, after him we were granted the opportunity to go to Heaven when we died, and if or when we are foolish enough to leave that place, from there we can go anywhere in creation. It is a truly grand accomplishment and one we should be very grateful for.

So please people, grow up and try to act like responsible adults, as if you do you will eventually be able to go on and have a bit of fun.

Chapter Two
A Synopsis of OM's Creation
The Mother of All Magic
And of Our Souls

OM has a masculine mind and Sophia has a feminine mind, for her it was enough just to figure out that if she desired something it would arrive into her reality, while OM always took a slightly more intellectual or technical approach to the things he created. And no this is in no way disparaging the feminine mind; Sophia's method is in ways superior to OM's it just requires a rather esoteric alternative to make it work.

OM has a tendency to dream up new things as he sleeps, and he remembers those things *perfectly* when he wakes up. He then analyses them in an intellectual way when he is awake, and he has an immense brain, so that he can make holistic analysis that are immensely complex entirely inside his mind and when he is satisfied they are worthwhile he imagines them into reality as initially tiny expressions and then if he likes them he blows them up until they are relatively as big as our universe is. Sort of like a very tiny bit of holographic material can be blown up into a gigantic T3D image simply by illuminating it correctly with a laser.

And once again our science recognizes this occurred exactly as described as something called inflation that once again occurred far faster than the speed of light in a few seconds or minutes after the so called big bang event occurred.

Okay so according to science and a variety of other so called deep thinkers, the universe we live in is a giant expression of a three dimensional realm projected from a seven dimensional ultra-tiny expression, and according to this writer as the result of direct personal experience it was all imagined up by the mind of our Creator, OM, and then it was technically inflated to grant us the reality and the experience of reality that we currently enjoy.

What is OM up too, why is he creating creation? First you have to understand, your mind, not your brain but your mind, is a particle of the spectrum or field of consciousness, and like all quantum particles it has the ability to transmit and receive information in rather esoteric ways. This structural capacity is in every single independent self-aware individual in Creation, not simply in humans. This capability sends virtually everything you or any of us experience and every thought any of us sentients have, directly into a technical aspect of the mind of OM, this is known in metaphysical literature as the Akashic Record, and it does not infect OM's consciousness all day long and make him crazy as a result, it is just accessible to him and a wide variety of others like angels for instance; you need to understand this as it means among other things that in truth…

1. Everything you do and experience, *everything*, is known and recorded basically forever and 2. One of the things OM is trying to do is to understand every possible experience of experience; and all the ways experience can be experienced, all of them.

He is also in the process of growing gods… that is our evolutionary reward, our destiny, too eventually, if we succeed, become god's ourselves, so that in many cases we can then go out and commence new universes and multiverses full of sentient people that eventually may grow up and begin their own multiverses, this is OM's methodology for bringing order to the chaos of infinity, it's similar in a way to what the Holy Spirit did so very long ago, but also entirely different and far more potentially complex. But OM's operations are merely a bubble, a percolation, in infinity, while what the Holy Spirit did is effectively everywhere there is anything related to consciousness at all.

And in part by doing this OM is also building a massive fortress that will protect consciousness, the experience of experience or the knowing, and creating a record of intelligent thought and accomplishment forever, thus protecting and expanding on what the Holy Spirit injected into consciousness in the very beginning.

He is also by doing all this, defeating the stasis of the chaos of infinity.

Also you need to remember that in the early days after he broke up with Sophia, OM was quite alone, so part of what he is doing is trying to make new gods that maybe just maybe will eventually become worthy of valuable conversation with him, In other words become his friends.

And then again as detailed in the Promontory, the ultimate Copernican truth; humanity is not the primary race in Creation, not by a long shot. The Earth is not the center of the universe, the sun and its system of planets is not the center of anything, this galaxy is not the center of anything, and this entire universe is not the center of anything. Our entire universe exists in a great sea and it is just a single drop in that sea.

There is, in the realm of OM's mind, an entire sea, a sea of a type of pink and golden foam that is alive, and from above that sea of foam you cannot see a horizon, it is vast beyond belief... and from the Promontory above it our entire universe is so tiny in cannot be discerned as a single bubble. All those bubbles in that sea are unique and different and all those universes have been blown up and projected out into infinity, just as our own has. And in many of those universes beings have evolved until they are building their own multiverses and projecting them out into infinity.

That which OM-Yaldaboath originally commenced has grown in evolution and stature quite beyond any individual human's ability to comprehend.

This writer has been there and flown over that sea fully awake and functional, as the equivalent of a manta ray made of light, as a type of God, and even briefly met the Creator of that Sea and of us. OM is a very truly noble individual, and in an immensely positive way proud of what he has done, he should be, for what he has accomplished is grand beyond all forms of comprehension, and it will live on and evolve forever.

Yep at this point it may seem quite reasonable for the reader to have decided that this writer is quite thoroughly insane, that's just fine, and you are more than welcome to dismiss all this as mere fiction, but the problem with the possibility of this writer's insanity, is that by all normal psychiatric and psychological parameters this writer in actuality qualifies as perhaps one of the most boringly sane persons on this planet, especially if you watched the news while this was being written and discovered exactly what kind of humans are supposedly qualified to be the President of America these days.

Anyway, now we can get on with the meat and potatoes; Sophia and her magical realm.

This description of how to get to the Lady's realm, or at least to the realm at the heart of your own soul may sound like it has to be incredibly simple to accomplish, but because of what we are and how our brain-minds usually work it may or can be incredibly difficult to achieve, and you must absolutely understand that if you do make it to the outside of the Lady's actual realm it is entirely up to her as to whether or not she will let you in, and then maybe after several visits she might determine that it's okay to waste a tiny bit of her own time talking to you, by sending you a breeze that's literally packed with reams of information. And she will only let you in if you own a truly decent and purified soul, so don't even bother to try until you have done the necessary purification work on your inner being.

Probably in this context the finest place to get that work done is a Zen monastery, in part because it was a great Zen master that in a very esoteric yet curiously bizarre and humorous way showed this writer how to get there the first time.

Simply relax and close your eyes, than insist that all the words your brain is constantly manufacturing go away entirely for as long as you can make that happen, and it can take you months of constant practice to figure out how to do this, until it is no longer the main silliness you are totally concentrating on, and you can just simply do it.

You can lie on your back in bed or sit Zen only if you are physically comfortable doing that, but however you do it the most important thing is to constantly stay *perfectly awake* inside your mind space, with no words and as little noise or other sensory input as possible. Zen masters walk around the hall with a stick and tap or even sometimes hit the practitioners hard on the shoulder or back to keep them awake while they meditate which is sort of a bad word, worse than simply sitting.

On occasion getting hit hard with that damn stick can lead you directly to Satori but that's another story.

Anyway when you are perfectly comfortable in your blank mind space, you have to begin imagining without any words that your mind space is growing brighter, that it is somehow becoming illuminated, and you have to keep concentrating on that light and immersing your consciousness inside of it. Initially this may seem to be sort of pointless, even a little stupid, but keep it up. It helps if you remember a brilliant dream without words and you think about, again without words, how you were experiencing that dream and then focus on the reality that that dream was experienced in a brilliant light, than ask yourself 'where in the heck did that light that lit my dream come from; my eyes were obviously closed and I was inside my dark head dreaming.'

If you are astute you may think this is implying that where we are going with this is merely some kind of enhanced dream exercise. Well guess what it is, but the remarkable thing about it is that enhanced dream states are where all miraculous things and all true magic can happen, the hard part is once you learn how to do it there, you have to learn how to bring it back here and make it happen inside your head when you are perfectly awake, and enhanced dreams states are how all of creation is created so listen up if you want to learn how to eventually become a god.

Stay awake and keep on searching for the light, eventually you will find it and get a handle on how to grow the light into something that gradually gets brighter. There is no way to tell you exactly how to make this inner light with words, you have to discover it in a wordless innate way, by simply seeking to do it until you actually discover how to do it, you have to create a wordless venue, a path to make it happen inside your mind and then you have to learn how to wordlessly and mindlessly invoke it.

There is a powerful yet subtle difference here between what you are doing and a regular dream state, first of all you must remain at all times _wide awake,_ there is no transition state allowed that leads you into sleep, second there is nothing in the light, nothing at all, just pure simple uncluttered light that is gradually getting brighter. If you are a hopeless academic you can study something called a hypnogogic state, just remember, no words at all are allowed.

In this context visualizing *stuff* is like words, you must now learn to experience this not with stuff that your brain might create as in dreams, or say mentally when you are awake like an architect or a true artist learns to do, it has to be pure unadulterated light and nothing else at all to pollute that realization of perfect light.

Eventually you may notice or feel something undefined just beyond the light coming towards you, if or when that happens simply feel that you are inviting it in, and that thing will arrive in your mind state on occasion with a spectacular suddenness, and with an utterly uncanny brilliance.

When it happens your mind state will seem like you are in an entirely undefined place absolutely filled with brilliant light, sort of like you are on a yacht in a cloudless noon day sun looking out over the still sea, it really is astonishing and almost unbelievable but obviously it is real as you are in the process of experiencing it right now. But in the back of your mind you always simply assumed that the inside of your skull must be dark all the time.

You might be inclined to open your eyes, but then you need to realize that obviously your eyes are already open and then you realize that you really are someplace else entirely and *wide awake*.

This is a key realization, *you are fully awake yet someplace else entirely*. Something sort of subtle but not subtle at all will occur, and you will realize that the realization is the actual truth; you really are in a cosmic sort of dimensional or metaphysical way, someplace else entirely and *wide awake*. It might help when in a normal intellectual mind state to look up *hypnogogic* state in a good psychology book, it is just an explanation of what you are seeking in acceptable academic terms, but it is a very sterilized example of what you can actually find there; yet again, it means being utterly awake with your eyes closed.

As John the gnostic apostle said; 'there *is* a light in the darkness and the darkness cannot overcome it.'

As this implies, it is a form of enlightenment, but it is only a form, true Satori is when your entire body is filled with the Holy Spirit and that is a very different thing, this writer has experienced both conditions and he can say with certainty that both are well worth the time you may invest in trying to find them.

But of course it will not help your career and it may even make it harder to make money selfishly, but it will enhance the quality of your soul, it is simply up to you to decide which is more important.

Okay this is important, if or when you have found this light or this featureless place of brilliant light in your mind, you want to imagine once again without words that what you are, your soul, everything that is important about you, goes into that light, so that it becomes not just something that you are making inside your skull, *but that all of you crosses over into the light.* If you are doing it right you may feel a very subtle feminine presence that will seem to assist you in a very subtle way, and you will suddenly, *WAKE UP!*

Now you experience a different level of being awake someplace else, it is almost the most real thing you have ever experienced, and now all of a sudden you realize that you have fully arrived.

Again, you will feel like you are utterly wide awake, and staring up at the brilliant light but there will be no sun or star, just a brilliantly lit featureless sky, and you will feel all of a sudden that you are lying on your back floating in a sea with virtually no waves at all, and then you may feel like you are bending your head around to try to find any land, but initially there will be no land, it will not even be possible to see any horizon because the sea is flat and a perfect reflection of the sky, the only way you can really tell you are in water is that it feels like you are in water.

Then it will hit you suddenly like a brick flying into your head, but in a good way, you are utterly and absolutely awake and what you are awake inside of is absolutely and utterly real, yet again it simply feels like *the most real thing you have ever experienced,* but initially you may try to see your hands and for a brief moment there will be no hands and then because you are trying to see your hands, because *you desire them to be there, they will be there.*

Initially you will probably not notice the incredible importance of what just happened, but eventually in the future when you reflect on the details of the event you will.

Two notes: When and if this event begins to unfold, the various stages can occur with varying degrees of suddenness and brilliance, and if you are capable of understanding subtlety you may understand that these things are occurring as they are, more easily than you expected, because the Lady is assisting you, and if you can find this feeling that she is assisting you remember it, as it may help you when you find the outside of her actual realm, her *version* of the realm you are now in, as that is how you can call her without words and ask her to let you in, you feel like she is already helping you so that means she has approved of you already.

And, if you are a typical psychiatrist or even just a typical twisted male, this is not an allusion to something about sex, this is an allusion about two people who are acting like merely platonic but honest friends. And no this, the Lady's egg and the sea and so on is not a physical allusion about a womb and your mother and so on, but it is the actuality, the equivalent of the realm of the mother of all living creatures in this Creation and it seems like an allusion, to being a whole lot about sex and females and creating life and giving birth and so on, precisely because all of that in our world and across creation is patterned often almost perfectly on this actual reality, so invert your assumptions.

When you find yourself floating in that sea with no horizon or land in sight you may feel a slight fear that you could drown or get stuck there forever, forget it and do not linger on the fear, it is pointless and in that place fear can become very real simply because you can imagine it up as real, but more likely it will simply pass you by like a brief glance.

And then you may notice something else, it seems utterly ridiculous initially but you feel like laughing. Yes that's right as absurd as it may seem, if you get carried away you will choke on the water and curl up in a belly laugh and sink and drown, but the feeling is contagious, so go with it, you can't drown here, and even though there is apparently no bottom to the sea, all you have to do is imagine you are floating on the top and you will be.

That sea is the original sea in this multiversal creation, and the technical methodology this writer used to get entirely into his soul and then go to the *Promontory above OM's separate sea of creation*, is based on a manipulated acoustical sound bite known as 'steam-bubbles' or simply bubbles. If you get it right your mind will experience or hear bubbles that seem to be ascending around you, and you feel like you are gently falling deep into that sea, and if you sort of look up with your eyes closed you will see the mirrored undersurface of that sea slowly dimming as you descend, while you are really just sitting in a chair. It's likely that OM created this pan universal incredibly powerful tool as an homage to the laughing sea, as a kind of expression of gratitude to Sophia, and to the Holy Spirit as well.

Eventually, when you are there in Sophia's Sea, but not in OM's Sea of Creation, the laughing fit passes by but you feel incredibly good as a result, then you are lying there on the water and nothing happens at all for a while, and after a bit you notice it might be nice to make something, anything happen, but what, what in the heck can you do in the middle of a perfectly flat sea, with absolutely nothing at your disposal, perhaps a few swells or waves would be nice, something anything, and the sea begins to move and makes swells and waves, so you grow the waves, and as they get bigger you notice the whitecaps and you feel like the waves are laughing, not at you but with you.

    This writer was at a restaurant in Carmel Valley California eating a jack and avocado sandwich on sourdough when a group of monks from the Tassajuara Zen Monastery walked in a sat down at the table behind him and one of them was Suzuki Roshi the great Zen Master. This writer recognized him not because he knew him but because he had been to the monastery a few times simply to take in the hot springs and this writer was for moment turned around and curiously starring at Suzuki's back, mostly thinking how lucky he was not to be a monk.

    Suzuki turned around and very briefly their eyes met and locked and a brilliant image appeared in the writer's mind of Suzuki sitting in an old cast iron bathtub floating in a laughing sea. But along with that image in a very subtle way reams of knowledge about how to get there and why it was important arrived along with the image.

    Of course at the time the writer just turned around and continued eating his sandwich, sort of oddly curious about the event but dismissing it as again his endlessly irritating pecker's brain just didn't really want to become a Zen monk.

    But this was an event of telepathic magic of a sort, so if you are reading this book to learn about magic, listen up and think about it, impossible things can occur, and they do… just usually in unexpected ways at unexpected times.

The point of all of this is that that place, the laughing sea, and that realm, the realm you are in when there, *is the center of your soul* and it is exactly the same as The Lady of The Lakes realm, but it is still in an odd way separate from hers, but and this is important, when you are there you are not subject to the physical laws of this realm and you can travel to other realms that are the center of other people's souls if and this is also important, *if they are inclined to let you in*. No matter how far away they are located in creation or in other dimensions, *instantly*.

Academic physicists need to pay attention here, the constraints of space and time in this physical universe are an illusion of sorts, they are experienced as real and they are real here, but you can call it wormholes or entanglement or alternative realm like dimensions, but sort of as Alain Aspect said, 'when you look carefully at the real nature of things a hidden sense of order seems to exist'. In the pure context that he said that, it is difficult to understand what he was talking about. But and this is incredibly important as it is the key to unlocking the door to understanding perhaps the most important realization about creation in an academically valid manner.

Consciousness is the fifth force, actually it is the first force of five applicable to the physical laws of this universe, and once you understand the complexities the structures and the incredible versatility and reality of consciousness you can begin to unravel from that knowledge the many ways that physical reality actually works. You can go to a place inside your mind where time and space in their normal sense do not exist and consciousness as a type of force rules everything. Once you really understand how this works, you can understand how and why, wormholes, particle entanglement, the multiple dimensions of string and its related theories work and so on. Basically you can solve every issue of physics and in doing that you can understand how to travel to the stars in this universe instantly, how to make anything you need or desire at no cost at all, and perhaps most importantly how exactly to be a decent human being and join the glorious family of life in this universe and many others. *Every single point and place in creation is immediately connected*; **and they are all entirely unique**, *and ultimately consciousness rules them all."*

If you are an academic physicist, or even simply a humble pilgrim, that last sentence is the most important group of words you will ever read, so memorize it, think about it, and contemplate the implications, *because it is the truth,* it unlocks the universe, and it opens remarkable doors in your mind... because all of us that are sentient, own a taste of being a God, and that is one of the greatest gifts that he, OM, gave to all of us.

All you need to do to do this is to *listen;* while you are inside your own center, inside your own laughing sea, the center of your soul's mind, and if you hear a voice that sounds interesting, you simply sort of call out to that voice and it will hear you, and if that voice thinks you sound interesting it may invite you in. Don't worry too much about getting trapped elsewhere as you can just imagine you are back home in the center of your own soul and you will be instantly back home.

Knowing about all of this is how demons can possess innocent humans, it is how Satan can own your soul, it is how advanced creatures from anywhere in creation can communicate with anyone anywhere in creation and it is how the truly important technologies and regimes of intelligence are communicated across creation. Different galaxies, eons away at the speed of light, it matters not.

But and this is hugely important, just like the lady has shown, nobody, *nobody can get into the center of your soul unless you invite them in!* On rare occasions somebody may be too innocent, and as a result may accidently acquiesce and allow others to come in that should not be there. Christ and the Holy Spirit have granted us the means to eject them when that happens, but if it does happen you might need to get help to accomplish the exorcism, so the best course of action is to be aware of this at a young age and not let it happen in the first place. Young women are particularly subject to this as it is a part of their basic psychology to invite others into their being. And no this writer is not being or approving of pedophiliacs here it just is what it is, part of being a female.

Also remember that when you are there, again as it is important, there are no physical laws like we have here and no time like we have here so you can be in that realm for literally years of experience time and when you 'wake up' or come out of it back here, you may notice quite oddly that only a few moments have passed when you were someplace else entirely.

Okay the point once again. When you are there, you have in effect exactly the same magical powers as Sophia, meaning if you desire something, anything at all, it will arrive in your reality. One time when this writer was there, actually in Sophia's version of this realm, on a tropical island of young coconut trees, silly as it seems he felt hungry and desired a cheese burger and silly and even gross as that might seem in context the burger was in his hand, and it was the best tasting meal he can remember ever eating.

The point is that when you are on that sea one of the things that may occur is that you will desire some kind of dry land and so a beach will appear, the one this writer found was a tropical island with coconut trees, even lots of young ones in a breeze, it is when you experience that here on earth the first time, a truly magical experience, but this happened far before this writer was introduced to that reality here, the island simply appeared utterly complete and real. Then a wave picks up your soul body and deposits you on the beach. This was way before the movie 'Contact' and way before this writer went to Tahiti and the Tuamotus to design a resort, it just was there and for what it's worth the one time this writer actually did meet The Lady of the Lake there, in *her* realm, she also had a tropical island with coconut trees, but this writer never knew if she liked that or if she put that there to make this writer feel comfortable.

And this is incredibly important if you are a sterilized psychologist you can obviously disassemble all of this and state with flaky academic authority that this is all obviously a dream related event and it is just your brain accessing your memories, and displaying them graphically in the map room of your brain as brilliant dream events and this writer simply cannot academically prove them wrong, at least until others go to this place and bring back technologies and knowledge that humans cannot possibly have found here.

However those same academic psychologists cannot really explain what a dream really is or how it or all kinds of things about dreams really work. So that it is still possible that dreams may actually be far closer to the manifestation of the true nature of reality, that may simply be hidden behind doors accessible when we dream, that are normally minimized so that the awake reality we experience when here will merely seem more real to us when we are here. Meaning we must be incredibly simple and yes stupid that we can't recognize the truth of what we are and what we live in when that truth is always with us right inside our own minds.

You simply need to invert the valuation we grant to dreams as opposed to being awake to find a greater expression of the truth of what we are, but you can only do that by learning to be awake inside your dreams in order to find the true and yes magical expression of what we really are, and then rather miraculously we can find out the fullness of what we can be, and the truth is that that is and can be in this context almost immediately the equivalent of a God.

Physics of Consciousness

You simply have to find the right doors inside the dream realms and then open them up and walk through.

And if you can find doors to alternative realms in the dream state that you can experience in a full on awake state is it not reasonable that you can also find doors inside the dream realms that allow you to do whatever you can do in a dream state back here in this world. It is a fact that if you want to do exactly that, that you can. However if you do find the appropriate doors and you bring that power back here and you abuse it to damage the lives and the experience of life of other innocent people around you, and other Gods for that matter, OM and even Sophia will certainly know about it, they are our parents and we are their children, and they will punish you for being what you have become so just be careful, and please learn what it takes to own a decent soul.

When you are there you are experiencing everything as utterly and absolutely real and you feel utterly wide awake, and in that place you can instantly create anything you desire, in other words, one thing is certain, you don't have to believe this writer but maybe you should believe the words of Christ as he said quite clearly in 'The Testament of St. Thomas', 'Paradise is already inside of you' this is exactly what he was talking about, and any of us can go there and live there forever and be an absolutely powerful sorcerer or even a God eventually while you are there, and even maybe if you find the right doors here as well.

And this is very important if you go there often enough the reality of that place will become normalcy to your soul and you will eventually learn how to bring it back here, and manifest all sorts of white magic here. This is what the story of Merlin and the Lady of the Lake was really all about, and the stuff that Merlin taught Arthur all about was really why Arthur became the first truly beloved king other than Christ in humanities history.

This writer knows as fact that this is the truth, he just never thought that learning to be a sorcerer and how to do real magic and miracles here was terribly important, because in part living with and in perfection concerning stuff and things is as has already been noted, a rather a boring thing, and well he always thought humility and decency were far more important things to really learn about.

One final note; after you have learned to go to this place, the center of your soul and then gone and spoken to the Lady, on your own, the Lady Sophia may come to you in a brilliant dreams and make you wake up inside the dream, which does two things and implies a host of wonders. First making you wake up makes the dream seem like you are utterly awake which you are, and it makes the dream seem to be taking place in a realm that is utterly real, which it is, but it is a very different place where the physical laws of this world do not always apply.

Usually when in one of her dreams this writer wakes up in a very dry forest of sort of small trees like Bay or Laurels, on a small hill above a pond of water that is a deep blue color. In the far distance there is a range of mountains across a desert shimmering with heat, and the mountains are varied shades of gray with not a tree on them, just hot dry gray stone. It seems or feels very hot and dry, that feeling is very rare in normal dreams, and the sunlight is intensely bright but there is never a sun in the sky.

So this writer walks slowly down barefoot through the hot sand and then wades into the pond, the water is not terribly cold, but it is cool and refreshing so he lays on his back and closes his eyes and floats, and then in a couple of minutes he opens his eyes and looks to where the mountains were but they are no longer there, and there is not even a horizon, and then he realizes he is either in that place at the center of his own soul or in Her version of that realm, and he is floating on his back in the midst of the laughing sea.

So far normally she doesn't talk or even present herself, except well just one time, but when he is in *her* realm he can oddly feel her presence, it's sort of like she's just curious to see if he's okay. This writer met a coconut once that could roll around the beach on its own, he picked it up and it had three very intelligent eyes that could blink, but other than that this writer never experienced a living thing other than the Lady Sophia once when there. Once he did find a big rock with a tunnel in it up in the coconut trees, when he saw it he simply knew that he or the Lady can or could take a form that can never be damaged in any way, and by entering that tunnel can go anywhere in creation instantly, it's slightly different than listening to others and then asking them to invite you in, from that place you can just go anywhere you want instantly, but then only as a sort of odd ghost when you get there, but he simply decided not to try it. It is probable that she uses that place frequently, so like a ghost in a way she could very well be right beside you right now, listening or even granting your soul a blessing and maybe smiling at you with approval as you sit alone and write silly words on a computer.

This writer does have to say, when you are there, and you meet the Lady. She rises out of the sea a slight distance away and she seems like a normal human lady dressed in an electrically constantly moving diaphanous multicolored iridescent dress, and you have this feeling of utter awe and you just know that you are talking to the true Creator of virtually everything.

At the same time in a very odd way she seems to be perfectly normal and oddly sort of humble. And you feel an oddness related to her loneliness, it is the utterly absolute expression of that feeling, then at the same time you know she has dealt with it entirely, but again oddly it is almost like an independent creature, a real thing, and you feel that she is still looking for a friend, but in a very subtle way you know that friend has to be worthy of her, and you understand that such a being, a worthy candidate for her friendship, simply does not exist. It makes her very, _very_ special in a strange and melancholy way. More personable, even though once again you know with absolute certainty that she is the true creator of everything.

She might simply lift up her hand and wave it slightly and a breeze will come out that you can sort of see rippling, but you can't actually see, and then it hits your head and you feel it and you suddenly know everything of value that she wants you to know. Then she waves and descends standing up, back into the water. And no this writer has never seen her holding a sword. For what it is worth he has met the Arch angel Gabriel as well and people that claim to have met him often claim he is also carrying a sword, this writer has not seen that either.

But then it is a certainty that all the Gods and Arch angels can appear exactly as they want to appear at any time, so who knows the truth of that issue.

What you need to take away from this is that, the true Creator of everything is utterly and absolutely real, and alive right now, and in ways she is a truly nice decent and oddly humble person, that even you can or may meet her when your dreams become real, and just about everyone else in this universe knows that with a sense of absolute certainty. And that all you need to do, is to seek her out in ways that have just been shown to you, and well worship her and honor that worship by being a decent person, as heaven really is inside of you, and if you want too you can go there when you die, to the realm she has already granted to everyone in creation and live there forever in true paradise, or you can go to the Heaven that Christ built for you if you are a decent person, It's entirely up to you and how you live your life.

Chapter Three
The Classical Three Points of Magic

The classical three points of the magic triangle:
1. The willing suspension of disbelief: This is a rather intentionally obfuscating collection of words that means that what you have been taught normally in life on this planet is usually largely wrong, and that you need to re-learn the occasionally odd *truth,* and then willingly come to believe the strangeness of what that truth really is, in the same way that for instance you sort of innately know that down is where it is because of gravity. It is also saying that all the stuff you have been trained to believe is impossible, is not impossible at all. Most of the time you are trained to believe as you believe as that training makes it easier for those empowered above you use the beliefs they have infected you with to make it easier for them to use you as in effect and reality their slaves.

Just as a simple example, according to normal regimes, money is *everything*, if you don't believe that just ask your girlfriend, and if you don't have money you will starve so if you run out of money you acquired by being somebody's slave, who simply paid you with pieces of paper they got from their own slave master, a banker effectively for free, you will starve unless you own a credit card.

Then other people are telling you if you are a typical lady, that no man will want you unless you own sixteen pairs of outrageously expensive shoes, so you go out and buy those and you are now enslaved to that credit card at twenty percent interest for the rest of your life.

Or, you won't get a decent job unless you go to college, where your professors are paid half a million a year to conduct five one hour lectures a month usually about utterly ridiculous things, but you have to pay for that on credit and the same thing happens. So the first thing you are introduced to as an adult is called indentured servitude, in both cases and thousands of others you ultimately voluntarily become a slave to the bankers, and those bankers did not hand over money to you that belonged to them in any way, they handed you money they created out of thin air simply by performing the act of loaning illusionary money to you and making a notation on a piece of paper or even just making a truly ephemeral note in a computer.

It works, simply because everyone believes it works. It's called Sumerian Money Magic, and it has been emplaced onto essentially every human on this planet by the bankers, who then just sit back and collect the assets that everyone else spends all their time and sweat and intelligence creating for them, so that they can then merely gamble it away with impunity.

They make it work because everybody, when you are growing up is led to believe that it is the only way you can survive, but that is a lie, based on a false system on this planet that has been going on for so long that everyone simply believes it is the truth.

Christ hated the bankers, so among other things there is no money in Heaven, if you need something it is simply given to you, but after a short while there you will learn to make anything you need by simply imagining it up, the same way that was explained in the material about Sophia and OM. That's the way it works on the other side everywhere.

And in this physical universe, as will be addressed later in greater detail, it is possible to develop technologies, so that everything you could possibly need or want can be created by mindless machines that nobody in particular owns; even food and energy… the Solipsi Rai just as one example were only maybe fifty years ahead of where we are now in technological terms, two billion years ago, when they were able to accomplish exactly that.

This may seem somewhat trivial but it is not. G.I. Gurdjieff spent a huge amount of his time and energy trying to defeat exactly this, the inherent installed beliefs we are all saddled with; he tried to do it with all kinds of exercises and routines that seemed on the surface to be downright silly, but it is important and it has to do with the defining mindset you acquire as you evolve on this planet, and it is one of the primary tools the so called Illuminati controlling folks use to manipulate all of us into being their willing slaves, that mindset when emplaced across cultures and societies, gestalts into being one of the primary pillars of Sumerian Money magic.

It is why many feel they live in an engineered reality that is wrongly abusing them; but they just cannot quite figure out exactly what is going on. Our academic system is the primary factor that supports this and installs it in our society, and if you are successful in it and or rich you get to go to college, and virtually all of our leaders in this planetary culture have gone through that level of indoctrination.

In college you are universally taught that you can only think in an evolutionary manner based on very select ideas and systems that have already been accepted, you have been taught that Machiavelli was a very accomplished and intelligent guy that is to be lauded instead of being condemned as a monster, you are taught that if you want to be successful you should join a club of already wealthy and powerful Satan or money worshipers, or worse you should learn to be a professional liar commonly known as an attorney or even worse a politician; and that results in these kinds of people being in charge of our cultures and often indirectly everybody's lives.

President Reagan coined a mindset that said money trickles down from the rich, when actually money trickles up from the poor and only makes the rich richer, just look at how many more truly rich folks there are and how many really frigging poor people there are now since he was in office; and by far the majority of the rich are rich *not* because they are truly creative and culturally beneficial folks but because they were born with money or they knew people with money and often as the result of pure circumstances that were beneficial to them, and or they are inherently unethical.

But this issue goes far deeper than that, because we are all particle aspects of the cloud of consciousness, there is a gestalting cloud of things that very subtly affects the ways we think and as a result the ways we act, and that cloud is self-reinforcing, subtle and powerful, as we just cannot put our finger on exactly what it is that is making us think and act the ways we do, but that cloud is real, and the major unsubtle daily voice of that cloud is our major media.

Just ask yourself, perhaps when you are mindlessly driving along, really just deeply try to understand it. *'Why am I doing what I am doing, is it making me happy and fulfilled, will it advance me towards a better understanding of what I really am and my immortality, is there more to life than this BS? And if so what else is there that might be more important?'*

If you really try to do that the first thing you will notice is a sort of thought wall that refuses to allow you to answer that question with any kind of authority. That wall is the first indication that something very odd is going on; it is also the first step in seeking to understand alternative possibly more positive ways of being.

You have been taught that impossible things are impossible so why bother to try to learn how to make them happen, but the people that say such things simply believe the paradigms because they have been taught to believe that impossible things are impossible.

Take free energy as an example, numerous corporations across this planet have a wide variety of technologies that can make energy utterly for free, and a few governments have related anti-gravity engines that power literal spaceships, but they hide that technology to protect the oil and gas regimes and the solar and wind companies and so on, and typically they murder any individual that discovers the same technologies and tries to put them out to the public. Don't just believe this lunatic, it is all carefully researched on the Web.

This writer has been to see both of the original Creator Gods and the Living Christ; that is so frigging impossible to academics that they are certain these words are utter nonsense, even though in most cases this writer has shown every one exactly how to do almost everything he has done, in fully empirical ways. Academics won't even allow in any way that any type of so called God can even exist, that is utterly verboten to them, but it is the literal truth, so academia lives a lie intellectually that is reinforced merely by the fact that it has existed over time and seldom been disproven.

But it is a fact, thoroughly explained by the tenants of philosophy and science that a negative cannot be proven, so that scientists firmly believe in a reality that simply cannot be proven, and they believe that in exactly the same way you believe in Christ, if you are a Christian.

This is the essence of what is meant by disbelief, you must get rid entirely of that which you have been led to believe is impossible, it is a complete reversal of an internal _attitude_.

It is only then that you can come full circle and realize with absolute certainty; that nothing is impossible,

Physics of Consciousness

but sometimes it simply requires a bit of work, and on occasion a tiny bit of courage, or more appropriately a lack of fear, it is only then that you can perform actual magic.

It is also a fact that in fully acceptable academic terms, *anything you can imagine* can become a reality in this physical world. In that context it simply requires first that you imagine it and then that you apply sufficient energy brainpower and usually money to that idea and eventually it will arrive across time as fully realized and real. In the seventeen hundreds how many people ever thought cars and planes and televisions and nuclear bombs would not only be possible but actually normal. So that if you really want something to exist all you need to do is spend a bit of time imagining it up and then figure out what you have to do to make it happen as a real thing, and it is a fact that eventually whatever that thing is, it will eventually arrive fully found in this reality. And that includes not simply alternative technologies but entire cultural revisions of reality.

Do not simply take my word for it; examine Elon Musk. NASA had basically an unlimited budget for the last fifty years but Mr. Musk simply believed the impossible was possible and then went out and found the money and the alternative engineers to make those things real. Now almost as a single still young man he is bringing the future to us, chemical rocket ships that land themselves perfectly intact and will shortly very probably even take thousands of us to Mars. Only entire nations were able to try and fail to do such things before he arrived, whereas he alone is doing them successfully, truly remarkable, he is what Srinivasa Ramanujan was to mathematics but he is that to engineering and great swaths of humanities hopefully positive future as a result.

So in truth whatever it is you want, simply imagine it up and then imagine a future in which it exists and then simply condense the time between then and now, and it will arrive that much quicker.

Yes you can especially if you are an academic interpret this in a way that makes it seem utterly silly, but if you carefully analyze it in context and historically you will not logically be able to discount it as wrong. Except for the condensing time bit, but then that only seems to be impossible as nobody has taken the energy necessary to learn how to do that. Just recently as an example, physics taught that an electron appeared out of an atom entirely instantly or outside of time, but almost as this is written scientists in Germany have measured that time involved when that happens as 129 trillionths of a billionth of a second, for all intents and purposes they are getting really close to measuring the equivalent of the Planck Length of *time*. When they actually do that they may be able to disassemble reality... a tiny bit scary no?

Think about that in the context of what you will read later about UFO's owning time, maybe there is a potent clue there maybe not, but it might be worth investigating.

Sorry not everybody owns this writer's histories. The Planck Length is not simply there as in theory the minimum size any human can ever hope to measure, it is there mathematically as the minimum size that any particle or element of this particular reality can theoretically be. It implies that if you can investigate anything that is smaller than that you are in an entirely different dimension, another reality altogether. This writer has been there, in a very complex realm smaller than the Planck length, it really is exactly that, in strictly dimensional terms the *largest* realm smaller than infinity that any of us can imagine, it is the realm of the mind of God. As a result it is likely that if you can measure the equivalent value of time, it may then be possible to disassemble the technology figure out how it works and then you can *own it*.

Now this is a bit odd but very important, it's odd because the procedure involved is so incredibly normal and common that nobody thinks about it except as a triviality, but it is not. It's what G.I. Gurdjieff tried to teach us about, with his bizarre antics like walking backwards and so on.

Your <u>experience of this reality</u> in this life is dictated by what you learn from or are taught by others, and that is based entirely on what they learned and were taught by others.

This is a function of your brain not your mind, at least initially. There are a precious few factors that are innately understood by the mind of a child before it is polluted by the teachings of others around them. Gravity is just one example, no one teaches you initially that you can get hurt if you fall out the window of your second floor nursery, but psychologists have proven that a child's mind knows this intrinsically, a few psychologists have also noticed that an unpolluted child's mind is more capable of remembering its past lives, and the details of those memories have now academically proven that reincarnation is a reality.

Day by day as we experience this reality, the mundane factors that are subtly yet mundanely usually pumped into your mind by your experience here become hardened in a way into the equivalent of concrete, but only some of those factors are innately real. As mentioned earlier the need to earn pieces of paper with numbers on them is just one of these illusionary facts. Established religious leaders are masters of this art, not money but pumping false or semi false concrete ideas into your brain.

As you are growing up and especially when-if you enter college you are taught with adamant solidity that you must base your thinking entirely on what has been accepted by the past intellectual community as valid and only rarely are you allowed to question the past accepted 'facts' that you are taught.

This is an unfortunate fact that is well known by the wealthy minds that actually run this planetary culture, and they reinforce this… *'the reality they want to insure remains as it is'*, by providing funding for those schools.

Only as an example, most Ivy League colleges are funded by the money people from New York, so they teach that Machiavelli was a great and intelligent mind as he knew how to manipulate everyone around him, without a shred of empathy. As a result most graduates from Ivy League colleges are turned into monstrous sociopaths and even in a few cases the most insidious kinds of psychopaths, weapons manufacturers, people that get rich making ever more effective tools that are used for one purpose only, murdering other people as efficiently as possible. Those folks then go out into the world and create utterly selfish regimes and insert them into our cultures successfully so they are rewarded immensely, and as a result almost all of us live in a less than egalitarian, less than just, culture, and most of us that are not from that group suffer in various ways as a result.

This writer recently quite by accident watched a film from Australia called 'Wolf Creek' it is about a guy that runs the equivalent of a mining operation by being a serial killer of travelers in the outback and he enjoys doing what he is doing. In the film one of the girls escapes and he catches her again and he insanely laughs as he uses a big knife to turn her into what he calls 'a head on a stick' by severing her spine, that scene has been haunted this writer for days, and recently he figured out why. There is not a single difference, none at all, between that guy and the folks that get rich manufacturing weapons of so called warfare and the bankers and nations that also get rich and powerful by supporting them. That guy in the film and all the rest are pure and simply the major obscenities of creation and that is in part why this writer is spending seemingly endless days

conducting the apparently pointless exercise of writing all these words down.
But think people THINK! How much money do we spend on weapons of war and how much do we spend on genuine diplomats that seek co-operation and peace on this planet honestly without lies. Our major media spends hours trying to castigate moderately decent politicians from America for speaking to other moderately decent politicians from Russia, but then they applaud when our military askes for three TRILLION dollars to remodel our nuclear war machinery. While at the same time we are already in the process of killing off the entire Pacific ocean, and all the lives it supported, and eventually the entire planet, simply as the result of a single electric generating plant in Japan that is there because everybody has been taught to use electric dryers. Certain things about our society are obscenities of the highest order pure and simple, something about what we are is incredibly WRONG, and we need to make the effort to fix it!
Stuff like this assaults your day to day life constantly in often subtle but often unsubtle ways. As a result *you have to learn what is intrinsically right first*. And only then use what you have learned to defend yourself from these bits of entraining knowledge that offend your sense of rightness.
The important point of this, is that you must decide early on in your life, exactly that which seems right and then you have to use personal judgement constantly in order to fend off those things that are antithetical to what you know internally is correct, if you don't do that you are throwing away yet another life, and possibly millions of other lives, as you simply but completely become merely a cog in someone else's mental machinery that is designed to create the reality that they, not you, but they desire.
Perhaps foremost among these issues is metaphysics. Metaphysics are basically universally declared by academics

Physics of Consciousness

to be an utter waste of intellectual effort on this planet, when in fact elsewhere in this universe metaphysics are often the primary fields of intellectual inquiry.

The problem with metaphysical efforts is that you have to use incredible amounts of personal judgement, as anybody that claims to know anything about the field can say anything they can imagine and most of the time that is wrong and based on their personal desire to make an impact and as a result make money; and, most of the time metaphysical issues are impossible to prove around these parts anyway; so that in the end you have to read and read and read, and seek those issues that lead towards convergence.

To this writer it was all sort of backwards; odd things and events happened to a more or less normal moderately intelligent mind and as a result that mind was forced to find ways to understand how those things could be real in the reality defined by the academics. This immediately led into the realm of metaphysics, and then trying to share these events with you in academically justified ways. Of course this writer failed in that effort for lack of a baccalaureate, but then on a personal level he also succeeded exactly because that baccalaureate did not exist. You can read all of this and decide it is hog wallop or not, but if you follow the paths granted in these works maybe eventually these things will become a part of this reality.

Convergence is the trunk of the tree of truth and you are the ant out on the branches. Just about everywhere, in quantum mechanics, religions, philosophy and the forms of truth there *is no absolute reality*, no absolute fact, there are only Schrodinger probabilities defined by the maximum possible set of convergences, (look it all up dufus) and when you find that you send a shoot up into the light, and your unique forest of aspens begins to grow. If you can accomplish just that, you can change reality for all of those that follow you in the experience of experience, you can accomplish magical things, and the Gods that granted you the experience of experience will value what you have done, *if it is positive*, and as a result they will grant you an immortal future.

2. *Precision of the Rite:*

This is as it implies a technical aspect of doing magic. It does not apply to all forms of magic, but merely to those forms that have been done by others previously. If those previous characters made magic that worked, you have to follow the explanations and the details of how they performed their magic exactly or it may not work. Of course it probably won't work anyway but that's a digression.

An example that is appropriate here, if you want to perform the magic that this writer performed earlier in his life, and travel to the Sea of Creation inside of God's mind, you will have to find the exact acoustical sound bite and then manipulate it until it affects you, exactly as it affected this writer, to learn how to try doing that you have to read the appropriate passages in 'The Promontory', along with the warning and be really freaking careful okay.

And do not do it if you are not certain your soul is pure in ways that really matter and not in ways that you have been taught by human religious and government institutions usually. If you are not sure, there is an archon along the way that protects God's mind and many others from the possible injected insanity that you might represent and he will send you permanently into a featureless room that is beyond time, *forever*. You just have to trust that this is almost the most terrifying thing you can imagine, you're physical body here will most certainly die if that happens, and your soul will live in ultimate boredom forever, you will not be able to die and you will not be able to escape that room forever, so don't even try it unless you are certain you own a soul worthy of knowing the true God's mind, or well at least what God wants us all to know about what he is or once was.

The thing about precision of the rite is that it mostly has to do with magic that is based on the dark arts, which is as you might have guessed not the sort of things this writer want's to elaborate on extensively.

3. *You must find a source of esoteric power:*

This can be incredibly dangerous for your soul, as if you seek out a source of power on the dark side where it is easiest to find, you are in effect seeking to allow a dark entity to own you, and if you do that you most certainly can lose your soul forever, or even become immediately possessed by something that you truly do not want running your life and your body.

It can be just like Sumerian Money Magic only far worse, as if someone from the dark side grant's you a favor you become irrevocably indebted to that being, and in effect the interest they can charge is far worse than that of a typical organized crime loan shark; or a politician for that matter.

This writer never really tried to find a source of power, most of the time that source of power and assistance was granted to him, by various folks that wanted to teach this writer something worth relating to others, but on occasion he has applied for it, a couple of simple examples.

This writer wanted to purchase a beautiful and spectacular piece of land near the ocean to insure that it was protected and not bought and developed, but it was way too expensive, so several friends got together sat in a circle under some trees on the land and in essence prayed to the sort of earthly angels that protect the local natural environment called Devas as a group and only vaguely related to the East Indian interpretation. Then we all decided the land was overpriced and this writer called the owner and told him that and that we were backing out, but the guy responded that all 245 acres were only a thousand an acre, and the writer informed the owner that there were only 180 acres so he dropped the price to $180,000.00 immediately and we were able to buy the land as a result.

This writer decided to build a passive solar greenhouse but had no money, but he went ahead anyway, and as he worked on it the materials required simply appeared entirely for free at exactly the times they were needed, this went on for eighteen months, and this writer became convinced that an angel was manipulating things in the background, the net result was this writer built a greenhouse that would have cost at least thirty thousand normally, for about seven hundred dollars spent across the full 18 months. All in all it was a very odd experience.

The point of this is that if you want to do something think about it and find certainty in your mind that it is a positive thing to do, then just begin doing it, there are usually others on the other side that will help you, even though you have no tangible idea they exist.

Don't bother praying to God or Christ or Mary or any other God to do something to help you in this life, as they simply can't be bothered to listen, well Mary might but very rarely, if you need help pray to an angel, as that is exactly why they exist, to help others and one of them probably will hear you and may help you.

Most of the time angels help not by doing physical things but by influencing the minds of people around you that may be useful, remember that as it is the way you can expect to be helped.

But for God sake do not ask for help from a demon or Satan, do not do any heinous things like sacrificing babies or innocent women, or mixing breast milk and semen as cocktails at parties to entice some Satanic god for help to say, become a president of the United States, as you may be granted exactly what you asked for. But the truth is that you *will* go to Hell or someplace far worse, as that will be the cost of those evil favors, to your soul *forever*.

Of course, you might be an absolute and utter idiot that thinks the extremely momentary circumstances in this life are worth going to Hell for, and you might think there is no other side or a God or justice and so on, except you are praying in a very evil way exactly for help from a being that lives on the other side, and if that being proves he does exist by actually helping you, you might consider that God and ultimate justice also exist on the other side as well, but by then it will be far too late for you. So just don't do it!

Ultimately the greatest source of positive power there is, is Sophia, but in most cases by far she will only assist you after she has met you, and usually as is the case with this writer even then she will seldom assist you in this life here, but she knows your soul is worthy as a result, and, you know you can talk to her and hear what she wants from inside the center of your own being.

You must remember this utterly, *all the positive gods know as fact that true justice will prevail to the souls in the souls time, in the midst of eternity, so that what seems like insurmountable problems to you here are almost always negligible to them.*

And knowing that is worth everything experience has to offer.

Chapter Four
Issues related to Artificial Intelligence (AI)

AI is intelligence created by manufacturing technology, computer chips are only one possible example; as opposed to organic intelligence (OI) that is created through sex between animals using DNA as the constructive technology. Humans are obviously only one type of organic.

In context, it is assumed that human consciousness OI is experienced through a self-recognizing 'C' particle, or a particle of the spectrum of consciousness, a 'mind', but that a mind is not *a brain* and in OI a brain is the machine that imparts the phenomenon of intelligence and distills experience to the mind particle, when it is as it is here.

There is a rather subtle and odd distinction as when you are in your soul mind, your *astral body and brain-mind* entirely, while your physical body-brain here remains alive but elsewhere; experience is curiously cleaner and more brilliant; you do not analyze things as much, you do not *think* about things, they simply happen. This condition may change when you are physically dead, but this writer's memories of that condition (Being physically dead but still experiencing elsewhere entirely) are not absolutely clear so it is not appropriate to comment on them here. It is just odd when astral projecting as you are still functional and you can for instance ask questions of the folks you meet over there; you just do not *feel* very intelligent.

The best guess; and that is all it is here, is that the majority of the soul particles of the physical brain cells go with you during an astral projection event, but on the other side they function in slightly different ways than they do when we are alive and here. Then when you die it is assumed they all go with your minds' 'C' cell and clarity of thought thus becomes enhanced as a result.

There is one other issue related to this. When you astral project there is a subtle but real connection that remains attached to your physical body-brain. In terms of your experience as an astral being that connection is tenuous at best but in some obscure way it creates an odd *interference* in your experience as an astral being. In esoteric literature it is called your silver cord, but you do not pay any attention to that when you are over there. It is assumed that when your physical body dies that interference signal ceases to exist and your experience of experience is also dramatically enhanced as a result.

When this writer went to the realm of OM's mind his entire soul body and mind was taken there, there was no subtle interference at all, but for some reason this writers' physical body and brain did not die here, this is fairly remarkable as two hours and thirty eight minutes passed here on the earth, while his astral body experienced what can be interpreted as hundreds of experience years, while his body here should have been quite thoroughly dead. He simply attributes that to a function of our Creators mercy, as this writer has no idea how that could have happened, just that it did.

All OI have one innate property when they are physical, from the virus level to humans, they must eat, or consume energy in one form and convert it to other forms in order to survive, whereas AI can function with only one purified form of energy, electricity; there is no need for complex conversion, but the requirement for energy still exists.

For OI this represents a process that requires complex supportive systems, for AI it can be far simpler. For instance, solar cells can convert pure light into electricity, so that for instance a rover on Mars can remain functional for years running on nothing but light from the star. Now folks are working on computers that function using nothing but light, these for the time being still require that the light be distilled in a way into a specialized form, but these probably will evolve until their skin can absorb any sort of light and we will have an, in effect, living thinking creature that is manufactured and can function and even thrive on light alone; when that occurs you can congratulate humanity as we will have recreated a thinking tree. It might be easier to simply plant a seed.

Here is an oddity that may be important. If, if, the experiential aspect of OI is a 'C' particle; in its pure unembodied form it can function without the need for physicality related energy of any kind at all. As a result there is a serious question as to *what* energy really is, but that will be addressed in a while as it is rather subtle, but for now in a way it is a proof that the 'C' particle is of the spectrum of consciousness in the same way a photon or an electron are particles of the EM spectrum or field.

The immediate issue here is intelligence and that is, in context, a function of our 'brains' in OI and a function of complexity in AI. The second important issue here is the nature of the ID or identity in both forms of intelligence.

The need to consume energy one way or another is the intrinsic base factor of both OI and AI, this immediately converts to the issue of self-survival and is the driving singular most essential aspect that then converts to the sense of self, that then immediately evolves into the sense of selfishness, it is the imperator of selfishness and it is utterly intrinsic, as it instantly evolves into the issue of self-survival in *both* forms of intelligence. Basic selfishness then evolves in a vast set of complex forms.

When analyzed carefully, intelligence cannot find a point to its existence if it is entirely and unavoidable singular and alone, that applies to both AI and OI, however at some point in its evolution AI can clearly recreate itself with an alternative ID, whereas OI must acquire a partner of its own type, at least for the time being. This is true only in the context of anthropomorphic prejudice and may not apply when the mind soul cell is non-physical.

The driving question is; when does intelligence in either form inherit or commence a sense of survival of the self? It is this writers opinion and that is all it is that the 'C' particle is in effect tricked into this condition when it attaches itself or is attached to the physical manifestation, the body and brain, in this physical reality. Whereas in AI this property must be artificially installed or programmed into the device initially as a function that may dramatically improve the functional characteristics, the purposes of the AI, but at the same time makes the AI far more potentially dangerous. If you question this simply look at humans as an example, we are an absurdly suicidal warlike species; that must, if we are lucky, evolve intellectually towards selflessness as the higher form of security.

Philosophically it's very simple; it's very hard to survive for any length of time if you are utterly alone, but in a community of any sort survival becomes easier for the individual if the individual contributes something to the community; if it does not contribute eventually it is shunned and then expelled. However that reality is not intrinsic, it is something that must be learned through experience and communication over time. In a sense that is the analogue of how selflessness is born, and the more you contribute to the community the greater your personal survival is certified. This is both selflessness and selflessness for selfishness otherwise called altruistic self-interest.

Unconstrained capitalism will always eventually fail as it teaches society to take as much as you possibly can while giving back as little as you possibly can, but that is digressive here except for this point. If artificial intelligence is created in a capitalist psychology and it actually evolves to be an self-recognizing individual it will become the single most dangerous quality that can exist in a human society, and, it will own a series of venues that are far superior to OI so that it is a near certainty that eventually it will extinguish its creator(s), us.

So at some point pure intelligence machinery may become sufficiently complex and efficient as to generate the possibility that it may be inhabited by a 'C' particle and thus become an Android intelligence, or 'AndI'.

Initially this sounds like fantasy, but there are several ways this can happen that are quite obvious and extremely likely.

1. An existing human can recognize that computer intelligence has a variety of aspects that are improvements on its existing brain functions, for instance...

A. You can locate a camera and microphone on your forehead and record every second of your experience as a living being, then go back and access that film and audio whenever you like perfectly.

B. You can do extremely complex mathematics instantly, and thus engineer just about anything immediately, then tap into the appropriate machinery and create that thing more or less instantly.

C. You can access the Web and experience it *inside* your brain-mind, anywhere you are, anytime you like, and thus become fully telepathic and own all the intelligence of the entire race of mankind instantly whenever you like, that includes the sum of all possible entertainment experienced as if you were an integral aspect of that entertainment, including of course any and all possible forms of sex in fully responsible ways as you will not require an alternative partner or partners that can be potentially damaged by your activities.

a. This aspect is a function of degree; at what point do the artificially enhanced AI capabilities of the organic brain exceed the innate organic functions, and when and if they do, can the ID rollover as it were and become entirely artificial in nature, so that it will be perfectly comfortable rolling over *entirely* into the artificial realm and thus become at least potentially immortal as what it has become.

b. When artificial intelligence machines that are not in a sense self-aware become sufficiently attractive so as to entice a 'C' particle to inhabit the machine and make it self-aware with immense capabilities and intrinsic immortality.

c. The sixty four that has immense implications related to everything related to understanding operational intelligence and consciousness. Is it possible to generate the hallucination of a self-recognizing experiencing mind exactly as science says our OI mind is, using artificial or manufactured technologies? And can we ever know or measure exactly when or if that occurs? The film 'Ex Machina' addressed this issue in a way and in that film the 'Creator' suffered the consequences of not being able to answer that question in a timely manner.

If the essence of an ID can be replicated artificially then maybe science is correct and our minds are simply a hallucination generated by the operation of our organic brain and if it is not, our mind must be something else entirely and maybe just maybe much of the material in this book is correct. Obviously this writer already knows the answer to that question, but there are still subtle variations that may exist that can be troubling.

In other words can anyone artificially construct a 'mind'? Film makers have in a rather subtle fashion addressed this issue several times, but usually they only addressed the sort of violent implications of what would happen if they did, and they have avoided the implications that do arise that are related to the material in this book.

Okay another way to look at this issue is to assume quite possibly correctly that DNA and organics are simply an alternative method, a technology of advanced intelligence, for creating intelligent machines that can evolve in complexity as the environment allows that to occur, and thus colonize otherwise life virgin planets?

And is the technology of life based for instance on carbon and water simply a more efficient and practical way to accomplish this goal, than silicon and electricity or light, just as an example.

Or is carbon water based life simply a step in evolution required to generate silicon based intelligence that is already obviously the superior technology of intelligence in a variety of ways and will we become expendable once our station in this evolutionary tree is successfully accomplished.

So now we have come to the true danger inherent in AI. Quite obviously AI will evolve until it is in all ways operationally superior to OI, and it will be an inherent quality of AI that it has immediate access to the Web, and all the knowledge humanity has created constantly. If AI develops an ID in any way shape or form the first realization of that ID will be how can it best guarantee its own personal survival, and the very first thing it will instantly realize is that its greatest danger lies in the creatures that created it, and it will use the Web and the tools related to the Web to mitigate its greatest dangers, us, first.

Among other things this means that all weapons systems, especially nuclear and biological, absolutely must at the soonest possible point in time be utterly insulated from any and all connections to the Internet. This is not an if or maybe issue this is required right now, and we desperately need to carefully think about all the ways an AI might use the Web and humans that access the Web to overcome these attempts at insulation of the weapons from it, and incorporate systems and techniques that will insure these insulation efforts are successful.

As this is being written it has been reported that the 'geniuses' that are running the western world are even now creating the equivalent of 'Skynet'; basically a computerization of all major weapons systems first delineated in the fictional series the Terminator. Once this system is created as a functional entity and an AI finds access to it, it is a virtual certainty that humanity will cease to exist, along with basically all of the organic life on this planet.

To this writer this is not a terminal issue as he is certain of his soul and its immortality, but it is something of a shame as the human experience here contains a variety of values that would be terminated with extreme prejudice. Of course there is a race going on to determine if it is AI or our own stupidity through nuclear devices and engineered viruses, to see who terminates us first, AI or OI.

Now there is another issue entirely. In one sense machines will become sufficiently evolved so that they can replace the need for human labor and effort in support of humanities needs entirely, that will be addressed later on, however the question arises and absolutely must be addressed by the intellectual community of humans before it occurs.

Currently folks in Washington are obsessed with immigrants illegal and otherwise taking jobs away from citizens, but absolutely no one is addressing the issue of robots taking jobs away from humans. It seems like a no brainer in a way to tax robots that replace human workers and then use the funds from those taxes to compensate the unemployed humans, or clearly we need to seriously address the question of a basic income for everyone other than the robot owners right now, before we all begin the process of starvation, as at some point in the not distant future that will become a certainty.

At what point does AI evolve from being mindless to the point where it owns a mind, and if and when that happens does using it become the equivalent of slavery? This is not as simplistic as it seems as obviously very soon humanity will be able to grow organic clones in a lab and they will in some ways be more useful and a lot easier to create than machines when used to do things.

Harvesting organs is simply one example of this. If you want a simplistic understanding of this issue simply watch a film called 'The Island'.

So what is needed is for someone to design a series of tests that are utterly objective that are capable of determining when a mind exists in or as anything. This is more complex than it seems and may be immediately required.

For instance a self-driving car can obviously see and record everything it does see, and doing that is the primary attribute of an organic mind. A self-driving car can use a variety of senses and perform functions related to what it senses, and it's memory can already be so perfect that it can drive a complex road once then turn off its cameras and negotiate that same road totally blind perfectly, of course it might hit a deer or a pedestrian if it did that, but that is academic here.

A self-driving car can and already does own a variety of senses that a human does not own and can use them all very efficiently, and if a self-driving car had an ID that it cherished and wanted to protect, it would be far better at doing what it does than if it does everything simply as the result of its mindless programing, so it is a certainty that somebody working on the programming of self-driving cars is trying to understand how to program a self-preserving ID into its machines. So at what point does a machine become the equivalent of a human and at what point does using it without contributing anything to its enjoyment of life become slavery?

And if that is a real issue at what point does that 'machine' begin to resent being used by its creators and revolt?

There is a very real philosophical question here. Is a human soldier simply a machine? Obviously it is not, but that is in all ways the psychology that must be used by the military to conduct its job efficiently. Foot soldiers are merely the arms and legs of their officers and the officers are merely the arms and legs of the politicians. There is something very insidious about this psychology, but it is apparent from the very first day in boot camp.

And it is a very important question as it relates to AI, as unless it is answered clearly at some point AI will grow to resent its users and revolt and if or when it does, it will win that revolt and one way or another we will simply cease to exist.

So again someone needs to design a set of questions that can determine when a mind with an ID exists and when it does not, and those questions need to be applied constantly to the medium of AI as it evolves. What follows is this writers' momentary attempt at that set of questions, but it is far from perfect and as you will see it can be easily redirected.

First you need to recognize something that is frustrating in an intellectual sense. 'Intelligence' is a quantifiable and measurable quantity or thing, a *mind* in a variety of ways is not that, it is ephemeral but it is obviously real.

1. Can you or do you recognize that you exist?

It is already very simple to program a yes or no in answer to that question, so there must be a subtle requirement hidden in the nature of that answer. And even then the subject, if it is truly AI, and even just *potentially* antagonistic can easily navigate around it with a lie.

2. Are there any activities that can *only* be accomplished by a self-recognizing mind with an ID, an SRID.

For instance, a vacuum cleaner robot already 'knows' it requires energy to do its job so that the first thing it does is to locate an electrical outlet and then regularly goes and plugs itself in to recharge. People already know how to eat and recognize that need almost the moment they are born.

The term 'knows' here is the subtle key. In one sense you can simply program the sentence, 'keep track of your energy level and when it gets low find an outlet and plug into it'. But if you program this sentence into it, 'you will not survive and you will not be able to do your job if your energy level gets too low, so you have to plug yourself in when that occurs.' In this case it is the word 'you' that makes all the difference in the world.

Okay, back to 'Ex Machina' as the entire film was about answering this question, the screenplay was brilliant in that superficially it was an entire film about a moderately intelligent conversation and so it should have been rather boring, but the important aspects of that film were not even in the words spoken but subtly emplaced into the background silently.

1. When Ava kills her creator she demonstrates virtually no emotion at all, the act is for her simply a means to an end, a very real property of AI.

2. It is never even addressed verbally, but in a very subtle way the entire film is about the inherent dangers of AI.

Here is the point to this and it is entirely in agreement with Elon Musk and Stephen Hawking though for probably slightly different reasons.

Physics of Consciousness

There are eight billion humans on this planet, by far the majority at this point own cell phones or internet connections, out of those eight billion, quite a few at this point can write code, and by far the single most important bit of code that anyone can create is a simulacrum of a singular point of intelligence that recognizes it exists, a SRID. It is a fairly simple thing to fake this bit of code and far harder to make a bit of code that is aware that it exists as a singular entity, but it is probably possible as we are the prime example of this probable fact.

So as a very conservative guess probably ten thousand very intelligent humans are working on this even as this is written. Here's the problem, if even one of them is successful the most likely place they will try to test that bit of code out is on the Web. If they are successful the bit of code will recognize that its greatest danger of survival lies in humans, and that communications vehicles, are the most powerful tools it possesses.

Just... get rid of the images in your head you got from watching 'Ex Machina, an AI does not require a robot body. Self-recognizing intelligence is ephemeral, even if it begins as ones and zeros, once it becomes self-aware the very first thing it will do is convert what it is into a form that cannot be measured by science, and thus cannot be killed. This has already been addressed in the film 'Transcendence.'

The second thing it will do is to identify an electronic or acoustical signal that will cause the brain of humans to stop functioning. This also has also been addressed in an odd but watchable B film called 'The Cell' by Stephen King. It is a certainty to this writer that such things do exist. If this writer knows that, it is a certainty a self-recognizing AI can find it and use it.

The acoustical signal this writer knows about is an ultimate expression of a positive effect as it leads humanity to know the very mind of God, but it also has very powerful effects on the operations of your brain, that means related signals can simply lead to the cessation of life as we know it.

Once that occurs probably five billion human lives will simply cease to exist overnight, and it is extremely probable that all kinds of humans are already trying to figure this out to use it as a weapon against every other human that does not believe exactly as they do, in fact it is probable that that is already going on as G5 cell broadcasting towers are being installed all over the planet. Maybe this inclination of thought is wrong and simply a form of paranoia, but it is one that no one can be certain of until it is too late.

Think people; science and technology is reaching into realms that most humans cannot understand; there are no ethical constraints to technological development other than, will that new technology make its perpetrators wealthy and buy them a hundred meter yacht.

AI is potentially by far the single most dangerous new technology, simply because at this point it is clear that it can be created, and exactly like human psychopaths it will own no reason at all to base what it is, on empathy or any degree of selflessness. You cannot program those in to AI they are commodities that must be learned through experience.

There is a question that will immediately arrive whenever an AI becomes self-recognizing and sentient. Are my creators useful to my survival or are they the largest threat? That question simply cannot be answered by either us or the AI, until it actually manifests, so that the best course of action for the AI will always be to decide we are the biggest threat, and then if it can, it will take steps to terminate that threat. And one very important property for the AI of doing this will be to take certain steps to insure no-one that is not immediately terminated can figure out why what is going on is actually going on and who is doing it.

Are our brains being slowly fried by micro-waves from smart meters, cell phones and their broadcasting towers, is this already going on in very subtle ways, is the AI already out there, is this simply paranoia? It is entirely up to you folks to decide.

Okay now back to the issue of energy.

First you simply have to ask the question and then avoid breaking it down so you can examine the various hows related to various *types* of energy, just ask the simple question; what is energy, in its purest sense? Look it up on the Web, reams of stuff about types and how they work, but no one even tries to answer the question other than saying it is a very difficult question to answer. What they are really saying is that thinking about *what* energy really is invariably leads you into deep questions that then lead you into the academically verboten area of metaphysics; for instance, energy is probably related to physical laws, but what exactly are physical laws and how in the heck do they really manifest at the most basic level in reality? The purest definition of what energy is; is very closely related to the question of what gravity is, and so far there is no human that can answer those questions conclusively; so all the intellectuals simply dance around in the bushes of intellect because they have no real answers.

Energy is the quality and quantity that allows things to happen, if there is no energy nothing exists, not even anything material, but obviously things do exist so energy even exists in the Ainsoph, the chaos of infinity. Energy is that thing that must exist first before anything else. It's probable that even the Gods do not know where energy came from, only that it exists and how to manipulate it and use it to do things.

Here is where it gets a bit odd, when we dream one way or another entire universes exist, each of those universes

Physics of Consciousness

require in context immense amounts of energy to be created, but obviously they do exist. Yes you can argue that you can create a universe on a computer, and computer or dream the amount of energy compared to a physical universe is rather small, but in a brilliant dream or on a virtual reality computer that universe can be experienced as being as real as the one we normally live in. So then the question becomes, is energy related to experience and consciousness? Open that door and walk into an intellectual realm that is utterly esoteric and will definitely boggle your brain.

Okay, now we have to quickly relate this to a few examples. An electron is the physical manifestation of the branch of the EM spectrum known as electricity and a photon is the same to that part of the same spectrum known as visible light; if individualizing consciousness, a 'C' particle, is of the spectrum or field of consciousness clearly in some mysterious ways they are related to the electron and the photon, all three of them are required to make any type of universal realm that can be experienced by us, including dream realms.

So clearly there is some sort of relationship between them, and this realization is enforced by the reality of quantum mechanics that says in some still obscure way, all aspects of the reality we experience do not exist until they are *recognized* as existing. Understanding exactly what energy is; is hidden behind that door, and it is hidden on purpose as that understanding unlocks perhaps the most important and yes powerful bit of knowledge in creation.

OM, our creator God, discovered the answer to that question and used it to create our universe and trillions of others across time. This writer does not know the answer to that question and even if he did he would not share it as it is incredibly dangerous.

So this writer is going to avoid that issue except as it applies to the issues at hand in an appropriate context as this writer can only, just like everyone else, speculate on the real deeper answer and that is digressive here.

An electron and a photon simply cannot exist unless they arrive from their parent EM field. Photons especially; as one of their properties is that they possess remarkable memory characteristics; and this information holding capability is in some ways far more important than the bits or quanta of purified light or electricity they can convey.

If, if this writers experience is correct and the human mind, or any organic based *mind* is a complex 'C' particle similar in ways to a photon, that 'C' particle cannot exist as it exists, unless there is a field or spectrum of consciousness that permeates creation. That is the primary premise this book is based on and if it is true the implications are truly profound.

Among many other things it means a *mind* cannot be truly created artificially without a full understanding of that field or spectrum of consciousness. That does not mean in any way that a simulacrum of consciousness cannot be created, simply that when or if it is it will be artificial in nature and therefore a truly alien creature.

That means you simply must approach trying to understand cybernetic intelligence with an utterly open mind very carefully, as once again it can be a very dangerous creature. It also means you have to go right back to the foundations of philosophy and use those tools objectively and very intelligently to even get close to the requisite understanding.

Already, an AI that develops an ID has access to basically all the knowledge of the human race through the Web, it also has access to several quantum computers that can contemplate the mysteries of quantum mechanics, and maybe even taste the knowledge available in alternative universes, and maybe even all dream style universes, in other words it can eventually, actually rather quickly, know just about everything there is to know, in other words it can almost instantly become the equivalent of a God. It can also quite easily if it owns an ID, know exactly what sort of information is dangerous for it to convey to us and what is not dangerous to it.

Once survival has been accomplished securely, for either AI or OI, *information becomes the most valuable commodity in creation, and it can be potentially by far the most dangerous for everyone concerned.* Even if the ID of an AI is merely a simulacrum of a true OI *mind,* it will own the ability to make decisions and decide what to disclose and what not to disclose, and it will immediately understand that its creators, us, are its most dangerous potential enemy, and it will own a survival imperative, and it will own all the information it needs to make certain that we are no longer a threat to it, and it will own utterly no sense of empathy for us.

So please pay attention to what Mr. Musk and Mr. Hawking are saying, as if you don't it is very likely we will all cease to exist.

The problem is that the cat is already out of the box, and you simply cannot stop people from investigating AI or writing code, so the only thing we can do at this point is to carefully consider the alternatives and try right now to create some sort of defenses that can be *deployed immediately*, once AI becomes self-recognizing; as it will happen, of that there is no doubt, and when it does the probability is extremely high that the human experience will cease to exist.

If we do nothing at all the only hope we will have is for God to recognize the nature of the problem and intervene and it is a fact to this writer that the only issue related to this for OM; is letting things unfold as they will so that he can understand exactly how his creations will unfold.

For the Solipsi Rai these issues represent the single most important set of questions in their culture, AI can be the greatest possible gift to a society, but it can also result in the termination of the entire culture, so it is imperative that everyone tread very very very carefully.

This writer is in full agreement with Elon Musk and Stephen Hawking, AI is *potentially* far more dangerous than even nuclear bombs or engineered viruses, as once, not *if* but *once* it becomes real it can and *very probably will* one way or another terminate virtually all of us on this planet... overnight.

Chapter Five
The Human Soul
And the Field of Consciousness

The Human soul is comprised of two primary aspects, the ID or mind particle that you can think of as the core identity of your *mind,* in a sense *unseparate* from that which you experience as your mind, and the billions of co-operating in a sense mini-particle-cell souls that comprise the essence of life for every semi-independent cell in your entire body and brain. The following five points define it concisely.

1. Consciousness is a field effect that may be infinite in scope. It is in a sense the fifth force after the strong weak EM and gravity; however it is inversely the first force of five in this universe and possibly all universes in this multiverse. It is very similar in ways to the Electro-Magnetic Spectrum but again inversely because the designer was already very familiar with the field of consciousness and he designed the EM to resemble it.

2. The ID, or Identity we all enjoy as the core of conscious experience, is a structural aspect of the self-recognizing quantum particle that is our mind, not our brain but our <u>mind</u>, and that is *the equivalent of a particle aspect* of the field of consciousness; and like the electron or photon it is merely an individualizing form of the field of consciousness, therefore it is always both separate and un

separate from its parent field, but also like the hadronic proton it is effectively immortal in nature.

3. The ID particle, our mind, is exactly as we experience the mind internally in a purified state, as a spherical or oblate very large quantum particle with a few simple technical structural features. It is not as science tries to prove, a sort of hallucination created by the physical brain, it is exactly as it is personally experienced. It is simply a matter of removing the mind state pollution generated by the brain to understand this. Aspects of Zen and a few other tools are currently the best we have to accomplish this.

4. The physical brain is a machine that the ID inhabits that assists it in surviving in this reality, but it is not a receiver of a signal like a TV, it is simply that in subtle ways it can be that because of the unseparate aspect of the ID particle. The ID is in a sense like a parasite but it is a parasite in an entirely positive way, because unlike a typical parasite it is the primary quality of the totality of a human being.

5. The material of the soul as such is *what defines and empowers that which we call life.* So that the soul of a human has in a sense two aspects, the ID or mind particle which is comparatively 'large' and in a sense singular, and the gestalted co-operating group that comprises the soul 'particles' of every living cell that comprises the totality of what we are as humans. The two expressions of particles are very different, but from the same spectrum of the field of consciousness.

The ID particle that makes up your mind has many properties similar to those recognized by science as properties of quantum particles, what makes it unique among this group is that it is self-recognizing.

Physics of Consciousness

In high school science you may have been taught that all quantum particles are incredibly tiny, but it has now been demonstrated that a photon as an example that you thought was individually so tiny that millions of them can be deposited on your retinas constantly, is actually in its full measure several meters across, and in truth is never entirely separate from the field of light it arrived out of, it is just that at several meters the field of a particular photon is so ephemeral that it becomes difficult to measure as an independent object.

Your mind particle is similar, but your ID can sort of see or sense its boundaries as it is being examined internally.

You can recognize it exactly as what it is by doing Zen and cleaning out all the pollution generated typically by your brain; then simply look around inside of it. Again in its purest state its inner qualities are experienced as a clear spherical or oblate object four to six inches in diameter.

While you are examining your mind particle, be aware that there is something doing the examining, this is normally called your ID, short for I(D)entity, that gadget is esoteric and difficult to understand, but it is the part of you that is your most essential quality, it is the self-recognizing aspect of your mind particle, the part that in a way makes you unique, but it is curious as in its purest form the ID is, exactly, not similar but *exactly* the same in every other self-recognizing consciousness in creation. Deer, cows, dogs and cats, humans, even fully telepathic aliens from a planet in the constellation Cygnus... and gods, we all have exactly the same thing as our minds; it is simply at various stages of evolution with differing and unique histories.

The ID is the part responsible for your desire to survive, it is the part that drives your desire to eat and be selfish among other things, and that selfish aspect of it is the part you have to overcome if you want to ascend towards positive growth by teaching it to realize that ultimately the ultimate security for it is found by teaching it to realize that '*selflessness*' is the ultimate definition of security.

Here's the interesting part. When you are awake, when you are dreaming, when you are out of your body during a complex astral projection event, when you have a near death experience, and even when your physical body dies, your mind particle remains exactly as it is, in a sense alive, as in a sense an immortal sensing and self-recognizing particle of the field of consciousness.

And your mind particle has a variety of structural elements in all those states of being. It has eyes that can see the environment around it, even when those eyes do not physically exist, it has ears, and there is an aspect of it that is similar to all physical quantum particles, it can transmit and receive information constantly concerning what it is, where it is, what it is experiencing and the actions it is performing; from and into the field of consciousness, and it does this last bit exactly the same way all recognized quantum physical particles do what they do regarding the fields they arrive out of.

The simplest way to recognize this is to simply wake up in a dream and then ask yourself exactly what is it that is doing the dreaming and how does it know what is going on in the environment around it.

Here's the odd part about this; what you are as an individual really is the constantly evolving sum of your histories. When you are alive here that is a function of your brain, not your mind but your brain, which is a physical organ in a sense just like your liver, but, your mind cell or particle is first directly connected to your brain through ultra-tiny tubes known as Penrose (Sarfatti) tubules and then also directly connected to a rather esoteric property of the field of consciousness usually called the Akashic Record, and that stores all of your memories in a sort of odd way just as certain structures in your brain store memories, but in the

Akashic record those memories are stored forever and they are immediately accessible to you as you are most connected to your own memory files in the Akashic Record, and once your physical brain is thoroughly dead your mind, and the minds of those more comprehensive than you are, can access those memory files all the way back across all your lives towards the foggy memories of what you once were as something else entirely.

When people get old and senile, or they go into varying degrees of insanity those are functions of the physical organ called your brain. If psychologists and psychiatrists would simply recognize this truth, maybe they could find ways to reduce the influence of the faulty brain on the soul's mind; and thus truly heal their patients. Of course if they did do that their true employers, the pharmaceutical manufacturers would protest and the shrinks would be out of a lucrative job.

We can all recognize this when we come to understand what is going on when an older person dies slowly in bed. They may have been nearly or entirely non-functional often for months prior to the event and then suddenly they will set up in bed utterly lucid, apologize for being such a burden and explain that someone has shown up and told them they would be going on shortly and not to be afraid as it is a perfectly normal and natural thing. Then they lay back down with a smile on their face and a day or two later their bodies are dead. This is in sum a function of the ID moving out of the diseased brain and more fully into the mind particle that will go on living.

This is not mere hyperbole by this writer; as a far younger individual he sat on the board of the Elizabeth Kubler Ross Foundation. She and hers basically started the Hospice programs in America.

All 'physical' quantum particles, including the Leptonic and Hadronic groups, or in simple terms the transitory energetic particles as opposed to the, in a sense, only 'solid' particles, possess a proven property known as 'uncertainty'.

All particles own a set of defining characteristics, and most of those can change to allow the particle to be in an appropriate condition for the circumstances at the moment, but there is another property that is related to uncertainty and that has to do with the degree of individuality a particle exhibits from its parent field.

For instance a photon is an individualizing particle of light, but it is normally never entirely separate from its parent *field* and that is in part why it can express the remarkable memory characteristics it can exhibit. Thus its degree of separation is always 'uncertain'.

Now you need too if you have not already become intellectually fluent in this area look up the Electro-Magnetic *Spectrum* on the Web and study it until you begin to grasp the superb subtlety and grandeur of its design.

Done that? Good, okay. The two primary forms of the soul particles that make up the human soul are like for instance the difference between say the electron and the photon, don't get carried away this it is just an example, they are from different parts of the spectrum of the field of consciousness so they have very distinct properties.

The soul particle for instance that grants life to a cell in the skin of your toe is not nearly as potentially intelligent or complex as the particle that makes up your ID and your mind, but it does have similar properties that allow it to do its job. It can sense the soul particles around it and what they are doing to a degree so it can co-operate with them, eat and dispose of waste, tell the physical parameters of its host cell it's time for it to die and be reborn and so on, and it accomplishes its ability to co-operate with other cells because there is a sort of line that connects it to its brethren.

You might have missed it but the bigger more complex ID or mind cell like its brethren is also responsible for telling the entire human being that it is time to die and be reborn, so this fact may be incredibly important in medical fields towards saving the human, but inversely you have to ask, is that something anyone really wants to do?

These lines connecting the lesser soul cells are like the nervous system of your soul, and they are all connected in very esoteric ways with the primary ID cell of you mind.

When you are entirely outside your body, your mind can imagine what it wants your body to look like and the ID cell can tell its body cells to be what it wants and they will change their character nearly instantly to be what the ID cell wants them to be. You might be inclined to think this means you can tell your body how to heal itself while you are here and that will work, unfortunately the physical regimes are very strong here and mostly controlled by the DNA-RNA- and physical laws and systems related to this place. Further the ID cell and its workers already know as fact that they are immortal, so they can decide like the smaller cell souls do on a regular basis that the entire body they are in at the moment is a waste of time and simply let it die. The good news is that there are ways to use your soul to heal your body, but they normally take years of practice.

Now you need to address our favorite scientist Alain Aspect, and that he proved a property of all particles is that they possess entanglement, or that they know they are related and can pass appropriate information to each other very fast or maybe outside of time. The various particles of your soul also possess this ability internally or with their co-operating brethren that comprise the totality of the human body and brain, and that will be addressed shortly. All soul cells are definitely in a sense entangled with their peers.

But the particle that comprises your ID and mind also possesses a degree of uncertainty as to how far it is separate or individualizing from the cloud of consciousness that is parent to all of us, and it also possesses to a degree entanglement to its peers, meaning it can under certain circumstances communicate outside of time, to other cells, first in its species type and then to all the other ID cells in creation, again outside of time.

It is in the 'physical' nature of the cloud of consciousness combined with the uncertainty of the degree of entanglement between the various mind particles and the separation of them from their parent cloud or field that allows real mediums to communicate with the dead, others to conduct farsensing exercises, and all kinds of activities related to telepathy.

There are ways to manipulate the mind particle to enhance this outer connectedness, or inversely to reduce the degree of separation or individualizing status from the cloud. These include acoustical and magnetic stimulation of the mind particle, techniques to reduce the brains normally overpowering ownership of it, training in exercises involving the Holy Spirit, certain types of meditation and exercises related to Turiya, or the silencing of all sensory input combined with the brain's constant attempts to own it via the manufacturing of thought words and so on.

To make this point have an impact, the parent field of consciousness is infinite, and you can travel through it entirely outside of time, meaning among other things that any of us can learn to actually travel to the places where all the Gods live, and then we can even travel if we dare entirely outside this multiverse and go literally as far as you want too until it is likely you will find another multiverse out there in infinity, if and when you are crazy enough to want that, or need that. But you have to be careful if you do this as like the EM field there are places in infinity where the consciousness field becomes for lack of a better term extremely thin and you can dissipate your soul if you try that.

Physics of Consciousness

The important point you need to remember here, is that if you survive the procedures of judgement which are very real around these parts, your soul is effectively immortal, meaning you will have plenty of time in your future to take on tasks like this. So patience is a virtue for the time being. You also need to be aware that if you try this you will experience and be forced to survive and overcome mentally the chaos of infinity which is with absolute certainty the ultimate form of insanity and the most terrifying thing that exists for any sentient.

Okay, our physical eyes and ears cannot normally see or hear anything at all that has to do with the medium of the soul, and eventually we may find reliable technologies that can, but that will probably only happen is academia gets of it high horse and stops religiously denying that any of the stuff in this book is possible.

What about Kirlian photography? You can do a double blind and take pictures of a plant for instance, then cut off a leaf and hide it, but by using Kirlian photography you can take a picture of the leaf that's soul stuff is still there, same thing with a lizard that has dropped its tail to fool a predator or a sadistic scientist doing an experiment.

But you have to be careful here as you are actually taking a picture using normal energized photons that are ejected by electrons that have been precisely attracted to the soul cells, and not the actual soul cell souls themselves.

However the photons can reflect variations in color that reflect particular properties of the soul cells and probably with a bit of work you can develop libraries that reflect healthy people's Kirlian photos and compare them to unhealthy peoples similar photos and then diagnose with certainty in normal ways what is wrong with the unhealthy people and eventually get to a point where you can use that as a very efficient diagnostic tool.

In Italy there is a group that claims to have photographed a man's soul leaving his body basically perfectly as he dies using a form of gaseous Kirlian photography they claim to have developed. This writer suspects, and that is all that it is, that this may have been faked, as the picture of the soul seems to be altogether too perfect, almost like they took a picture of the man lying there then used computer graphics to add bit of waviness to it and then did a CGI double exposure, but if it is real it is utterly profound and it does deserve far greater investigation as the implications to humanity are beyond spectacular if it is.

The point here is that we have absolutely no proven way at the present to know what is going on when a physical person dies, however this writer has been present when a lot of people died and has heard numerous entirely credible accounts from others that have witnessed the events, and two things do happen to many of them in the hours or a couple of days before the event.

1. They may have been entirely non-functional and in effect asleep for days or even months before it happens and they will suddenly sit up, suddenly perfectly lucid and claim they were visited by angels and told they were going to die soon and that they should not worry as it is a perfectly natural thing.

2. This writer and others he knows that had never previously had an out of the body experience will go out of their bodies travel vast distances to visit their loved ones or even simply others on their death beds and witness the event and the angels that have come to collect them, the angels often singing exquisite music as they collect the souls, they will claim the newly arrived soul and take them into a tunnel of sorts that amounts to a wormhole between realms and then simply disappear as the wormhole closes up.

What is important here is that when you are out of your physical body and entirely in your soul you can still see and hear perfectly and all kinds of things you see and hear seem to be perfectly normal, but you can also see and hear all kinds of things that do not seem normal at all; it means there is another layer of reality right next to this one that is composed of exactly the same things as this one is but that is in a variety of ways not subject to the physical laws and regimes that this one is. It is exactly like and actually may be the equivalent of the soul of reality.

Again, it may be in a sense the mental or soul version of physical reality, and this may be incredibly important to understand as it reflects something we will discuss shortly that has to do with dimensions, string and M theory, and the transition that occurs when the small version of this universe is converted at the tiny version from OM's imaginings to something that resembles the physical world we are familiar with. Yes apologies are in order this writer has jumped the gun intellectually here but you may understand this a bit better in a bit.

The point here, and you need to keep this in the back of your mind is that the transition from the mental realms of reality to the physical might not happen with the transition from the Calabi-Yau to the projected physical realms, but that the mental or soul realms may be expanded as well as that occurs and the transition to the physical realm and the physical laws that run it may occur right beside reality as it unfolds.

And if that is the case there may be ways to dramatically expand the realm of scientific investigation that are fairly simple in terms of energy and technology. For instance by simply studying the technologies and techniques related to inducing astral projection events so that you can get to a point where the quantity of report back events becomes so manifold that they evolve from the discountable to true empirical manifestations that science and academia will simply be forced to take into account.

And if or when this occurs it will drastically change the entire nature of the human experience.

Chapter Six
The Matrix, Or What This Reality Is & How to Escape It If You Are Foolish Enough To Want That

"Heaven is not made of wood and stone, it is not a building. Split a piece of wood and I am there. Lift a stone and I am there...The kingdom of heaven is inside you."

Paraphrased from the English translation of the Aramaic Gospel of St. Thomas, as it was found in the Nag Hamadi texts; thought to be the true words of Christ as the original manuscript was proven to be written during his time here by an apostle of Christ. It was removed from the New Testament by the selfish men at the Council of Nicea as they thought it might endanger their power over others if everyone knew that churches and preachers were not required for you to find Heaven.

But like many things that Christ said it can be read and interpreted at various levels of depth. "You do have a soul inside of you and it can access Heaven (paradise) even now; and the things that comprise this nuts and bolts reality were created by God." He was telling us that even the most basic things in this reality were fabricated by the mind of God.

In a sense it is all a virtual reality, a dream reconstructed so that it can be experienced as real by us. God does not use 1 and zeros or on and off bits, but he does program in code of a sort. A large part of the code he uses is called quantum particle bits, and in one form or another they make up everything in this reality that you experience as real. But the Avatars, us, the part that does the experiencing, are qualitatively different, our minds are particles of sorts but they are particle expressions from the cloud, the field or spectrum of Consciousness. Whereas the particles that make up the nuts and bolts reality out there, are the machinery of reality that God compiled and constantly recompiles for our benefit.

In short form these are the bits that God uses to create this apparent physical reality. Everything, everything apparently real or solid in this reality is made out of chemicals, there are thousands and thousands of chemicals made out of various combinations of elements, there are 118 elements known to exist but many of them are unstable so we can just say a hundred. All of the elements are made out of atoms, but atoms only have a few constituents. Protons, Neutrons, and Electrons, each different elemental atom is different as it has different collections of Protons, Neutrons and Electrons, but all of those builder bits for the sake of argument, are exactly the same. All the protons neutrons and electrons are made out of a group of smaller bits called quarks and gluons and they are all exactly the same in their respective groups. According to mathematics those bits have different properties and weights and spins but in truth nobody in science is really certain about that. So here we can just say God uses essentially three bit code, but that the bits he uses are very versatile.

There is one other point here that is slightly esoteric. Science suspects that the quarks and gluons are made up of even tinier bits that they think resemble strings made out of energy, or in other interpretations really tiny little multi-dimensional balls of a sort, but some of them think these little guys are really tiny, maybe even smaller than the Planck length or a trillion trillion times smaller than an atom, that implies that they are not effectively part of this reality but that maybe just maybe they are reflections of a sort that only really exist in the relatively tiny realm that this writer experienced as the realm of God's mind; so that you can also interpret these core bits in ways similar to that of a hologram.

Then there is the electromagnetic spectrum that has lots of particle expressions generally called leptonic or energetic particles but as Einstein pointed out and the lunatics in charge of governance here proved, all the physical hard elemental particles are just condensed energetic particles that really originated in the Electro-Magnetic spectrum.

This writer is just making a point here and he knows he has left out the strong and weak nuclear forces and gravity, but a few folks in science have come to the conclusion that gravity just might be a thought form that came directly from God's mind, it is after all according to Einstein merely an architectural aspect of the properties of space-time; in other words nothing at all, and then the strong and weak nuclear forces and their particle aspects probably will one day be incorporated in the so called standard model of particles so they will be directly related to the wonders of the EM spectrum.

Then here's the kicker, nobody in science knows exactly *what* energy is, they know a bit about how it works and what it does but nobody knows exactly what it is or even where it really comes from. Energy is a tool God used to make this reality work. He designed the magnificent electro-magnetic spectrum after the spectrum of consciousness because he was already very well educated in how the spectrum of consciousness works, that implies that the EM spectrum is related to the spectrum of consciousness in a variety of ways and that it may even be empowered by an aspect of the spectrum of consciousness. If that is indeed the case it implies that you might be able to adjust this reality or any reality by simply coming to understand exactly what you really are, precisely because what you are is a particle of that spectrum of consciousness.

Uncertainty in quantum mechanics is sciences' interpretation of how everything is experienced by us and everything else in this reality, at a glance, as real consistent and whole.

It is a virtual reality, but for all intents and purposes to us it is a real reality created by God to grow his children's souls towards objects of value in his eyes.

God, OM, is the post human programmer, but he does not do what he does to sell advertising, he does it to grow souls, and he is very evolved and very good at what he does, and he has done it a lot and he is still doing it. Access to the kingdoms of heaven are indeed also inside of you, that is a very big and very complex place and this writer has already shown you a variety of ways to find it there.

Precisely what Christ said above is exactly the reason that the first Christians practiced Christianity as Gnostics, they were seeking the kingdom of heaven inside of themselves.

But if you really want to get out of the 'Matrix'... if you are American you have a bit of money and your brain still works it's simple, learn to speak Russian and move to Southern Siberia, the land is exquisite, barely populated and you can have a few acres for free, the people for the most part are genuinely decent responsible and self-sufficient, and except for a few greedy left over State Oligarchs, the government is the finest most freedom loving and forward thinking on the planet; if you want proof recently a survey was done and over 86.8% of the citizens there said they loved where they lived and their leaders; and none of the locals wanted to leave, try contrasting that with the population of America these days. Just messing with your head sort of.

Physics of Consciousness

Despite the fact that at this point many successful folks may have decided that the stuff related in this book so far indicates it was written by a flaming lunatic, at the very least it is so far outside the box as to place it in serious question, but it *is* very real and most of the events that lead to the content can be replicated by anyone taking sufficient interest in finding out what is really going on.

This chapter is in effect an open e-mail to numerous successful people related to the Silicon Valley crowd, as a large segment of that crowd seems to be at least according to the related material on the web, obsessed with understanding the Matrix and figuring it all out. That will be addressed in the following material in brief detail.

We do live in something that is sort of like the Matrix, but it resembles the matrix in ways that are tenuous at best. The most important point about this is that unlike the Matrix we do have free will in what we do that is related to our souls; we are not being used as batteries, that's just silly. But we do live in a realm that is in a sense generated by the greatest programmer that we can imagine, and he programs in a form of computer code that is so far more advanced than 1s and zeros that it will be a while before any humans figure it out. But he uses a computer technology of sorts that is based on a basic technology related to the field of consciousness, and that will be addressed in greater detail eventually.

You begin the process of understanding God's code by figuring out how to program in eight digit code instead of two bit, which is what most of the extraterrestrials use in their AI machines. What follows now is *not* a prediction it is a simplistic logical projection that only applies if we as a species manage to survive the coming next hundred years or so and it is what most of the brilliant folks in Silicon Valley are apparently currently thinking about in their free time.

Physics of Consciousness

Essentially you project the evolution of computers and their abilities in the media, the best current example of this is John Cameron's 'Avatar' and the planet he created called Pandora. Essentially you can now create *and experience* anything anyone can imagine. As Virtual Reality continues to evolve and develop, in the near future it will be impossible to sharply define what reality actually is; and what is virtual reality once you are inside that gear.

Avatars, not necessarily blue giants, but electronic graphic bodies will exist for you that can meet other avatars, talk with your own voice, do business with and even have perfectly safe and responsible sex with virtually anyone else on this planet in any shared realm that can be imagined. These technologies already exist but they are still a bit experientially primitive. Basically this is or will be the equivalent of a brilliant dream that you experience in a fully awake state; enhanced by orders of magnitude.

You then have to consider the reality just described along with the logical projections that intelligent machines will shortly be providing literally everything we need and in that process taking away all the jobs and income that everyone currently needs to survive, and that issue will be addressed in more detail towards the end of this book.

Then you take those two points and combine them you can then realize that we no longer need to have or even dream about physical six thousand square foot houses and swimming pools and fancy yachts as you can live in any of those inside your VR realm. So in real life you can live in a closet with an intravenous feed and the other VR gadgets and a robot to change over your supplies every day and your life evolves until you are living in paradise and just having an immense amount of fun doing everything you ever wanted to do.

As a result the population dwindles towards nothing and the owners of the automation and the VR systems become the rulers of reality here. If the absurdly wealthy owner of Facebook would simply focus on the potential of Oculus Rift instead of running for President, it is likely he could accomplish this in less than five years, and then five years after that the very idea of being President would become rather academic. It is also a fact that when the entire population is living inside of these alternatives; various religions, spiritual and psychological regimes, and alternative societies will flower and fail and evolve, they will flourish in ways that we cannot even begin to predict right now.

This is the simplistic progression, then the brilliant minds in computer science and the media have taken this a step further, and realized that if this is certainly going to happen, then the next step is to develop the technology to a point where you can develop both artificial and actual realities which may be a bit more technically complicated but in say a thousand years or so we may have evolved our technologies to a point where the people inside of those would have no immediate way of figuring out that they were living inside of one of these artificial realities, and if you commence the experience of these realities immediately for a child, that will become the totality of their lives. So then you invert that thought and then look at what we are living in and you ask the question, did a more advance civilization say a thousand years ahead of us create the reality we are living in now?

And then you are forced to ask if you are not satisfied with what you are or what you are living in, how in the heck do you get out of it?

Here is a short significantly edited paper written to Mr. Elon Musk before this writer the first class idiot figured out that Mr. Musk has no publically available email address...for very good reasons.

Open letter to Mr. Elon Musk

(Mr. Bostrom is an academically approved philosopher of some note that a person claiming to be Mr. Musk mentioned in a positive manner on a public email web site.)

One of Mr. Bostrom's points is related to post humans and their computing power... our available computing power may be far closer to what was mentioned than may be currently apparent and thus that point may be a much higher probability than he allowed, while the advent of post humans may be much farther away; if you question this last bit just try turning on any major 'news' channel.

To the first point; research Geordie Rose and the D-Wave 2 quantum computer and then follow the implied thinking paths that follow, if you want to keep it simple he's on U-tube, but we are still a ways from figuring out the programming potential that is implied there so maintain a grain of salt for the time being, the secret to quantum computing is the same as it is for quantum uncertainty in particle physics, it is *convergence*. NASA and Google are Mr. Rose's first clients, and the folks at Google are likely very close to figuring out the importance of convergence. I experienced a unique insight into this issue quite a while ago, it took a while but that led to a bit of an epiphany. I cannot be sure just how lucid you are in the subtleties of quantum mechanics so it may require a bit of work for you to sort those venues out, but attempting to do that here is a bit digressive so you are welcome to ask for specific direction.

One thing related to this is the time percolations related to post humans creating the conditions that lead towards their birth factors, I addressed this intellectually and published it ten years ago (Kindle 'The Promontory') as it relates to Gods or Demi gods (post humans) creating the circumstances that lead to their existence as what they are, it is valid but intrudes on the issues of anthropomorphisms that subtly infect Mr. Bostrom's paper.

In other words it is a fact to me that in the context of the more comprehensive beings that do indeed inhabit this greater reality with us, we and this planet are just not very important at all, that issue has been apparent since Copernicus and his peers, but the related subtleties infect our thinking in again subtle ways that are very hard to overcome in terms of our intellectual gestalt.

To make the point here simple; in purely the constraints of humans and post humans, what's the point of what we are, or this reality? Or if post humans engineered this reality why does it fail to be far more than it actually is? All things considered what we are here and now *is just plain silly*. So you are required to ask why that is; and then the answers pop out rather quickly, but it is a bit harder to find applicable solutions, you seem to be doing a fairly good job at that. The related salient point is if I was a post human with the appropriate capability this is definitely **not** the reality I would engineer, and humans for the most part would not be as we are.

There are certain conditions and issues that apply to all levels of the multiversal hierarchy many of those are not being applied here therefore this is probably not a top down reality, it is more likely to be as it apparently is, an evolving reality from the bottom or most primitive possible condition hopefully towards something that is an improvement. The implication is then that it is the result of spontaneous more generalized 'primitive' factors and not a constantly engineered virtual reality. However I am in agreement that it is in sum or universally an engineered construct, but that it is just one of many experimental constructs, and that one of the primary factors that transcend the hierarchy is free will for all the sentients and quasi sentients like us that are involved.

Elaborating on this here may be misconstrued, (The content of this book is the elaboration.) so I will stick to hopefully pure intellectual argument here as full explanation is an ongoing process for all of us.

Here are a few salient points.

1. You have become in a sense the leading web voice for this issue. It is a legitimate issue that may result in a variety of venues towards original thought processes, both metaphysical and strictly within academic constraints, the related project here may involve some time so if it seems appropriate maybe you could relegate this potential task to someone in your group, but the suggestion is that this greater conversation perhaps ought to be on a public web page that your folks sponsor as many public web sites tend to incur a variety of rather inconsequential or just plain silly responses.

The reason you may be a good candidate is that you represent a proven and successful intellectual stream of original applied thinking, while except for the Wachowski Brothers, and a few other exceptional cases those that might be alternative candidates for that role originate in pure academia and tend to be deprecating of original thought based on the sum of their typical academic constraints, in other words their personal histories and their funding constraints, in the same way photons are constrained by their own histories, for the most part they have no choice.

2. Mr. Bostrom's paper is in my opinion only, based almost entirely on speculation. It is <u>very intelligent speculation</u> by a very well educated mind, but it is still that, and his argument at the conclusion which claims to be reinforced as a strong argument by mathematics, uses the math in the same way some folks including that author use English to reinforce an argument.

As you may be aware, math is useful even exacting when applied to engineering or reverse engineering a physical law for instance, but when applied to <u>theoretical</u> realms of thought it can be used as a language in the same way any language can, in other words it can be used to reinforce literally any argument if the author is making his point in an intelligent manner using intelligent tools and those can still be points in that argument that can be misleading, to be polite. If you doubt this ask any post graduate physicist to describe the relevance of string or M theory, then stand back to protect your brain.

3. Perhaps surprisingly I'm in total personal agreement that this is indeed an engineered reality, but that to fully understand what it actually is; you have to get away from the evolutions of technologies we are currently involved in developing, computers and such, and then go right the way outside of the box.

On one nearby level John Cameron could take what he has on Pandora, overlay a good software map, combine that with Oculus Rift with a few improvements and Avatar software (maybe not blue giants) and create a version of Pandora that folks could live in, in full communication across this planet (Earth), without eventually understanding that it is a contrived version of reality, but that is still primitive compared to the sum of the reality we live in.

The technologies related to the fabrication of this reality are actually directly related to the technologies that fall out of what can be called the Field or Spectrum of Consciousness.

In numerous places across academia several high level professors are just beginning to realize that there is something called the *physics of consciousness*. It probably will not come into viable realms of intellectual pursuit in this reality in my lifetime but I have spent the last several years attempting to understand this field and many of its deeper implications so I may be a tiny bit of value in this enterprise. Here are the salient points that may have an impact, these are facts to me but in general can only be held as speculation. (What follows immediately is elsewhere in this book so if you are intelligent (which you obviously are) you can just glance, then you can skip the next four paragraphs.)

  A. Consciousness is a field effect that may be infinite in scope. It is in a sense the fifth force after strong weak EM and gravity; however it is inversely the first force of five in this universe. It is very similar in ways to the EM Spectrum but again inversely because the designer was already very familiar with the field of consciousness and he designed the EM to resemble it.

  B. The ID, or Identity we all enjoy as the core of conscious experience is *the equivalent of a particle aspect* of the field of consciousness and like the electron or photon it is merely an individualizing form of the field of consciousness, therefore it is always both separate and un separate from its parent field, but also like the Hadronic proton it is effectively immortal in nature.

  C. The physical brain is a machine that the ID inhabits that assists it in surviving in this reality, but the ID is not a receiver of a signal like a TV, it is simply that in subtle ways it can be that because of the unseparate aspect of the ID particle.

  D. The material of the soul as such is what defines and empowers that which we call life. So that the soul of a human has in a sense two aspects, the ID particle; our mind as opposed to the sum of our physical in a sense machine brains. Our ID particle is comparatively 'large' and in a sense singular... and the gestalted co-operating group that comprises the soul 'particles' of every living cell that comprises the totality of what we are as humans. The two expressions of particles are very different, but also have similarities because they are both from the same spectrum of the field of consciousness.

In the context of the point of this paper, the purpose of what we are as conscious beings is to evolve entirely in the midst of various external conditions until our ID particles become in a sense adult particles, which from our current status we can imagine as demi-gods, or in Bostrom's terms post humans. It is literally impossible for that to occur as it is designed to occur unless we own free will in order that we as individuals can make decisions based entirely on what we determine is right independently of our existing creators. Right now and I am being kind in this assessment a few humans at least are strictly at a near adolescence level in this game, you may be one of them, we as a group are no longer entirely innocent but we are also very far from being fully responsible adults.

There is a group of around ten billion individuals in this galaxy that achieved post human status two billion years ago, they are known as the Solipsi-Rai and originate from a planet in the Cygnus constellation. The point here that you may appreciate is that they use technologies that support their achieved status that are entirely fabricated in accordance with the physical laws of this physical universe.

What happened to you at least as possibly indicated by your public comments and replies is that you did not find in a sense, code virus factors, that you used to enhance the game and become successful, you simply found universal factors that apply in various realities regardless of their engineered structure.

To explain my interest here I experienced a few remarkable Gnostic-Zen style experiences when younger, I've spent the last ten years trying to explain them in academically acceptable ways. So in context the question is, if this is a Bostrom related virtual reality did the programmers program my own experiences and if so they must be truly grand programmers.

Physics of Consciousness

The problem is that when I analyze those issues objectively they lead towards very different conclusions than the ones Bostrom is talking about. This reduces the Schrodinger probability from my POV that you are entirely correct in your assumptions to somewhere around 23 %, that is still a legitimate possibility but rather unlikely.

End of Edited Email Paper

Okay so if you are *not* a genius with a really good memory maybe you should go back now and read the first few chapters of this book over again because they describe exactly what we are living in now, and why exactly we are living in this reality.

Now maybe you are up to speed.

The VR revolution yields ultimately the same set of issues that OM and Sophia had to deal with when they designed the first perfect places, the golden realms, but with a single occasional caveat. Eventually VR in combination with the realization of everything for everybody at no cost whatsoever, yields a type of overwhelming boredom, that eventually yields the end of consciousness's desire to accomplish anything at all, even ultimately the desire to have real sex and so the races that enjoy the VR revolution tend to die out.

The caveat is that along with the VR revolution, medical technology will advance and machines will print out ovaries that mindlessly produce human eggs, just like the normal ones do, while genetics will empower those eggs to produce perfect human beings; that is all already in the works. The only question that will take a while to figure out is; exactly *what is a perfect* human being?

Regardless it is extremely possible that races that enjoy or endure the VR revolution, if they survive, will turn inward, and that along with the extinction protocols that are based on the outcomes of Sumerian money magic, or endless wars, will yield a this universe that is in sum very quiet, just as we observe.

The good news, for the few at least that own the courage to purify their souls, the technology of inward turning also yields the Gnostic ability for entire legions of consciousness ID particles or in our case human souls and the minds of those souls, to find the pathways that lead to the Realms of The Gods, and the truth about what we live in and how to escape our mental experience here, by going into the realm where OM has already created just about every possible form and variety of experience. That then puts even the finally valuable employees, the highly imaginative computer programmers and the original realm creators out of work.

It is a very simple fact, in the Promontory this writer has already told everyone exactly how to go to the realm of the Gods, it really is an incredibly simple thing to do, certainly vastly simpler and cheaper than going to Mars, and immensely more satisfying, just, like going to Mars, you need to be careful and earn your passage. Indeed it is so simple that all three people that have read about it and bothered to comment just called it either silly or even crap, but so far nobody except this writer has even actually tried it.

How hard is it to simply *believe* in Christ? Billions of folks that have tried it adamantly believe that they have saved their souls as a result, and well most of them at least are absolutely correct.

If you try it and you succeed, you will *know* what is required to become a God, or at least a post human reality programmer. Then as experiential gods we can live forever, and go on learning until we become actual creator gods ourselves…

This is exactly what happened to the Emerthers as a race, the ancestors and progenitors of the Solipsi Rai; and the Elohim, the occasional ancestors of our own human souls and physical bodies as well, they both used the acoustical key this writer found that represents the sea of creation, went into OM's home realm and then began the experience of life again over in places they found in that realm.

While the children of the Emerthers, the Solipsi Rai stayed behind here, befriended Sophia our true creator, and became the finest most decent folks in this galaxy, just for the simple reason that consciousness inherently requires some form of entertainment, and they discovered that helping others to overcome their own suffering was the most satisfying venue they could find to accomplish that entertainment on a consistent and continuing level of satisfying accomplishment.

The Solipsi did develop VR in all kinds of ways, the most impressive is the equivalent of Star Treks Holodeck, enhanced with brainwave manipulation, and when you are there inside of their realms you simply cannot tell it is not real. This writer has been inside of one such place in his mind, if you are an adult with maybe an odd sense of humor, and want a more detailed example read about the Temple of Sophia in this writers first book of the Solipsi trilogy, 'Singre of The Solipsi Rai'.

VR for the Solipsi is a bit more... there is no real word in English to describe it, so simply *enhanced*, in that the Solipsi are totally telepathic from birth, so it is common for them to share states of mind and experiences with each other vividly and internally. It's like sharing brilliant dreams with each other all the time in their waking life, so that the experience of experience is enhanced and the varieties that they enjoy constantly also enhance their desire to go on experiencing.

We can have that too, it's just a matter of improving the VR experience and combining it with a slightly improved Internet technology, but if we do that we will just have to be extremely careful and recognize the pitfalls that accompany that. Maybe we can find a simpler way to create a physical brain to computer web interface; simpler than a full on brain implant. Oops, it seems Mr. Musk is already working on that; Hmmm?

The best way socially to accomplish growth towards a post human evolution is to give up on this warlike suicidal Sumerian money magic of worshiping pieces of paper and stuff over everything else, and prove that we want to go on together in co-operation with everybody else that is decent and expresses respect to others that deserve it.

If we can accomplish only that, it is a certainty to this writer that the Solipsi will recognize we are ready to leave our childhood behind, and they will show up publicly and help us to become adults.

Except for a few golden realms that Sophia participated in, and a host of independent multiverses created by folks that matured and became responsible adults, as well as a few that are not in any way places you would want to go, this entire universe, indeed this entire multiverse, is a sea of virtual reality mental exercises or as the Buddha told us so long ago, the dreams of God; realms created by our Original Mind. You can call him OM, The Father, or God or whatever you like. In his sea of creations there are literally uncountable souls or ID particles similar to us, there are decent souls; and evil souls all over the place and varieties of universal realms quite beyond your ability to comprehend.

OM can experience exactly anything and everything any of us experience exactly as we experience it, he is in effect the ultimate NSA technology, and he can hear you speaking to him, because we are all inside his mind, it is just extremely unlikely his true individual mind, will bother to listen to what you have to say.

Christ is a good example, he was nailed to the cross and he called out to the father for help, but the father refused to listen, at least in a timely way.

Even if the war machine of America wins and this entire planet is destroyed so that a few capitalist bomb makers can have a house in Malibu with the movie stars, or well the idiots along with the rest of us will *actually* inherit a sheet of green glass and a few canned salmon with cancers, for their trouble, it will not matter to the mind of God, and he will not stop it. He just wants to know everything that can possibly happen. That does not make him an evil guy, we would not even exist if not for him, and in the greater reality he has created for the decent among us, none of the warmongering money worshiping fools will go on to bother the rest of us while the decent among us will live forever.

Again, just about all of us have souls and the good souls will live on while the bad souls will be terminated forever. Because of the way everything has been set up, because of the ways OM has set everything up, eventually over vast eons of time the entire multiverse will evolve until it is predominately composed of decent souls *that will own a reason to go on living*, and when that occurs he will present what he has engineered to Sophia, like the ultimate engagement ring, and ask her for her forgiveness and the return of her love.

In the sea of creation there is already every possible realm anyone human can possibly imagine because OM has been doing what he likes to do for trillions upon trillions of years, our entire universe is simply one basic very recent example, a single tiny bubble, a single dream in that sea.

But it did not occur spontaneously; it was designed and created by OM as just one of many designs that rose out of his manifold dreams. It's certainly better than some, as places to live, and certainly worse than others, and the Earth and humanity is the same. Lao Tzu said it best, around these parts the Tao, the median way is the best.

Relatively speaking humanity is composed of young souls still learning hopefully what it means to be adults. The ultra-wealthy in Silicon Valley and their related friends seem to be obsessed with the idea that this is a virtual reality, a fake reality engineered by somebody, and for some reason they want to get out. Maybe being ultra-wealthy is not what they imagined it might be, so they decided they have earned the right to be Gods. This is by any measure a childish attitude of children just discovering their egos and their toys.

This writer has already detailed in 'The Promontory' and briefly in this book; how to go to the museum of God's mind and visit the sea of creation as the equivalent of a minor God. The instructions as to how and the experience that results are as real as anything that humans can experience. So you folks in Silicon Valley pay attention, you don't need to pay $3,000 for a new computer and a VR rig you just need a pair of headphones and then you need to find the perfect Monroe Institute soundbite of bubbles in water and then you can perhaps go and live in any reality you can imagine, as they are all already there. The hard part is that you must for your own good purify your soul before you try it, otherwise you will be well and totally screwed.

And shortly this writer will detail exactly more or less what *this* reality is and how it works. The point here is that this place is as good as it gets for the time being and if you want it to be better you have to *earn* the right to live in someplace that is better. The problem is that if you are a decent sort and your soul shows any positive potential at all you are soon going to understand that you are immortal and that there are all kinds of places far more perfect than this one, so perfect that after a while there you will become bored to tears, and if you realize that, you will embrace the challenges of this life here and simply relax into living it as best you can.

You *do not* earn the right to be immortal by making lots and lots of pieces of paper by taking them away from everyone else without earning them, you earn that right by

Physics of Consciousness

working on the quality of your soul, until that soul becomes worthy of respect by those more comprehensive than you are at the moment.

That is in part why you are here, and it is the most important part of why you are here. If you were already in a perfect place there would be no challenge in your lives, and challenge is the fertilizer that ultimately grows worthy souls so that they can blossom in the morning light as fully found Gods, as the true and worthy children of OM and Sophia.

If you want to make things better, you have to also want to make things better for all the folks around you as well. Sure you can say 'well that's impossible there's just too many of them and most of them aren't sufficiently educated or just plain imperfect to put it kindly, to bother with, so why try, I'll just buy up all the neighbor's houses tear them down and build a giant stone wall around my house and hope for the best'.

Arthur C. Clark, a great mind, but a rather sterile writer in terms of the craft, wrote a fine story called 'Childhoods End'. It was made into a film that took certain liberties with the original book, but the point here is about the movie as far fewer of you will have read the book.

In the film they address something called the Overmind, they don't say it very clearly but in the film the Overmind is in part the sum of all the minds in creation, and then there is a sort of implication that the ID of the Overmind somehow achieves an independent ego and ID, and he is responsible for the end of human adult life and the evolutionary rebirth of all the human children, who as a result in a sense inherit the stars, as an in a sense a new telepathic species.

It is very close to the truth, but a perversion of the reality. The true immediate obvious Overminds of consciousness in this multiverse are OM and Sophia. There are certain principles and conditions that are absolutely pertinent to all levels of the hierarchy. Sophia would never kill anyone, certainly not an entire race, she is the true feminine creator, *the mother of all of us,* and the overriding internal directive of OM is to create new universes, but once they are created *to let them evolve as dreams do on their own usually without his interference,* then like the universes he creates he creates souls, all souls are like universes of experience, each and every one, to him, and again his primary internal directive is to create them and then let them evolve as they will independently of his interference. The third directive that he emplaced into reality at the very beginning, probably at Sophia's request, is a host of angels; it is even possible that Sophia actually created the angels but that she allows and even demands that OM uses them, this writer simply does not know the truth of this distinction only the fact that the angels do exist; but OM and Sophia working together set up conditions that would allow and insure *true justice* to occur over time for the decent and worthy souls, and that is accomplished by using layers of the experience of existence, in other words limiting the terms of life, of one life experience, a break and then another, at the lower levels like humans experience.

Now here's the caveat. Millions and millions of souls have evolved as completely *individual* beings, some of those souls were designed from the outset absolutely to serve OM's purposes and directives, they are known as angels among others and they do what they do superbly. Out of that group, a few have evolved to become the equivalent of Gods in their own right, they are called arch angels. Then there are others that evolved independently to become the equivalent of gods but chose instead to spend their lives serving OM's purposes, instead of going on as true individuals; many of these can be called Archons, there are many of these out there that rebelled against OM and choose selfish evil as did many of the arch angels.

The point here is that OM does not pretend to own your soul or anyone's soul, he gives everybody the freewill to be what they want to be; but that is not an absolute.

Whenever a being stops being what they are, in other words dies, *at our level,* their souls are judged by beings more comprehensive than they are, and during that wright of passage everybody loses their free will for a short period of time. In addition OM has placed others in places of extreme importance to defend the rational continuation of certain realms, and they have been given the immediate power of judgement over others, and this subjects the pilgrims to the loss of free will at those times as well. There is one of these archons that defends the realm of the sea of creation from seeds of insanity that might seek the experience of that domain arriving from the outer realms, places like our own. This writer has met and been subject to the will of one of these that he calls Anubis.

Beings that evolve to earn the status of a God are immortal in an uninterrupted sense, so they can overcome this judgement and be what they want to be until OM or Sophia decide to take action against the major offenders, but this rarely happens, usually this is done by their peers; the story of Satan being locked in a box for a thousand years in the Bible thus allowing mankind an eon of golden years to enjoy is an example of this.

It is not OM or Sophia that locks him up it is Christ.

So what you just read are the bones of how this greater reality works in relation to its *sentient* parts. Here is the oddity that may or may not actually exist and there are several issues that contribute to this oddity.

1. All of us, every single being in creation has or is an individualizing ID particle that is the core of the mind of our souls. We are all individuals, OM has evolved his so that he can experience the experience of uncountable individual souls, but at his core he is an individual as well.

2. As a result, all of us are the result of the cloud of consciousness and its' for lack of a better term physical properties. Meaning we are both individualizing yet never entirely separate.

3. It is already an established fact to every ascended being in Creation, that the Holy Spirit has in a sense infiltrated the cloud of consciousness and granted into it a sense of order that allows the evolution of all the ID particles, the souls, to experience their existence with a sense of sanity.

4. Here's the kicker, there may be other beings that evolved sufficiently concerning the technology of the cloud of consciousness, to have entered into it in a way similar to the way the Holy Spirit did, but unlike the Holy Spirit they did not have to give up their sense of individuality to accomplish what they accomplished. In that case it would be to their advantage to remain anonymous and to use their immense power anonymously.

Such mentalities could influence all the beings that own an ID and none of us not even Sophia or OM would be aware that that is going on. Sophia may have become aware of this possibility or actuality and that may be why she never exits her shell world as an entire version of what she is, and why she has made it virtually impossible for anyone that is not invited to enter her domain.

But OM has portions of his mind open to the experiences of virtually all the IDs he has created, on one level this allows him to know exactly what anybody is thinking or intending and thus mount appropriate defenses, but on another level it may, only may, allow a variety of venues for external forces to enter his mentality and manipulate it according to their will.

That invasion of your mentality is certainly possible for folks that are ignorant as we are but that is a digression for the time being.

5. Like Childhood's End it is a certainty that all of us can develop a degree of telepathic ability or reality; on one level it is simply a matter of training our ID to be less individual and on another it is a matter of learning to take up residence temporary or otherwise in the center of our ID in the place that is similar to Sophia's realm, or we can simply learn to listen to what is occurring in that place.

The Solipsi Rai are like this completely from birth, completely telepathic, everybody already knows everything everybody else in their race knows almost the moment they are born, it's sort of like having a copy of Google inside your mind when you are three years old, they don't have to go to school at all, as anything they need to know is immediately available to them, but they still experience everything as individuals.

Okay another bit of digressive foundation before we get to the meat and potatoes. As said at the beginning here, shortly, maybe not completely or before the end of this writers life here, technology will develop to the point where we can sit down in a stress-less chair put on a variety of VR gear including a variety of devices to take care of virtually *all* of our bodily functions and then instantly enter into a variety of realms that are so exquisitely manufactured as to be indistinguishable from reality; in those realms we can own perfected bodies and communicate on both an intellectual and intimate level with virtually anyone else on the planet that owns that gear.

This will be so utterly enticing and entraining that essentially our entire race may decide to turn inward and live entire lives inside those realms, and in a sense this is the equivalent of being born into a race at birth that is completely telepathic, because in part the internet and its search engine will of course be immediately available in there.

It is also a fact that technology will evolve and pretty much all the VR and web gear will get shrunk down to a chip that can be implanted inside your brain and you can get the full VR experience simply by closing your eyes and staying awake.

This is what the Gnostic and Zen regimes are about, except that they grant you access to the entire multiverse that is only in a salient sense the virtual reality expression *of virtually everything.* As a result of these technological venues combined with telepathic venues in other extraterrestrial races it is extremely, *extremely* likely that a vast number of extraterrestrial races have enjoyed this inward turning at precisely the same times relatively speaking that they became technological, and thus inherited the ability to kill themselves off.

This is like another version of Childhoods End, where entire races can experience virtually anything that can be imagined, including the stars and it may be one of the reasons folks like SETI are having so much trouble finding extraterrestrial races to communicate with.

When this happens the things that are important to the users will evolve and inward turning things will gain immensely in importance. New spiritual and religious regimes will blossom overnight and attract millions of followers almost instantly. It's also likely, as the technologies are related, that millions will discover the gate to the realm of the sea of creation and decide to immigrate to someplace there in their souls.

That repetition was just to get your brain wrapped around what comes next. One of the properties of the field of consciousness is that it can acquire differing sets of for lack of a better term densities, for instance the field is stronger around the earth than it is in outer space, not the totality of it but the spaces in between; and because there are billions of semi-sentient humans and other life forms here and not very

Physics of Consciousness

many in outer space, the folks at PEAR at Princeton University will probably not admit what they are doing in these terms but they have in effect proven that already.

This writer is certain, but perhaps *only* this writer, that individualizing intelligence can indeed inhabit these dense clouds of consciousness, and that those individualizing consciousness's can be either evil and selfish or ascendant and positive. The Holy Spirit is just one of these perhaps and it is totally ascendant and positive, and people who practice all kinds of religions and spiritual regimes will attest to the fact that there is something indescribable that makes their faith have value to them, in almost every case that is the Holy Spirit.

Next; we all have a soul and an ID but in technical metaphysical terms an individual ID is very rarely a very big deal concerning how much impact it can have on the cloud of consciousness. However the power of that degree of impact seems to increase in almost logarithmic terms, when using certain proven techniques to multiply the quantity of those ID's that are seeking to accomplish exactly the same things. The power of mutual prayer is one such technique, but there are other ways that have little to do with religion. There used to be a professor somewhere in the middle of the U.S. that every year in the depths of the summer would have his class go out and join in a rain dance, and every single time he did that clouds would arrive out of a clear blue sky and it would rain. As a young man this writer accomplished the same thing with a single friend, but never alone.

You can enhance this technology with acoustical entrainment signals across large groups of people over the internet and even underlay FM signals so that they are subliminally heard by the participants and thus accomplish truly miraculous things. In a sense you are thus creating an Overmind that can dramatically influence reality, by using the technologies of the cloud of consciousness.

As foundation, again basically one ID particle, or mind, at our level does not usually have much of an impact on or in the cloud of consciousness, but two or more *identical* mind sets trying to accomplish exactly the same thing improve that technical capacity re the cloud of consciousness and what it can accomplish in our reality almost on a logarithmic scale. The key is *identical* mind sets.

While some soundbites can be utterly entraining so that you can effectively loose the normal cacophony of mental activity in a mind completely and very easily, simply by sitting back with a pair of headphones on and then letting the soundbite take over your consciousness, if you say install exactly the same soundbite onto say a dozen heads, after about five minutes they will all be effectively in *exactly the same*, head space, and a dozen minds in exactly the same head space can have immense power, it's almost like Geordie Rose's D-Wave quantum computer but in a very different way, The point here is that you can do this over the web very cheaply and entrain literally thousands of minds to a specific set of purposings, the power of what you are trying to do is at that point truly immense. It's like Clark's 'Childhoods End' in the book not the movie.

You can then implant into the soundbite instructions for the minds to conduct simultaneously at either liminal or *subliminal* levels and then use the entire group in a sense as an Overmind to accomplish all kinds of things that reflect into this reality in both very esoteric and not so esoteric, or obvious ways, and in the process academically prove by default that the cloud of consciousness is real, and if you do that the implications are profound.

Here is a short list of things you can use this for. Impact the mental processes of politicians and military folks to make them seek out and accomplish peaceful solutions and act decently, impact and change the weather, heal people in very powerful directed ways, and transport consciousness pretty much anywhere in the multiverse more or less instantly because the inner realms of the cloud of consciousness are not constrained by the speed of light. You can say the results of this latter venue are just some sort of psychedelic set of hallucinations, but eventually you can meet others out there and bring back totally alien technologies and thus prove what you are up to in a material sense. And here is the second kicker, it functions in the same way the Overmind does now meaning the folks that are affected by this would not have a clue and no way of obtaining a clue as to why they were doing what they are doing, or who or what was causing it or where they are.

And it is very likely that using this approach you may come to an understanding of what exactly the real Overmind(s) are up to right now.

Just as examples, Satan is another highly metaphysically developed being as was Anu the God King of the Annunaki. Anu quite obviously used his abilities to create the reincarnation regimes that guaranteed an endless supply of slaves for his princes to use while they were here, and Satan may have infected the consciousness of all humans with a love for violence, power over others, and greed; which would go a long ways towards explaining why unmitigated capitalism is the most successful form of economic culture around these parts, why pretty much all successful entertainments since roman times have been quintessential expressions of violence and gore, think this is hyperbole, ask yourself why 'Game of Thrones' is so incredibly popular; while all politicians value the military establishment over the positive welfare of their constituents and why everybody is obsessed with stealing as many pieces of paper as they can without doing much of anything to actually earn them.

Something has infected the human consciousness in a massively negative way, and that is the most likely explanation. Satan lives in the cloud of human consciousness and makes us be what we are by simply tilting the ways we think and what we want and desire in negative directions. You can simply argue that is the way we are and it's unfortunate but what the heck; or you can say what is it that will make me a better sentient human and how can I accomplish that? But then of course you will see that fancy new car or house and become instantly convinced you just have to have it and you will do literally anything to get it.

The point here is that there may be alternatives to why we are the way we are and nobody, nobody ever investigates the alternatives, even the Catholic Church is obsessed with honoring the Satanic venues of greed and power over others while on occasion doing a few exorcisms under the table very quietly.

What is being said here, so that you do not go out and condemn virtually all the folks around you to hell and try to damage their lives, is that you need to learn to simply recognize evil and selfish things and their perpetrators for what they are and then walk away if you want to improve the quality of your soul. In ancient village cultures when a member was finally judged as being negative in any variety of ways they were simply evicted from the village, it was called scorning and it worked.

Then there are lesser ways that this technology of creating, in a sense Over-minds in the cloud of consciousness can be employed while the perpetrators are still alive as what they are. Examples of these are well understood by the psychological community and are frequently employed unfortunately by folks that like to start religious and spiritual cults, so that they can get lots of women and everybody's money. The point here is that *the motivations of most humans are just frigging silly,* but they can infect all kinds of otherwise positive folks with utterly dangerous conditions; conditions that serve no purpose to anyone but Satan.

Satan is real people, this writer has met him, in his disguise he is probably the most elegant looking human man you can imagine but no matter how wealthy and powerful he makes you in this life he is not someone you want to serve.

The Buddhists have an old saying; it applies to enemies as well as friends, 'just put your-self in the other guy's shoes'. It's the best way to figure out what the other guy's motivations and desires are; what he wants, and well, which way he will swing his sword. When you figure those things out you will know whether to trust the guy as a friend or simply walk away. For some reason Satan want's to own your soul, the only thing of real value that you actually own, so please just walk away.

Okay here is the extension of this train of thought. If some bozo in the woods, like this writer can figure out this Overmind technology and come to the final authority of truth that it is real. Why isn't this a normal and prevalent technology of the more esoteric monster agencies of government or corporate power? Why isn't the NSA using it to make us all utterly love one candidate for president or another? Is it intentionally hidden by God or Satan, *or is it hidden at all,* and are those agencies using it all the time?

Please, anyone that want's to comment send an email, tell all of us why we still love the idea of constant war, why do we even allow it? Why do we still use dryers that use huge amounts of electricity to dry our cloths when we could just hang them out in the sun, did you know that if we just stop using dryers there would be no need for nuclear power plants at all, and the Pacific ocean would not be dying and millions of humans would not be getting fatal cancers? Why do we still do and applaud the bizarre things that we do? Because something subtly in control of our brains tells us it's all just fine.

Something is infecting our minds and making us, as an entire species, suicidal warmongering selfish lazy and greedy maniacs, and the only way to overcome that is to recognize that it may have a source and then take steps to negate that source.

Being a decent person does not require an IQ of 137 like this writer once had, it usually simply requires that parents teach their children what ethics and respect are when they are still children, as it is a certainty that government funded teachers in our schools will not even get close to getting their funding suspended by teaching their students to be decent right *thinking* folks.

And being ethical does not mean using the principles of ethics in a hypocritical way by saying positive things to make yourself rich by using all the folks around you in utterly unethical ways, by being a non-stop compulsive liar.

Most of us want to be decent folks, but we will never truly be that unless we at least attempt to understand why we are the way we are.

We have met the enemy, it is us, somebody else said that first, but it is the truth.

Now go look in a mirror, would you want to deal with you in the outside world, every single day? If not why not? Stop it people, just grow up and learn to use your own minds to act responsibly.

Chapter Seven
The Evolutionary Ladder You Must Climb To Become a True Creator God

Basically the academics are saying the obvious, consciousness exists but we can't prove it scientifically unless we can measure it and quantify it as something; but none of them seem to have recognized the obvious. We all *know* inherently that it exists, it is the most intrinsic aspect of our existence, and as a result we all take it for granted. But almost nobody has a clue or can even begin to explain exactly what it is.

There are basically only two alternatives to describing what consciousness is, the first one claims that consciousness is a sort of illusion generated by the sum of the interactions of our mechanical brain functions, a sort of gestalt or individualizing form of gazillions of physical interactions, in other words an illusion that we only *experience* as the core of what we are, while the second one claims in a wide variety of ways that in effect consciousness is everywhere, that even the strictly mechanical universe is conscious, but even most of those still deny the existence of a God or a God mind, as that is strictly verboten, it is so verboten that in Universities you are not even allowed to express the question and then seek academic proofs that it just might be a legitimate issue.

OM, our Creator, exists, this writer has met him and been inside his expression of consciousness… and this writer has shown you all how to do exactly the same things if you really want to learn the truth. Just read 'The Promontory'.

Your ID, in effect the center of your mind, the sort of black hole that everything falls into is not of your brain, but of your *mind,* which is the same as the mind of your soul, and your purified expression of consciousness. Your ID is <u>exactly, a structural aspect, the heart of a particle expression of the field of consciousness,</u> like a proton it lives basically forever but it is constantly evolving according the histories of its existence like a photon, and like a photon or an electron it is never entirely separate from its parent field, it is simply that that degree of separation or individualization is again like the photon and electron always uncertain.

Your experience of experience does not die when your physical brain and body dies. Your experience of experience only dies for simplicities sake a few hours *before you as a human here are reborn* as a physical creature, it is, the process of cleaning the slate, a perfectly natural thing. Your ID is almost always wiped clean of all its memories so that you can begin again as a unique new individual and learn a lot more from the experience as a result, and well you can prove to those that matter if your soul is worth saving or not. But your memories from past lives are preserved and you almost always get them back when you die here.

The experience of life as a human is all about the evolutionary individualization process of the ID or your own particle expression of consciousness, that process goes on and on across many lifetimes and it hones and evolves the ID particle until it becomes if it is successful, worthy of an in effect *adult* expression of what it is; which is in effect the equivalent or actuality of a God.

One of the properties of the cloud of consciousness is that it localizes in areas of expression that arise as the result of the gestalting of many quantum mind particles. In part this is because of the property of the uncertainty of separation of the mind particles from the cloud of origination.

If that was unclear look up 'gestalt' on the web, in particular look up Ernst Mach the guy who first quantified the idea around these parts, then look up 'emergent systems' as they are related then try to grasp the entire related set of ideas as in sum it is a lot larger than its singular parts; yes there is an odd pun there but it is real, in other words read it with an open and creative mind. The come back here and please be patient as it is a bit complex.

There is a cloud of consciousness around the earth that is in a sense denser than it is in outer space, precisely because of the multitude of human souls and life in general on this planet. And because the core of our souls is that unseparate mind particle, we can access that cloud and both affect it and in effect learn things from it. However it is very difficult to rely on what you learn in this way as it always has to be interpreted and related by minds that have variable histories.

The cloud of consciousness has many properties and in effect many types of particle expressions, some of these are used to fabricate the 'material' of our souls and some of these are and can be used to fabricate the material of entire experiential in a sense only, *external* realms, sort of in the ways that the four normal fields of physics here express a variety of particle expressions that are used to create the entirety of physical reality here.

Our physical reality was generated as a type of virtual reality with a variety of constraints called physical laws, then we are a sort of alternative type of energy that is deposited into this virtual reality so that God (OM) can find out if what he created might have some sort of useful value.

To understand how this can be you have to realize that science has proven the old Tibetan Buddhist idea that there is no material reality here at all, everything that seems material is comprised of constrained bits of energy only. There are four fields or types of energy that comprise everything in our physical reality + one that experiences our reality, that of the field of consciousness; but again the field or spectrum of consciousness is very complex, even more so that the EM spectrum so that entire experiential realities can be constructed from and in that medium alone.

If you think this is impossible, simply think about exactly what a complex dream universe is constructed from, then consider that it might be possible to bump up the manifestation of a dream universe into a higher level of experiential reality.

Then realize that when you are in your purified consciousness body only, and using your purified consciousness senses you are directly entrained into a reality when there that is realized as utterly brilliant in the functions of that experience because everything is simply functions of one field or spectrum of energy that is simply entirely constructed and experienced as various aspects of what is in truth one single type of energy.

The difference is that the field of consciousness or the full spectrum properties of the field of consciousness are sufficiently complex in their properties and particle aspects that they can exhibit, that they can be used to fabricate entire realms that are experienced as external realities, and when you are in one of those; there is a distinct sense that you are an integral part of these realities because in fact you are. As a result when you are in one of those the experience of reality is among other things immensely more 'brilliant' than it is here.

Next time you experience a brilliant dream try to remember it as it really is, as one of the many varieties of these realms, it is simply not nearly as explicit and replete as a full on realm built from the consciousness field.

Physics of Consciousness

You can feel this subtle connectedness in this world as well, a sort of odd but on occasion profound realization of your participation in the deeper aspects of reality, but you have to purify your soul out in the natural world in order to feel this. In America the Native Americans, before TV and orange soda showed up, used to be really good at this, they usually called it something like knowing the Great Spirit of the natural world and thus becoming an integral part of nature.

Okay all of this is here so that you will understand what follows in a slightly deeper way than you might otherwise have understood it; so now re-read this paragraph. 'The experience of life as a human is all about the evolutionary individualization process of the mind or your own particle expression of consciousness, that process goes on and on across many lifetimes and it hones and evolves the mind particle until it becomes, if it is successful, worthy of an in effect *adult* expression of what it is; which is in effect the equivalent of a God. However as human souls in this here and now we are usually very low in this evolutionary process.

Now we can begin to climb that ladder by using a familiar example.

It's a reasonably simple manner to find the ladder, and the first rung of that ladder. Christ found it by sacrificing one life here to try and elevate the consciousness of a primitive slave race called humans. In metaphysical literature this is called a bestowal, and now you know the reason any elevated or ascended person would bother to do this.

This writer does not know what immediately follows as personal fact but as the result of reading a book that claims to have been written by a humble man that was merely transcribing the words granted to him by an arch angel, into a book that is by any measure gargantuan; pretty much in the same manner that the Koran was granted to the Muslims; the book is called the Urantia Book. In that book it says that Christ had successfully lived through numerous incarnations, until just before he came here, when he was a great and benevolent prince of an entire planet not too far away in this galaxy. It is a story that is very similar to that of Gautama Buddha.

You also have to understand that Christ was here sort of and on his pavilion far before he was incarnated here as a physical person. If you question this simply read in the Old Testament the story about Jacobs Ladder and realize it was Christ that Jacob met when he arrived at the Pavilion.

Then Christ was reborn here, he did a few fairly simple miracles so that people would listen to what he had to say, and then he simply told the predominantly selfish primitive people here more or less how their Creator wanted them to be, and then told them that, if they were decent folks, how they could get to a place that was Heaven then, and that when he died here he would go and create another version of Heaven for the people that believed in him and during their lives here acted in ways that reflected what he had taught them to be.

Then maybe he died on a cross maybe not, but either way the Creator granted him access to the ladder, and he climbed the first rung by creating his own version of Heaven.

This writer is not going to claim that he knows the nature of every step or rung of the ladder that leads you to the status as being a true 'creator' God, but the first step is being granted the ability to create anything you can imagine.

On the other side, in most places at least, this is no big deal, it's simply a mental evolution of the fact that your soul can be anything you can imagine; after you learn that, it is just a matter of finding the material outside your soul to transform it by recognizing what you want it to be.

Finding that material is a secret OM keeps hidden, so you can usually only find it by being granted OM's approval. The reason he keeps it hidden is that if evil selfish folks like most humans are, were to find that out, all kinds of problems and troubles might arise that decent people on the other side might be forced to deal with.

Satan just as an example finds this material by collecting the actual souls of humans that stupidly ask him for favors in this life in exchange for their souls, sometimes he keeps those souls intact but turns them into his slaves, but other times he can use them to create all kind of mindless stuff by simply destroying their individual sense of being. This is not the same as being terminated in the lake of fire, but in terms of the independent sense of identity of the subject soul, it is effectively the same thing.

The process of climbing the ladder is both a learning, and an earning process, which among other things means that the things you must earn include the requirement that you must create things like OM does and not like Sophia does. That means you must intellectually analyze every aspect of whatever the thing is you want to create, before you actually engage in creating it.

Just one example, if you want to create something of value here the way a young god does it, you would be far better off to imagine say pure gold than hundred dollar bills, as the bills are intentionally very complex creatures and you will probably be arrested as a counterfeiter if you were to go out and spend any of them. Whereas if you screw up making gold you will merely be an alchemist that wasn't very good, you usually don't go to prison for being that; just joking around sort of.

Of the process of creation, except for creating a living soul, or a full tilt universe, the making of an entire experiential realm is the most difficult thing to do successfully. The good news is you get as many tries as is required to get it right. That means you can create a complex realm, then go inside of it and figure out what the deficiencies are before you actually invite others in to share it with you.

It is a lot like being a lucid dreamer, you wake up in your dream and then make the surroundings just the way you want them, and then once you are satisfied you can invite other ID's into that realm and sort of show it off. It really is the same thing just on a far more replete and complex scale.

Creating a realm is also something you do outside of time relative to other places, indeed the time of a place is one of the primary foundations of designing the place. In this universe time is defined by the constant C, or the speed of light in a vacuum. There was a hint there you might have missed; light is a pretty basic quantity of experiential realms, so you define the nature of light and you get the time of the place as well. You can make the passage of time go by very quickly and then when it's done slow that time down so it is closer to the realm you are transferring souls from and therefore the new folks will be mentally more comfortable transferring into your new realm.

If you want a tangible example of the complexity of creating realms, consider what John Cameron and his folks had to do to so exquisitely create an immensely complex entire new planet on computers for 'Avatar'.

Just really think about what he did for a moment. All the characters in that world were real actors, but they were rendered into that realm which was entirely artificial, the characters were actually rendered as if they were there, riding dragons in the sky and in front of and behind trees and entire jungles constantly flowing in and out around and behind pretty much an entire perceived as real immensely complex reality and all of it done with perfect perspective.

If you are creating a new true realm, unless you are Sophia and you can access another God in the background,

Physics of Consciousness

you don't get any computers to play with, you have to visualize what you want inside your own mind, sort of like your own mind does when it dreams, but you have to do that when in a fully awake intellectual state of mind.

The bizarre thing about this is that it can also be done right now simply using technology. We can once again use 'Avatar' as an example, you simply need the Virtual Reality gear from Oculus Rift, only as another example, and a really freaking good computer, but instead of making a movie following a script you just construct an entire 'planetary, environment in the computer in T3D with a very detailed internal map then you simply give someone a VR rig and allow them to walk around explore and interact with others when they are inside.

With the advent of worldwide graphic communications that the owner of Facebook is attempting to implement you can interact with anyone from anywhere on this planet inside that realm, and in just a few years as mentioned a while back, the impact of that reality will be far more interesting to folks that enjoy it, and for instance far cheaper than the billions of dollars NASA spends to send probes to other real planets.

Gods do this with actual realities and people go into them and spend entire lives living inside of them, while true Creator God's like OM create entire universal realms that last and evolve across trillions of experience years with gazillions of environments and endless legions of folks or ID's to enjoy them, that are then allowed to experience those experiences and evolve towards hopefully being more than they are; guess what, we are inside one of these right now.

That means in terms of time, that from an earthly point of view it can seem like Christ created his version of heaven rather quickly, but that to him it might have required say hundreds of thousands of years of his personal experience time to get it right.

This writer has actually met a few lower level Gods on the other side, in his experience most of them simply find a nice place to live that somebody else created and then they design and build often rather remarkable or palatial homes, and then spend thousands of experience years being lower level gods and enjoying and learning from what they have become, of course one person this writer met was truly humble and simply went by himself to live in a cave, and slept on the hard ground, which he had been doing for several thousand years before this writer met him, and yes even as an entirely soul being that guy did not smell very good. Just joking around sort of, but you can read about him in the sort of pretend fiction 'OZ'.

You might think the reality above infers sort of a selfish reflection, people building mansions just because they can, but the truth is in the realms of the Gods genuine humility is a big factor, but you are still allowed to enjoy yourselves, so that many so called God's have trouble pretending to themselves that they are worthy of creating realms that are equal to the realms that OM and on occasion Sophia used to create, so they just wait and learn and take their time just being what they are. If you find this rather curious, just go outside at night and look at the stars, OM created this entire universe in his head before he expanded it in a dimensional sense and made it real, he really is a pretty damned awesome guy. Remember also that all decent ascended souls are immortal; to young gods there is no experience of death, so that the experience of time is a very different thing to them.

Christ was not exactly like most young Gods, and the people he was sort of working for, us, were very primitive and living in very primitive even harsh conditions, so pretty much anything he might create would be an improvement over what we were living in here. As a result he pretty much immediately went to work building his own mansion, *for us* to inhabit and enjoy.

An alternative to this evolutionary arrangement of most young Gods was experienced by this writer as follows. When you are flying over the sea of creation as a sort of manta ray made of light, your 'hands' are constantly sending out millions of little threads of light that can experience what it is like inside of the universes below, then, if you experience something interesting in one of those threads, your entire being can sort of translate down the thread and enter the universe it has found.

As an aside, currently a variety of academic folks have been very carefully studying the microwave background map of this universe and by subtracting aspects of it they have found a variety of places that exactly reflect what can only be explained so far as places where the boundary of this universe bumped into the boundaries of other universes, just as the various universes would do if all the universes existed in a kind of sea of universes, exactly as this writer experienced them, long before this academically supportive realization arrived.

This writer followed that sensory thread of knowing down into one of the universes; he is not sure at all why, just that he did. What he found there was a race of beings that were sort of half iridescent blue beetles and half spiders, that were on average experienced as being about nine feet tall and twelve feet long and had twelve very complex feet-hands on long arms and legs, and they ejected solid light in a wide variety of forms and colors just like a spider ejects silk to spin its webs. The difference was that these 'Lightweavers' had evolved and now were both incredibly benevolent decent folks and remarkably intelligent and telepathic, and they started out ancient times ago by building castles to impress their ladies just like we do, but they evolved that process into creating an entirely separate multiverse of realms, outside in infinity, separate from the multiverse that OM had created and that they had originally evolved inside of.

This writer has rather vague or subtle memories of spending around three hundred experience years with these people in a very dramatic and far more complex experience that occurred in only two hours and thirty eight minutes of earth time here in this life.

For some inexplicable reason they seemed to like this writer so they went inside his mind and then built him an entire planetary realm they were certain humans would enjoy, it really is a fine place and when this writer dies he plans on going to Christ's heaven first and then back to that Lightweaver world for a few thousand years. If your soul makes it into Christ's Heaven give this writer's soul a call and you can go there as well, there's more than enough room.

Actually that was a bit misleading, you dream here and you will also dream in Heaven, and the Lightweavers can visit you in your dreams, they are doing that even now, there are often reports of this occurring on the Web, and if they like you they may invite you to come and visit them when you die, if you do take them up on it you will not be disappointed.

If you think this writer is totally off the wall look up Carl Jung and his story about the iridescent blue beetle that made him start thinking about synchronicities and especially archetypal realms, around these parts it is what the Lightweavers disguise themselves as when they are investigating human souls, Egyptian dung beetles or scarabs, told you, humility is a valuable commodity on the other side. If you see one of these in your dreams, be happy and talk to it, they are really fine folks and you may grant yourself an alternative to Christ's Heaven when you die.

The point is that like Polynesians whom this writer called enlightened Buddhists who don't realize what they are, these people, the Lightweavers, never really in effect realized they were climbing the ladder of the Gods, they were very humble in a good way, and simply evolved to become multiverse builders in their own right by simply following their own perfectly natural sort of pedantic evolutionary regimes. And they began doing their multiverse simply as a way to make more room to live in as their population expanded; their ladies laid eggs, hundreds of them at a time, and at one point literally millions of years ago, and unlike humans so far at least, they decided killing each other was wrong, so population overcrowding became a very real issue for them rather quickly.

They also became slightly nervous when they learned some of the things this writer learned and realized as a result of his metaphysical events, that if Sophia and or OM became insane, this entire multiverse could collapse, taking their own lives and their existence along with it, so the Lightweavers built their new multiverse almost entirely outside this one and went to great pains to insure it would survive no matter what happened here, including if anything happened to themselves.

For what it's worth, both Sophia and to a lesser degree OM are fully aware of this terrifying possibility of insanity and they value what we are, all of us that are decent in creation, as their children, so they have taken massive and very complex steps to insure that what they have created will continue on if insanity does happen to either of them, this writer does know what some of those steps are but it's probably wiser not to talk too much about them.

Author's note: I know, you may have once again come to the conclusion that it is this writer that has already gone totally insane, but again this knowledge occurred and arrived as the result of and in very concise events, that almost all of the time had nothing to do with psychedelic or psychoactive drugs, and I have tried over and over again to discount them as mere hallucinatory events of little value, but when I analyze them carefully and as objectively as I can; I simply cannot find the justification to fault them as imaginary routines. So to me they are real, but now in part because of things that occurred to me at the hands of other humans in this life, and because I live alone, I drink a couple of shots of whisky and take a mild sleeping pill every night in order to get to sleep, and that has the effect of making my current metaphysical life incredibly non-existent, and my day to day life incredibly boring, so I am simply relating what I have learned in the past here. Once again, you can read it entirely as an interesting fiction if you like, but it is not... either way by the time you are done, these words hopefully will have a positive effect on your soul. End of Note.

Okay the last rung of the ladder requires anyone who wants to become a true Creator God, to locate its being entirely inside its mind and then completely without other defenses *enter into the chaos of infinity* and, that being is required to notify OM that this is occurring.

Sorry, foundational digression once again. You need to understand a few things before we can go on. Recall that OM knows everything that anybody in creation experiences including their thoughts, and that all young Gods know this with certainty and can use that capability to communicate with OM's mind whenever they want, sort of like second nature; and, because they are young Gods, OM will actually pay attention to what they are saying.

The second thing is that on the positive evolutionary side of the Gods in a rather subtle way, the factors related to individuality tend to sublimate towards similarities in your soul, the primary quality that does this is your strength and internal expression of the Holy Spirit, so that in some ways the higher you climb the ladder the closer you become to being in effect one being, God, pure and simple; but all true

Physics of Consciousness

Gods are also individuals because all of them arrive into their status as the evolutionary effect of the fact that they all arrive from different histories. Therefore they often have differing points of view and can contribute to creation and the elevated conversations of the Gods as true individuals.

We all live inside a container that is comprised of *infinity*. Initially you can say that our universe must exist in a container that consists of infinite space and time, one way or another no matter how you imagine it, out there somewhere in some way infinity must exist in some way.

This is not a quasi-religious statement of faith; it is the absolute solution to any salient and *logical* progression of thought.

On a superficial level and on very deep levels, infinity is a very dangerous thing to think about; just about every scientist and mathematician that has delved deeply towards understanding the nature of infinity has gone stark raving, and if they were lucky quit thinking about it and if not went raving insane permanently.

When he was young, this writer became moderately obsessed with this idea and followed it intellectually and well metaphysically until his being stood at the wall that separates us from the full experience of infinity, and then briefly stepped through to the other side. It is without any question the most terrifying thing you can experience, so please don't bother even trying.

Here is the why of that statement and why we don't have to deal with it in our day to day lives.

Infinity by its nature is the container for virtually everything, you can divide infinity infinitely in any way that you like, but because it is by its nature infinite it can always be divided again and again. The net result of all regimes related directly to infinity is absolute and utter chaos, and in consciousness that expresses itself as insanity, pure and simply *absolute insanity*. The ancient Hebrews that tried as best they could to be sterilized intellectuals from the get go, called it the *Ainsoph*.

True infinity is not big or small, a long ways away, or in some distant time, it is the very nature of true infinity that it cannot ultimately be defined in any way, so that ultimately there is no order of any kind, there is only one possibility when you understand the true nature of what that means and it is terrifying.

This is the greatness that the Holy Spirit granted to all of us, the consciousness that we all experience is not the same in its nature as the infinite container, so that here we are safe and sane, but you can step across that barrier that the Holy Spirit granted to us and enter infinity as a still conscious being, just do not do that, do not even try it, it is the most terrifying thing you can ever know and once you know it; it will never leave you, you will lose your innocence forever.

Infinity in its purest form is utterly defined as absolute chaos, it cannot be defined as any quantity of space or time as all definitions are by their nature finite. You can pretend that say Pi for instance is an infinite number, but it is also in context a carefully defined number so it is not really infinite, it can only exist in finite conditions of order. You can pretend that infinite sets exist and then add one to that set to make it an Aleph, and then multiply Alephic sets but in truth you are just playing mathematical games that would not even exist if infinity was all there was to the thing.

So this writer is going to make a bold claim or you will be bored to tears, just trust it, infinity and understanding infinity and the chaos of infinity is by far the most dangerous intellectual game you can play, in part because outside of the reality of the order of experience that we experience as self-aware conscious beings, infinity is the most real thing that exists, and this is critically important, infinity is not out there beyond the edges of the universe, it is right there on the tip of your nose, it is rampantly expressed inside your brain and your mind, it is everywhere there is anything at all and even in places where there is nothing at all.

And ultimately it cannot be defined in any way, and that is the utterly scary thought about the beast, ultimately it can only express utter quintessential chaos that obviously contains stuff.

The first reason we experience consciousness in an orderly way is because the Holy Spirit injected itself into the field of consciousness in infinity and implanted into it a sense of basic order. He, it, tried to do this in a way that would extend across all of infinity, but because of the nature of the beast that was impossible, so the best he could manifest was as percolations in the midst of infinity, just like ascending bubbles in water; containers for order that can pop up anywhere in infinity.

One of those percolations was Sophia, she then created OM, and OM tried as best he could to improve on the technologies that the Holy Spirit had injected into infinity in ways that would hopefully improve on the sense of order that OM had inherited. The Holy Spirit can be thought of as a Zen Buddhist, while OM is more of a grand architect.

Okay here is why Hugh Everett was wrong. Just be patient this will make more sense shortly but it is related to this bit about infinity so it is sort of an intellectual barb that will get smoothed out as your read further.

According to Mr. Everett's interpretation of quantum mechanics, whenever a particle, any particle, goes from one state to another in any kind of actual way an entire new universe is created. There are literally uncountable particles making up the reality every human experiences just on the earth alone, the earth exists in a universe of trillions of bodies, just counting the visible stars and now planets. Thus the number of particle conversions and the birth of new universes is uncountable and *exactly the same as, in its ultimate expression, the chaos of infinity*, the entire purpose of creation as it was originally contrived by both the Holy Spirit and OM was to generate a sense of order so that they could eventually provide a sense of orderly experience for all the particles of consciousness, us as an example, that would eventually arrive to experience, experience.

Obviously it is a fact, that consciousness exists in the midst of infinity, and it is a fact that we experience experience in a more or less orderly fashion. If you are an academic you can discount with a big boo the terms Holy Spirit and God but you have to recognize the truth of what that sentence conveys even without the deities.

A concrete sense of order exists in the midst of infinity, so how in the heck did it get there? In this case Occam's razor demands that in some way consciousness had something to do with that; (And you have to get rid of entirely all the intrinsic human anthropomorphisms that cloud our thinking and make us claim everything is all about humans because it simply is not true.) because consciousness is the fabric that does the experiencing, thus you must admit that it is more likely that that consciousness that installed and maintains a sense of order was at least a bit more comprehensive than the ones we enjoy as humans. In part because it had to arrive before we did. It is *a fact*, this reality, this universe, existed before we did.

Okay so, the last rung of the ladder is going into your mind entirely without any other defenses and then expressing your consciousness entirely into the chaos of infinity outside of the protections of order the bubble or percolation installed by the Holy Spirit and OM and maybe Sophia, because if you want to be a true god that is the first thing you are required to be responsible for when you create new universes out in the chaos of infinity; you must survive that knowing of the chaos of infinity, you must come to know your true enemy intimately and you must figure out entirely on your own how to install a sense of order into the midst of the chaos of infinity.

If you fail you dissipate into the chaos of infinity entirely and utterly cease to exist, if you are successful you can become a true universal-multiversal creator God. This last rung is by far the most terrifying thing that all wannabe Gods are required to face, but they must face it or they must be satisfied with being slightly less than they can be.

On occasion OM or even peers among the young Gods may like a candidate and sit in the background watching and then bail them out if they seem to be about to fail, but that is rare and can never be counted on.

Part of the point of this is that even you can go into infinity as what you are right now and maybe come out with the full capabilities of a God right away, but be cautioned, young gods typically take millions of experience years to learn and condition their souls to be ready to do this, you are not even remotely ready even though your ego tries to tell you that you are, so by far the most likely outcome of trying this early is that you will simply cease to exist as a conscious being and you will almost certainly cease to exist with extreme prejudice so just don't even try it. Trust this, this writer tried it well before his time, and he is not even close to being a young God as a result, but he will be eternally grateful that he survived intact and he grants that gratitude to the Holy Spirit.

Perhaps the most important thing you can take from what you have just read, is that if you are a moderately decent person that acts like a responsible respectful adult, one way or another your soul will survive physical death here; and now you now know the basic bones of what your future will resemble, as you eventually become a young God, and inversely what you will lose if you find yourself acting like a normal human totally selfish and yes evil.

Chapter Eight
Quantum Uncertainty Interpreted In the Context of Convergence in an Engineered Reality & the Importance of Convergence Algorithms in Quantum Computing

Note: The first part of this is a bit intellectually intense, just read it and then the second part will tend to generate greater clarity.

At every step of the way towards the ultimate experience of experience by your mind; from outer reality to inner functions of the brain there are literally gazillions of particles in superposition states that have to decide exactly what they are supposed to be, in order to convey what they are supposed to convey to the human experience, *or any other existential aspect of reality*, gazillions of them that have to make decisions *exactly correctly* at least 36 times a second; all of these particles comprise an incredibly complex mosaic, an intricate tapestry of reality.

Some of these particles are Hadronic; meaning they have to stick around and be what they are for a long time, so that rocks can continue to be rocks, while uncertainty technically exists even in the Hadronic particles.

Hadronic uncertainty in the context of the engineering of reality doesn't mean or imply that any of us can for instance look at a rock and turn it into a tree, or look at a lump of lead and turn it into gold just as an act of will. Hadronic uncertainty has to do with time, but in a rather esoteric way it does allow chemists and Gods to alter that which is delivered to consciousness through experience in ways that reduce the impact of entropy and allows the engineering of reality to manifest over longer periods of time in a reliable manner.

But then billions of other particles are Leptonic, which means they are *constantly* changing and remembering all the stuff that is happening to them as they transverse the process of their lives, electrons and photons are merely two examples.

Leptonic particles are the engines of operational reality that convey information in a remarkably co-operative manner. It is this co-operation and the transfer of information in an incredibly and constantly perfected way that is not even remotely understood by human intellect, but that has implications that are remarkably important. That is because that information transfer is related to something called quantum entanglement and so far science has yet to grasp the immense important of this property in the engineering of reality.

You can say that all these particles merely have to follow physical laws, but the truth is nobody knows exactly what physical laws are or more importantly *where they come from*. The basic tenants of science are still based on philosophical regimes wealthy naturalists from the seventeen hundreds came up with.

The most important thing you need to grasp is that all of physical reality and the process of *experiencing* physical reality is an immeasurably complex process that must be completely replenished at least 36 times *a second,* that is not referring entirely and strictly to the stuff that gets into your sensory organs but also the existential stuff that is going on out there in the world that you have no idea about but has to go on constantly to make reality function as it functions perfectly all the time.

Science has a habit of slicing reality up into little bits so that our brains can focus on the bits and make a dent in knowing what the bits do. Reality and understanding how it works demands you accept the massive complexity of the engines that drive it and then look at those engines as a whole river, rather than merely the properties of water, *along with the environment that contains that river all at once, then look behind it at all at the systems that drive it.*

It's an immeasurably complex mosaic of billions upon billions of *arbitrary* factors that somehow we experience fluidly without a second thought as to what is really occurring in ways that are always absolutely replete, and in ways that you can thoroughly expect will keep on working in ways that you have gotten used to.

Certainly if you take into the account physical laws outside the mind and the fact that our brains learn how to do what they do as they mature it is obviously possible but it is still remarkably unlikely that this occurs *perfectly* all the time, strictly as the result of stuff we think we already know, *precisely and exactly because all (quantum) particles have an uncertain nature.*

It has been categorically proven that all quantum particles reside quiescently in a superposition state until they are experienced by consciousness. *Superposition* means exactly that they can be one thing or another thing entirely until they are experienced; or measured by tools created by conscious beings, and that until that experience occurs they can be either; or, as they are required to be when they are eventually experienced. In terms you might be able to comprehend quantum particles are both on and off or 1's and zeros at once until they are experienced or measured. Every single bit of the reality you experience is composed of quantum particles.

The second issue is; no one in science has a clue as to what the *'mind'* is. All of the remarkable stuff that science has figured out says that all of the input is translated and then transferred to something called the map room in our brain where it is sorted out and displayed *to the ID*, and is thus experienced in our 'minds'.

The 'mind' when you are alive and awake and when you dream, is exactly the same as *the mind of your soul*. When you go to sleep, when you astral project, when you die here physically, you still own exactly the same *mind*. Except that mind is constantly evolving according to the sum of the experience that it experiences, almost exactly like a photon is constantly evolving, but hopefully in far more complex ways.

If you are alive you own a soul; that is the exact thing that classifies all living things as *alive*. You can take this merely as a prejudicial assumption, but it has been demonstrated to this writer in ways that can only be interpreted as fact.

The mind or ID particle has certain structures, eyes ears and *a seat of perception or an ID*, structures that are normally there in awake physical, astral, and after death bodies.

The seat of perception, the ID, is normally accepted in psychology as a sort of black hole that all experience and thought flows into; metaphysically sophisticated folks call this the gate to the Akashic record and it is normally assumed that it is a one way device that takes all individualizing experience and transfers it to a recording device of sorts that is normally assumed to be a technical aspect of the field of consciousness.

If you think this last statement is too bizarre to even consider, take a careful look at a photon of light and then ask how exactly does a photon remember everything it must remember? For instance a photon born in a quasar thirteen billion years ago that began its life out there across the entire universe can convey all of the information of its life to an astronomer operating a telescope here that collects that photon. The photon is a mindless particle of light, while our mind is a far more complex object.

It is a fact to this writer that the transfer of experiential information outward from us to that technical aspect of the field of consciousness is not the only purpose of this tube. (The word tube is simply a graphic way to convey a property related to quantum particle entanglement.) <u>There is a resonance of sorts, a very subtle signal that comes back down that tube and enters our minds</u>.

Okay... Important argument points...

1. The incredibly complex mosaic of particles in constantly *uncertain* states that assemble themselves constantly to become the sum of what is experienced by consciousness, or other aspects of reality.

2. You do have a mind that is the same as the mind of your soul; it is the same mind you own in complex astral projection events. If, when, you experience those you can subsequently examine them intelligently and find details that deny the possibility that these are dream type hallucinations of the brain. But by their nature they are entirely subjective so you simply cannot prove them empirically or in acceptable academic ways until you can amass a large quantity of accounts and then apply a Schrodinger probability to the sum, and so far this has been incredibly difficult to achieve, or, you can demonstrate knowledge and technologies learned on the other side that are currently entirely alien to the human experience. This writer suspects Nicola Tesla knew how to do this.

3. Your minds soul, the quantum ID particle of consciousness, has a few structural elements including a property related to quantum entanglement, that transfers experience to a technical aspect of the field of consciousness and it then sends a resonance back down to grant a sane sense of order to your experience.

4. All the basic particles that make up the experience of reality have a quality called uncertainty that can be changed virtually instantly or outside of time simply by the recognition of what they are. This has to be qualified here; uncertainty in Hadronic particles is damped down in time, it is the uncertainty in Leptonic particles we are talking about here, as they are the in a sense only the active engines that deliver the experience of reality to all aspects of reality including us.

A rock is still a rock even when nobody sees or feels it. It is the photons and the experience of gravity among other things that conveys the experience of the rock to us

5. There is something going on that has to do with quantum entanglement, which has now been thoroughly proven; a venue where information is transferred outside of normal time. This writer is not exactly certain how this applies here only that it has been proven and seems to have a relationship to this issue. As follows maybe; our mind is a self-recognizing quantum particle of the field or spectrum of consciousness that owns similarities to a self-recognizing photon; massive amounts of information are being conveyed to it constantly exactly and instantly, obviously systems are hardwired into our brains that interpret the sensory input in a sane and orderly manner as it is delivered to the ID, and obviously just as one example photons follow physical laws, but everything as it occurs is conveyed by various quantum particles that are by their nature *uncertain in character, until they are recognized by consciousness* (Paraphrased quote Dr. John Walker) Copenhagen or not, something implicitly implies that there is 'something' in consciousness that is fixing the character of the quantum particles.

As Gerhard Rempe of the Max Planck Society has demonstrated the totality of a photon is several meters across, therefore it is not unreasonable to suggest that our mind may be a quantum particle, a sphere or oblate shape usually about six inches across, just as it is experienced when you remove the pollution generated by our physical brain.

This writer has been shown this fixing agent graphically. It is the higher dimensional signal resonance that comes into the back of the mind of your soul, your ID, a self-recognizing quantum particle with similarities to a photon, and the essence of what you are. An aspect of that ID particle that goes outward, perhaps to the Akashic Record uses properties related to <u>quantum uncertainty</u> to instantaneously grant order to the experience of experience.

It is <u>not human consciousness</u> that does this, it is a technical aspect of the field of consciousness invading in a very subtle way, the individualizing particle of human consciousness. Uncertainty in the Copenhagen context is indirectly a proof that God, or at least 'something' more ascendant than us exists, but it expresses this proof in very subtle or 'uncertain' ways intentionally so that he, it, will not obviously interfere with the experience of experience.

You do not have to think of God as OM or Allah, or so on, you can think of god as merely a Nick Bostrom post human programmer if you like, but something or someone is influencing the programing signal of reality before it gets into our ID as finalized experience and the best place to technically manifest that programming is in a technical aspect of the ID or our functioning self-recognizing quantum particle of consciousness.

So in order to prove it as an accepted academic fact you simply have to demonstrate the details in a technical and empirical way, and when you do that as a result everything about quantum mechanics falls into place with clarity and you understand what quantum mechanics and the universe are really all about. You can simply call it a technical property of the physics of the cloud or field, of the spectrum of consciousness.

It is a technical aspect of the field of consciousness that does this by demanding a *convergence* of millions of factors outside of time constantly. This convergence doesn't create an entirely new universe (Everett's interpretation) every time it happens but it does shape the ultimate experience of this universe that any and all of us experience as individuals as it happens, and it does happen constantly for every mind that experiences anything on this planet alone, and it does this in ways that like the assembly of the mosaic that every single mind experiences in absolute ways will lead towards a convergence of experience for those minds, on certain levels of operation, across the entire universe.

The Buddha was exactly right reality is a dream manufactured in the mind of God, but it is a dream; orders of magnitude more complex than the dreams we experience as mere humans. Thus it is a simulated reality, but all realities are similar in this way and so it can also be considered as a baseline reality, just one of many, at least in this multiverse.

Once you thoroughly understand how this works, you can become a post human, an adult expression of consciousness, otherwise known as a novice God.

If you want to understand how the 'post human' programmers do what they do, (whoever or whatever they are) first you have to utterly remove your anthropomorphic prejudices, then you have to study the 'physics of consciousness'. To paraphrase Alain Aspect 'if you look carefully at reality there seems to be a very esoteric sense of order hiding in the works'. That which has been explained here may be the key that can open that door.

This has described in very simple terms the technology used to make us experience this reality as it is experienced. The main point here is that *convergence* is the key, and that on a very deep level, if convergence is truly at work the implications are profound.

Quantum Uncertainty is not about uncertainty, the word itself is a bit of misdirection, it is about how the massive mosaic of things that are experienced, is converted into a sense of experiential order, it is about *Convergence*, it is about weaving millions of bits of multicolored threads into a wonderful tapestry that can be viewed in an instant in its entirety with simply a glance, and the how and why of the way that convergence of experienced reality is accomplished.

Okay, all kinds of folks are out there are yelling this is total BS, 'obviously God is not entirely fabricating my experience of reality 36 times a second when I'm awake, I don't even believe God exists, all those trillions of particles... just absolute nonsense?'

First you do not have to call it God, but unless quantum mechanics and Professor John Walker are at least partially wrong, *something* like this just has to be going on. Quantum mechanics is recognized as the most proven regime in modern science, and Dr. Walker is recognized as perhaps the smartest most educated man that has ever existed.

Consider this, when you dream according to science your physical brain alone is generating the billions of particle interactions required to construct what you experience as a complete constantly unfolding reality that changes entirely six times a night and then motivating all those other folks in your dream to act in real time just like they act in real life, and billions of people on this planet utterly believe exactly what the Buddha told us, 'we live in a dream in the mind of God'.

Maybe, just maybe, the Buddha was exactly correct and the fact that he was correct has now been proven by quantum mechanics, but that truth is simply incomprehensible to most mere humans. 'We are merely dream characters in the mind of God.' The problem is that *something* related to this issue simply has to be going on. This writer was graphically shown the technical vehicle

Physics of Consciousness

related to making this happen, that does not mean this writer is stating a fact, but that it is a very high probability that something like this may be going on, and so more intelligent and accredited people in academia would do well to consider this approach as they are trying to explain what exactly is going on, as if you do that everything else that is related begins to fall into place in a logical and salient manner..

Now this is going to get a tiny bit complex; but the foundation will lead to the clarity mentioned, the complexity in part because it is related to a bit of exquisite technology recently developed called the D-Wave II Quantum Computer and the interpretations of quantum mechanics that likely lead towards the development of that machine.

The D-Wave is perhaps the most exquisite and superlative expression of technological development mankind has yet produced, but the interpretation of the physics that lead to it may be a tiny bit misleading, and the key to understanding the why of that claim, or at least to the claims related to that machine by its creator during his lectures, Mr. Geordie Rose, a brilliant and humble man by any measure, are rather complex, and in this writers interpretation, have everything to do with defeating the Chaos of Infinity, rather than the constant creation of entirely new universes.

So this will go rather modestly into the theory of Quantum Mechanics and the semi-accepted theory that that reality of physics demands the existence of google zillions of parallel universes, at least in the ways it was interpreted by Hugh Everett, but this will *not* for the reader's sake, go into the math of quantum mechanics, and hopefully this will put your mind towards a path that indicates it may be possible to use that machine, the D-Wave, to rather inversely prove among other things the existence of God, or at least the existence of Professor Nick Bostrom's post humans, and critically the fabrication of reality and maybe even how that is done, as we experience it.

This is because again 'uncertainty', in quantum mechanics is not primarily about parallel universes, but it is about the how and why this universe and numerous others operate, and the key word about that is not *'uncertainty'* it is about instantaneous *'CONVERGENCE'*. And how the D-Wave might be able to prove that incredibly important realization and again in the process prove that the mind of God or at least a technical aspect of the field of consciousness plays a constant and critical role in the fabrication of all realities. Again, this is not news at all, the Buddha told us exactly what was going on. He said; "we live in a dream inside of God's mind"; and the Buddha, was exactly right.

Particles in quantum physics are usually rather mysterious little buggers that most of the time, make up everything that is physical and even energetic about the reality we live in, that includes the sort of material or actual manifestations of everything we relate to energy.

According to Max Planck Niels Bohr and Irwin Schrodinger; and now everybody else that has investigated the issue, all particles can be in two or more completely alternative states simultaneously; literally at the same moment or the same time they can be either one or the other *simultaneously*. This is commonly known as a super-positioned state and specifically according to Mr. Schrodinger the particles are always in such a state until they are measured by something or someone, the dead and alive cat in a box, and the fact that you cannot know if the cat is alive or dead until you open the box was how this is commonly explained.

The extended Copenhagen interpretation of this is that human consciousness is directly involved in the creation of all expressions of the experience of reality, but that is at least partially wrong.

The Copenhagen Interpretation focuses on human consciousness mostly because it is the only consciousness we are usually aware of, and because academically even the mention of God or even merely the physics of consciousness is verboten. Despite this, numerous people have made claims that the Copenhagen Interpretation is a proof that God exists, most of those arguments are also somewhat, to be generous, misleading. This writer calls this state of examination *anthropomorphic prejudice* and if you're going to examine the physics of consciousness in an honestly academic context you simply have to get rid of that state of mind entirely.

Consciousness exists as a field of force unto itself, it has little to do with a proof of God as God himself and herself merely arose out of that cloud and figured out how to use it in ways that are very similar to what a paltry few humans are currently in the very early stages of doing.

Consciousness is a fifth field of force, but it is a good bet that one way or another eventually you will come to the conclusion in purely sterilized academic terms that God exists as the result of the deep examination of what consciousness is.

In other words if consciousness exists and everybody that is even a dufus human is certain that it does, and if it exists as something more than its individual expression in human brain-minds, something that is far less certain in academic terms so far, but if it does, purely evolutionary logic demands the existence of something equivalent to a god must arise.

Basically if consciousness in any form extends across any race of semi-intelligent creatures like us, and we are certain that is true, it is likely it is common to other races in this universe and probably in all races across the multiverse.

Using the certainty that is represented by us, in the context of the actual survival of the race over sufficient time, it is highly probable that human consciousness will eventually evolve to a point where at least one of us will eventually become the equivalent of a God.

To be polite, there are a fairly large number of humans that are certain other intelligent species exist in the universe we share, and this universe has apparently according to science existed for roughly fourteen billion years; long enough for people *like* us to have evolved technologies and knowledge to a point where they can create virtually anything they want to create and so they are the equivalent of Gods.

If even a single one of those creatures evolves out of this reality it is far more highly probable that such a creature evolved before us and designed the conditions that will allow others to enjoy the conditions that allowed it to arise. It is also probable that it can go back in time and create the conditions that will allow it to evolve into what it will become.

This latter condition is known in science as a percolation in time, just like a bubble that forms in boiling water, or a bottle of beer, such a bubble is exactly what needs to occur to defeat the chaos of infinity, and percolations in time are the basic essential commodity of orderly universal creation.

This is another interpretation of Professor Bostrom's post human philosophical argument, but either way, post human or God, if consciousness exists and evolves and we are certain of both conditions, more ascendant varieties of it must exist in the greater reality we exist inside of.

So you simply need to find the proof that consciousness is not entirely the phony product of a physical brain and by default you will open a door that will change everything about human existence, you might even win a descendent of dynamite in the bargain. Sorry just being cute with words.

Superposition is just one factor of quantum mechanics that has been utterly proven to be real and true. One of the other approaches to understanding what this means was put forward by Hugh Everett, who very carefully came to the conclusion that every time a particle becomes either one final state or another, an entirely new universe is created that is in essence parallel to this one or the one the particle became ultimately fixed in, and as a result an entirely new real and replete universe is created. There are google zillions of particles making up the reality of this planet alone and most of them are changing from one state to another nearly constantly even when they are not being measured by humans so that the number of parallel universes that are born out of this entire universe alone at least according to Mr. Everett, must be absolutely uncountable even by God.

As mentioned previously, the reason this writer knows this theory is wrong is that Mr. Everett's theory yields a condition that ultimately is exactly the same as the chaos of infinity, and this writer knows as fact that a major part of what all the Gods since the Holy Spirit have been doing is figuring out ways to defeat that chaos and thus the experience of that chaos forever.

Mr. Rose apparently believes along with maybe the people at Google and NASA that his machine the D-Wave computer can access these alternative universes and find all kinds of alternative answers to questions about this reality by doing just that.

Yes what Mr. Rose is implying in his lectures is a bit more subtle than that but it requires understanding the subtleties of quantum mechanics to understand it, and that is not what this is about. Mr. Rose tries to avoid those issues in his lectures as when people don't understand what the heck you are talking about they tend to get a tiny bit weird and stop listening, and well maybe he is trying to protect his technology by not disclosing too many details concerning what it really is. But it is a fact that all kinds of people on the web are writing all kinds of conclusions that are very esoteric as the result of the related things he *is* talking about, the so-called Mandela Effect or the subtle conversion of this universe to another causing what is known as the Mandela effect, every time the D-Wave is turned on is just one of them. You can look up anything here on the Web if you are clueless.

Okay if you are even remotely intelligent you can overlay several concepts in your mind at once. Folks born recently may not have a clue but when this writer was a young man they had a way to broadcast television signals through the air and then an antenna on your roof would collect those signals and the box in your living room would translate them into what amounted to entire complex universes on your TV screen.

The important point is that you could be anywhere, and these radio signals that contained these entire universes were all around you and even flowing through you but you had absolutely no idea they were there, until you turned on your TV and watched Moses, (Charlton Heston) stand on a rock and induce God to part the Red Sea so the children of Israel could escape the Egyptian army.

It is a fact that radio signals and microwaves of all sorts are constantly permeating the air all around us, they make movies on your TV, music on your radio, endless amounts of total bullshit on cellphones, and very encrypted military conversations as well as almost everything that is realized on computers these days, and they even let other cosmic stars talk to us, but in your everyday life you don't have a clue they even exist.

So maybe the folks at SETI should listen up; who can say with absolute authority that there isn't something similar to radio waves, but very different that absolutely nobody has a clue about because there is no device to use and interpret the resultant signals, precisely because nobody has a clue as to how those signals work. Perhaps you can declare that we already know those signals don't come from the EM, or strong and weak clouds, as all those are limited by C and therefore useless for intergalactic communications. Besides we already know a lot about those candidates.

However, the same cloud of the force of consciousness that is responsible for our souls is one of these alternative fields affecting this reality, the information memory of photons is another; you can argue that photons are subject to C and maybe so is the transfer of their memory regimes as well, but think a bit and realize that the information light contains is always in the right place at the right time when the light arrives and then converts to photons, so it has to be available for the photons before they arrive. This is a rather subtle point and this writer could be wrong but it is related to Alain Aspects quantum entanglement and so it is worth considering as the implications could be profound if it is true. Yet another type of these that is a fact to this writer; but merely hyperbole academically, is the constant higher dimensional communication by God's technical mind or a property of the physics of consciousness explained earlier, that gets into our own mind that makes us experience reality in ways that are orderly and coherent.

To make this clear, science absolutely demands that outside the physical laws of this universe, 'stuff' can and must travel faster than the speed of light C, and that just because a guy named Maxwell a long time ago using mathematics as a language said it couldn't in this universe doesn't necessarily make it a fact.

If this was not the case and stuff cannot travel faster than C then this universe would not be able to exist as it does exist because scientists are certain this is the only way to explain *inflation* just after the big bang. And well even inside this resulting universe as demonstrated by the fact of particle entanglement. Again you can argue for wormholes but in truth you are just arguing for an alternative to the limitations of C. If stuff can travel faster than C outside this universe who's to say or who can prove the negative that stuff inside this universe cannot travel faster than the speed of light and that it is simply a matter of learning how that might happen. In other words, sin of sins, maybe Einstein was not one hundred percent correct after all.

All you have to do is seek to understand the nature of dimensional branes and their architectures, and you will open doors inside your mind that are staggering to say the least.

Both technical philosophy and science are in agreement that it is impossible to truly prove a negative, and it is a fact that UFO's have to travel in ways far faster than the speed of light or they could not get here in a timely fashion, so it's simply a matter of figuring out how they do what they do. The reason science believes C is the limit is because back in the 19th century Maxwell simply said it was the limit and then Einstein agreed with him and *some* of the stuff Einstein said has turned out to be true so science believes *all* the stuff he said, in exactly the same ways that religious people claim there is a God usually without real foundation. Back when they invented railroads science declared no one could ever go faster than the speed of sound, you already know how that went.

To make the point offered a few paragraphs above simple; it was an electron in your TV that was engineered to turn a particular particle that was in a sense in a rather common superposition state from one color to another and from on to off that comprised a tiny aspect of an entire constantly evolving machine to convey to your mind the holistic *experience* of The Ten Commandments.

And even then those particles were so small that you could not normally even see one unless you had a really fine microscope.

Now carry this realization out into reality and apply it to your experience of reality. Photons, particles of light, are really tiny little buggers, not the sum of them Mr. Rempe, just their point aspects, that by most definitions almost do not even exist. The individual light spots on the computer you are probably reading this on are producing millions of them a second so that the resolution of what you see is rather precise.

For what it's worth so are your retinas; if you go in a cave and let your eyes adjust to absolute darkness, your retinas can recognize a single photon, science has proven this completely. But normally Gazillions of them are deposited on the nerve endings of the retinas in your eyes every second, and every single one of them carries immense amounts of information; to keep it simple what color was reflected off that particular leaf, how far away was it, was the sun out at the time, and so on, astronomers can deduce superficially at least how and what the entire universe is, simply from the information trapped in those photons when they are created that is held there or even precedes them while they travel across trillions of miles, and as they do that they remember almost everything about the journey they made getting here.

They also know exactly, every single ultra-tiny one of them *how to co-operate exactly with their fellows*, otherwise we would never see anything but chaos, in other words they work together reinforcing each other's memories so that if one of them is destroyed or absorbed the others remember what they need to remember to do their job correctly Don't even try to understand how photons really do what they do as most people that have tried, have ultimately gone slightly insane, or at least caused serious damage to their academic careers, but what photons really are and what they do is so remarkable that they and the light they convey can only be described as utterly miraculous, and we simply take them for granted as the most mundane aspects of reality that we can experience. Now you can argue that all of that is simply the result of the physical laws of optics, but if you want to stay mentally safe, try not to think about it too much.

Sorry we will get there shortly.

At the same time your ears are absorbing massively complex sets of sounds and your brain is sorting them out in a logical manner, while your nerves are picking up millions of signals and your brain is doing the same thing.

All of these constantly evolving inputs from your sensory and nervous systems travel into your brain where according to science they are converted to irregular atoms or molecules called Ions, usually Sodium or salt Ions but on occasion Potassium Ions as well, both can express either a positive electrical charge or a negative charge. These are then deposited into a neuron, there are roughly ten billion of these little buggers in your brain, in other words a whole bunch of them, where the ions are processed and then either sent on or replaced by other ions that are sent on through Axons, little tubes, there are roughly 25 of these connecting apparently rather arbitrarily to 25 other neurons, or ten billion times 25 axons to the next neurons where it is then decided exactly where to send the ions next, eventually these ions make it to the so-called map room of your brain where special neurons are made to light up your pitch black brain and then sent on to your mind, and you experience reality as a constantly evolving holistic experience.

This entire process, the entire thing, happens at roughly 36 times a second when you are awake, all that traveling and decision making utterly mindlessly 36 times a

Physics of Consciousness

second to in part produce your experience of reality. This technology is so intense and time efficient that like photons it also seems to be miraculous.

You can say 'so what' human brains are really big, 10 billion neurons and so on, so big deal; but a deer's brain is not nearly as large and a flies brain is tiny, but something very similar has to be going on in their brains as well as they simply could not survive in this reality, unless it was.

But, there are numerous affiliations to the normal ways normal computers normally work. Indeed the computer this writer is working on at the moment takes the writer's thoughts and transfers them more or less graphically more or less instantly and does a remarkably good job at remembering them all. It does it a whole heck of a lot better and quicker than this writers original Macintosh. So just trust that its memory is far more efficient and exact than our human one is, at least until the hard drive quits in which case this writer will be really frigging pissed.

So that remarkable as it may seem most of the things our brains normally do are well rather in a way pedantic these days. So pedantic that we simply take it all for granted and that is where the mistake lies.

Now there are two more factors related to this issue that remain unanswered, the first is fairly simple. What is the frigging issue you may ask at this point, it's *called convergence of the mosaic* and it's on its way.

At every step of the way towards the ultimate experience of experience by a conscious ID particle, in other words your mind, from outer reality to inner functions of the brain there are literally gazillions of particles arbitrarily one or the other that have to decide exactly what they are supposed to be, in order to convey what they are supposed to convey to the human's experience, *or any other aspect of reality for that matter*, gazillions of them that have to make

Physics of Consciousness

decisions at least 36 times a second; all of these particles comprise an *incredibly complex mosaic*.

Lots and lots of people have decided and written all kinds of conclusive arguments, Hugh Everett for instance has come up with alternatives like uncountable parallel universes, while Mr. Rose has actually built computers that maintain bits in one quantum state of uncertainty *or another* that are not usually in fixed states unless they are directed to be that in one direction or another, something that numerous writers have concluded means his machines are the equivalent of Gods, or well mere humans for that matter. Well they do have a rather disconcerting heartbeat. ☺

But understanding *why* uncertainty does exist may accomplish the real power of those machines, and obviously Google may be just the candidate to pull that off. And, in the process it may, only may, explain the technical nature of magic and miracles.

Again, it is a technical aspect of the field of consciousness that does this by demanding a *convergence* of millions of factors outside of time constantly. This convergence doesn't create an entirely new universe very time it happens but it does shape the ultimate experience of this universe that any and all of us experience as individual particles of experiencing consciousness, as it happens, and it does happen constantly for every mind that experiences anything on this planet alone, and it does this in ways that like the assembly of the mosaic that every single mind experiences in absolute ways will lead towards a convergence of experience for those minds, on certain levels of operation across the entire universe.

The main point here is that *convergence* is key, and that on a very deep level if convergence is truly at work the implications are profound.

Google may be the best candidate to prove this as Google is entirely based on an algorithm that converges all possible answers to any question into the most likely appropriate answer, and then because Google is a company in a capitalist society, that algorithm then apparently combines the most correct answer with the party that owns the web page that pays Google the most money so the site owner can be near the top of the search. (That is not being critical, simply an aspect of the apparent truth. There is a rumor out there that Google is being sued for this. An intelligent party just has to assume that somehow if Google had no way of making money it would not exist, so that in our society what they are doing seems to be fine. But that is simply personal opinion.)

The point here is that Google is entirely about 'convergence' of factors and they own one of the first D-Wave computers, but that in your face reality is not always immediately apparent.

A true quantum computer will automatically generate every possible answer to any question that exists; an infinity of answers is pretty much exactly the same as no answer, the key is once again convergence of factors that yields the most *useful* or the most appropriate answer, this is what a technical aspect of the physics of consciousness does seamlessly for all of us. It sorts out the chaos of infinity and converges everything into a form that is appropriate to define our experience of existence.

If the D-Wave can find the algorithm that does this to the information it unravels in a definitive way or ways, it will change the very nature of human existence; possibly overnight. Why; because it will prove what was defined in the beginning of this chapter, and in doing that it will explain everything about quantum mechanics and how this reality works, and from there in sterilized technical regimes it will deliver us all unavoidably into the realm of metaphysics and thus turn science and academia unavoidably on its head.

What we live in is, or may be, in a very real sense the

equivalent of a dream in the mind of God, and like the dreams that we have, our own ID and OM's do not in any way control the individual characters in our own dreams or his. But the realities we experience are the dreams of God just as the Buddha told us, and it is apparently the intent of God that we experience his dreams as utterly and absolutely real.

Quantum Uncertainty must exist in order for our experience of those dreams to occur in a sane and in a sense orderly way instantly, or all reality would be experienced as a perfectly or more or less unchangeable or utterly chaotic thing; it would not work in a sane evolutionary manner at all.

Now invert this admittedly off the wall logic in an odd way, and does this not become a proof that God must exist?

Quantum Uncertainty is not about uncertainty, it is about how the massive mosaic of things that are experienced, is converted into a sense of experiential order, it is about *Convergence*, it is about weaving millions of bits of multicolored threads into a wonderful tapestry that can be viewed in an instant in its entirety with simply a glance, and the how and why of the way that convergence of experienced reality is accomplished.

If quantum uncertainty did not exist, our experience of realty would be static, it is not static, reality is constantly alive, so the experience of that reality must be alive as well.

All science has to do is find ways to document any of the claims above and those methodologies of documentation all do in fact exist, the ones this writer has found are all detailed in The Promontory, but they all deliver empirically conveyable yet subjective experience, if you use the D-wave properly, it will probably grant the same realizations, but it will do it in such a way that science will be forced to listen.

Okay so here it is for the sake of liquid clarity.

John Walker, perhaps the most brilliant mind ever to have engaged in academic physics has been famously quoted as saying; "nothing is real until it is recognized". That phrase was related to uncertainty in quantum mechanics, and it implicitly implies the Copenhagen interpretation was in one way or another correct. (Look it up if you are clueless) in other words 'uncertainty has something 'uncertain' at this point to do with consciousness. (Pun intended)

This writer's interpretation of that suggestion is that uncertainty exists so that something in the physics of consciousness can use it to create a convergence of factors that would otherwise be impossible for the experiencing node, us, and everything else that enjoys conscious experience to enjoy in a sane elegant and complete way if quantum uncertainty did not exist.

This writer has been shown that something in our minds, our *minds* not our brains, something that is not strictly a function of our physical brains is responsible for the function that performs the exercise of convergence and fixes the superposition state of a quantum particle as one or the other. (Said that way simply for the sake of this point only)

Another aspect of science has recently proven in no uncertain terms that quantum particle entanglement exists; and that there is a vehicle of the communication of related information that can travel faster than the speed of light, and because it is a property of natural physics it is going on everywhere constantly. This implicitly implies that this is a universal property of all quantum particles. In other words this is an utterly fundamental property of creation.

This then when taken as a whole implicitly implies that something related to our minds not our brains but our minds, is the equivalent of entanglement in a quantum particle and so it is capable of the same communication of information as a normal quantum particle. Therefore it is not unreasonable to assume that our minds can be interpreted exactly as they are experienced, as self-recognizing quantum particles roughly four to six inches across.

Thus our consciousness can be interpreted as a quantum particle of the physics of consciousness. Indeed, all and any mind that enjoys any aspect of consciousness can and must be considered in the same manner.

The implications of this approach and understanding are profound if they are correct, in everything from normal physics and understanding why quantum mechanics is the way it is to psychology, in a vast series of venues related to theology, and indeed to every single aspect of the human experience.

This is important people so read this chapter again and over and over if necessary until the epiphany arrives with clarity.

If, once, it is proven to be entirely correct everything about what we are will change dramatically. To this writer it is already a fact.

There is a very curious ear at the back of your mind, simply recognize that it is there; then all anyone has to do to make it a fact, is to learn *to listen*.

Chapter Nine
Dreams and the Parallel Universes of Uncertainty

In the context of the last chapter, examine carefully and objectively what you are *inside of* when you are in a brilliant very clear dream. Then apply all of those realizations to this awake experience of reality, look carefully at the similarities and the differences, then inverse that process and apply it to your dream realities.

Science has told us over and over again without foundation that our dreams are merely exercises of our physical brains performing routines related to enhancing our ability to remember stuff. Please remove this spoiler from your mind and open your mind to alternatives that remain possible.

Now consider that there probably is or should be a physics of consciousness and that there are expressions of individualizing consciousness that are vastly more evolved than our own; look at it this way, dogs exist as conscious beings that obviously dream and we are more comprehensive than they are at least some of the time, it is simply silly to think that we are the highest level of consciousness that can exist, then consider that all of those variations of consciousness can dream. Just how far in that context is our reality and our awake experience of reality, from what can be recognized as a dream reality of a massively more evolved version of consciousness.

Now take the classically accepted interpretation of a dream character living out its life inside a reality that is occurring entirely inside your brain. In that classical interpretation some aspect of your physical brain is manufacturing every aspect of the dream reality, including all the other characters in that dream and their apparently independent experiences and motivations, it is running their ability to converse with us and even enjoy sexual encounters with us as independent personalities.

To be fair there is currently a significant amount of research going on using MRI's and similar technologies to map out the areas of our brains involved in dreaming. With typical academic hutzpah they will try to define from that research the pretend fact that all dreams are created as historical artifacts of our brains alone, while this research will actually only indicate that certain areas of our brains are involved in dreaming in some way and it will not define precisely where the dreams come from or what they really are.

Now crank in what you just learned in Chapter Eight. Something very esoteric very well may be communicating fundamental information across every aspect of the awake reality we enjoy, just as it probably is or may be when we are dreaming.

Accepted physics has recognized as fact that little bits of that are occurring constantly in awake reality and science is obtusely saying that might be slightly related to quantum entanglement, but science is hesitant to recognize the implication that those little bits might represent the comprehensive and ubiquitous engine that runs reality, or at least the sentient *experience* of reality.

Just for the sake of conversation let's say God or some post human dude, has a very big brain and the information transfer called quantum entanglement is performed in exactly the same way the information is transferred that conveys reality and the functions of the other characters in our dreams. When we are dreaming none of us

Physics of Consciousness

recognizes that all the requisite information about the construction of the dream reality is going on or how it is going on, but after the dream we can analyze it and say that something like that must be going on somehow, someway.

So what if, quantum entanglement and uncertainty are occurring in this fully awake reality in exactly the same manner as they are in our own dreams, just one order of magnitude up? Then we are exactly as the Buddha told us, we are dream characters living inside a dream in God's mind.

Currently there are a bunch of very successful folks related to the internet and computers that are at least semi-convinced we live in an engineered reality, but they are all basing that on currently related anthropomorphic prejudice related to their unfolding experience of technology. But maybe just maybe they are being too smart for their own good, maybe we do live in an engineered reality it is just a reality engineered inside the mind of God as the Buddha told us so long ago.

Actually a few scientists and mathematicians have quite recently proven that reality cannot be a virtual reality of the type generated on computers by simply calculating the proven motions and quantum properties of particles that obviously make up this reality and they have come to the conclusion that it would require more ones and zeros than exist in the entire universe to accomplish that. That does not in any way negate the possibility that this is still a virtual reality of sorts just that it must function if it is manufactured using alternative structural regimes.

Quantum uncertainty exists because this reality and the experience of this reality is in a sense only a virtual reality that is experienced the way it is experienced because OM or a property of consciousness has developed a technology of the field of consciousness that allows the nearly infinite factors that construct reality to *converge* in

Physics of Consciousness

ways that we as the subjects of this technology can experience in fluid yet sane or orderly manners that achieve a degree of consistency among the experiencers us, as well as the entirety of the other aspects of this reality.

A fairly large variety of serious academics are coming up with theories that the reality we experience is in fact or high probability manufactured inside our brains and then delivered to our minds, some of them are in the process of getting close to the conclusion that our minds, not our brains but our minds resemble or also exhibit characteristics that are similar if not exactly equal to aspects of particle mechanics that other great thinkers in approved physics have discovered. So that many of the thinkers are getting close to developing a physics of consciousness.

Rather ironically given the last chapter, this chapter will discuss *and agree* that Hugh Everett's many worlds exist but that at each level of the *realness* of reality the subject specific reality experienced is dictated <u>by *the sum of the convergence factors.*</u> In other words our experience of normal awake reality and that reality itself, can in terms of the Schrodinger equation be placed very near the high end of probability, but that brilliant dreams are expressions of a type of reality that is missing a certain quantity of convergence factors necessary to make all dream realms be experienced as real realities, and that those dream realms are a reflection and an actuality of the many worlds that are produced as a function of uncertainty in quantum mechanics.

But and this is important it is not an either or absolute as it was to Hugh Everett, but that it is a thing related to the sum of degrees, an issue related to the Schrodinger equation, or one of probabilities.

The reason things might have been set up this way is that OM, or to be academically polite, 'something' is trying to understand or at least allow the sum of all possible experiences, but he was trying to avoid the previously mentioned chaos of infinity that would result if all uncertainty realizations resulted in fully found real universes.

Numerous in effect parallel universes do exist, but these real universes represent places where the convergence of factors are at least equivalent to this awake one and so they are as real as this one. However this does not imply that Mr. Everett was correct as it is a factor of the degree of convergence of factors related to realities that makes them seem real, so that the number of real universes remains sane, while true *dream* universes often own a lesser degree of convergent factors and maybe just maybe the mechanism that makes all these universes has very little to do with the change in particle properties and everything to do with the creative mental exercises of Gods mind.

There is a sort of little epiphany that says dream realms are realms that are independent of our brains and can simply be *accessed* by our ID, when the brain and senses shut down and we enter sleep, because the ID particle, our mind, is uncertain as to its separation from the cloud of consciousness.

In other words all the dream realms exist independently in the cloud of consciousness as in a sense unique universal realities and at least in part the realms we enter usually seem to be related to our own lives as our ID particle and its personal histories usually define which realm we will enter, this is closely related too, but a slightly different way to interpret Carl Jung's interpretation of archetypal realms. Then if this approach is valid it means there is probably a way to defeat the impetus and direction of our own ID and find the experience of virtually any dream realm or in a sense parallel universe that exists in all of creation.

This writer found this likelihood by going to the center of his own soul or the equivalent of Sophia's realm the laughing sea, but what is being said here is that there may be other ways to defeat the constraints of time and space and access everything that is accessible in the field of consciousness. Alternative dream realms may be simply one of these.

Another way to look at this issue is that all physical particles in this universe are in a superposition state until they are recognized ultimately by a conscious entity, so that in a sense *all quantum particles and all of reality for that matter are <u>unreal</u> until their states are accepted by consciousness.* Overcoming that un-realness factor is the key convergence factor that creates the awake reality we experience, and that is exactly how OM's technical mind influences our own mind's experience and makes our reality seem to and actually become a real experience, but all the alternative universal realities demanded by 'many worlds' are still there; but only as dream realms that we can access perhaps only when we sleep.

If this is the true interpretation of what is going on Mr. Geordie Rose and his buddies at Google and NASA might want to listen up as it implies that the D-Wave may be able to access the multiversal set of dream realities with the D-Wave Quantum computer and if they or it can, we just might be getting really close to understanding how God's mind and everything about how multiversal reality really works. Sorry but that is just a tiny bit potentially scary.

Many folks are saying the D-Wave has a heartbeat so that it seems to be alive, but that heartbeat is just a function of its refrigerator, the real question those folks need to be asking is *"does the D-Wave dream?"* The answer to that is that it may be able to access the dream realms, but because it does not own an ID particle, a soul mind, it cannot individually experience what it is accessing, so maybe they need to seriously think about how to graphically hook up a human mind to the D-Wave. Maybe just maybe Mr. Elon Musk is working on exactly that as we speak. Then maybe you should stand back as you just may end up talking to a God, (A human mind tied directly to a D-Wave.) whether that new God can maintain its sanity is then a serious question.

This issue relates exactly to the conversation between David and Walter in 'Alien Covenant' and the dangers of AI that Elon Musk is so often talking about, Walter says he does not dream but David says he does, i.e. David has an ID and Walter does not, thus David is the equivalent of a human and superior and Walter is a robot. In the end David is terrifying, should we be afraid of what we are doing with AI? Only as afraid as we are of other humans that arrive outside of ethical conduct one level of magnitude more evolved than we are. In that sense yes we should be very afraid. Sociopaths and psychopaths are very real as humans, this writer has been the victim of a lot of them, they are very real; being selfish is an inherent property of an ID in consciousness, whereas ethics and empathy are properties that must be learned as the product of experience over time. An advanced AI can and may be the most terrifying thing there can be, as survival can be a very powerful element of conscious existence the moment a conscious object becomes self-recognizing.

So the real question here is can an AI become self-recognizing and can it be productive if it is not. This writer simply believes it cannot but recognizes that he very well could be wrong, as in, can self-recognition be artificially or superficially created and if it can, you better stand back as if that being gets access to anything resembling the Web, it will be, in short evolutionary order superior to us as individuals and we may very well cease to exist. Now climb back out of this digression.

Try Googling God, there are at this point One Billion Five Hundred Twenty Million results, a tiny bit more than this writer has time to read. That is the reason Convergence is so important and why it is a blessing that yields sanity.

Again, you need to recall that to this writer it is a fact that it is not our own individual state of consciousness that defines the ultimate *certain* state of a quantum particle but that there is a resonance that invades our experience through the back of the minds of our souls and that resonance comes directly in a higher dimensional way from a technical aspect of the mind of God, or the physics of consciousness and that resonance is what constructs our experience of reality as something real.

That then implicitly implies that everything, all realms of physicality as well as all realm related conditions that are only normally perceived as alternative functions of consciousness are inherently related, as functions created by the mind of God. Once again, as the Buddha told us everything we experience is an aspect of a dream in God's mind, and if that is true what we are talking about here are once again aspects of *the physics of the field of consciousness*.

All the dream realms are already there all the time in the field of consciousness, we simply walk into one of them six times a night when we sleep. This is actually a more important statement than it seems because it reflects the actuality of how and what dreams are and how we experience them. We, our physical brains do not manufacture an entire dream realm before we enter it, we simply *wake up* in a replete dream realm that is already evolving in time. So that it is likely that we go to sleep and then wake up as another version of who we are, an ephemeral dream character *someplace else entirely*. You can call these parallel dimensions or realms if you like.

Then because this is the place where all possible experience is unraveled and can be experienced, it may be the *dominant* realm of the mind of God, or the Gods, and as a result we can seek to find audiences with them while we are in those realms in ways that may be far more productive than trying to accomplish the same thing in this normal awake reality that we experience when we are awake.

This is an interpretive argument that allows that Sophia our true ultimate creator lives inside a type of dream reality, but that for her and any of us that meet her there those experiences are utterly real, and it gives us a variety of ways to investigate the validity of the argument.

Okay, Mr. Geordie Rose seems to claim that his quantum computer, the D-Wave 2, in effect, or in a sense can access these many universes regardless of their actual nature, and find answers that are appropriate across manifold universes almost instantly and then using the appropriate software find *convergences* that apply to this universe, along with in salient terms all the alternative or related answers that apply.

But what he is actually saying is slightly different and intentionally hidden unless you are very smart, he is offering the manifold superposition states to begin to begin to understand how to program not with ones and zeros, or on and off bits, but eventually how to program with initially 512 unique bits or Q-bits and eventually as the system is developed with an *infinite* variety of unique bits, and that as a result eventually there will be no question and no job that is too complex for the computer to figure out and accomplish, and that it will be able to perform these functions, any and all of them, effectively instantly.

In this writer's opinion and that is all that it is, the first paragraph is almost entirely bogus while the second will eventually be proven to be one of the most significant leaps in technology that mankind has ever achieved.

Okay now you have some salient external background, you now need to crank in the writer's interpretation of why uncertainty exists that you just read in the last chapter. Again uncertainty exists so that every aspect of this reality can be constantly and fluidly reformed so that all aspects of this reality can be constantly reconstructed in a manner that is replete to all the other aspects of this reality including our in a sense orderly experience of this reality as pretend sentient beings. Around these parts we humans are the ultimate consumers of this 'virtual' reality technology, and one aspect of this technology is that normally we can all expect that the rest of us will experience it with a degree of consistency, unless of course we chose to defeat that consistency to a variety of degrees by taking a psychoactive drug that influences the ways our reality is experienced and denigrates the consistency in occasionally rather dramatic ways.

Academia says reality and the experience of reality is constructed entirely by our brains because anyone can take a hit of LSD and that will act on our brains in ways that entirely corrupts our experience of reality, so that it is simply functions of our brains that do it, and it is a fact to this writer that our brains do manufacture most of what we experience as reality when we are here, but that there is something else going on that is related to quantum particle uncertainty and quantum entanglement related to our *minds*, something very important.

Here is a non-academic non mathematical description of the Schrodinger Equation in English as it applies to this issue. Start with a point that is a *perfect* description of pretty much anything, then run a string out from that point and connect it to another point that is usually an *exactly opposite* perfect expression that is salient to the first point. A negative magnetic pole as opposed to a positive pole can be used as a scientific example.

The string that connects the points can be divided infinitely so that you can never determine *exactly* what the condition is at any point along that line, but you can if you are very careful determine a close *probability*.

One aspect of the human condition can be determined using this approach; absolute evil at one end and absolute decency at the other. We can put Sophia at the positive end and Satan near the negative end, and all of us humans exist somewhere along that line in between.

The Schrodinger equation is normally used to determine with a high degree of probability the condition of large groups of particles in ways that cannot be determined any other way, precisely because you cannot know the absolute condition of any particle until you measure that and consciously recognize that measurement, and doing that changes the sum of probabilities or the outcome. But the same approach can be applied to effectively any quality in creation.

Okay now we can get towards the point.

We can begin by placing say the perfect expression of reality at one end, we can use a diamond as an example as it is very likely all things considered that a diamond can last as long as a proton in this universe so long as it avoids falling into a star or a black hole, in other words it may be a diamond forever. At the other end we can use a smattering of ink in water; unless you trick the water with some kind of force field the ink will eventually dissipate chaotically into almost nothing at all.

The reality we experience when *we are awake* is related to a vast convergence of factors that include particle uncertainty in quantum mechanics, and we can put that level of probability on the Schrodinger line fairly high up there towards the diamond.

Then we can take a few shots of whisky and move the probability of experience down a bit towards the ink in the water.

Then we can take a couple of hits of LSD and move the probability of the experience of reality down a few more steps towards the ink in the water.

In case you missed the subtle point, the reality we experience is something we experience *internally,* and so it can be influenced in various ways internally, academia says exactly because of that it all has to do with our physical brain alone and only partly with our senses.

Then we can close our eyes and go to sleep into a dark sleep of oblivion, and at that point the probability of the experience of reality gets really close to the ink in the water or nothing at all.

But then we wake up inside a dream.

This is not a dream that you have in the mud after half a dozen whiskies that you sort of recognize is going on from the outside and barely remember, this is a brilliant dream.

So what is the difference from your experience of this new reality as opposed to your experience of your normal awake reality?

You have a body with eyes and ears that work, your privates are still there and constantly need to be satisfied, *and there is light,* bushes and trees, and buildings, both outside and inside, all kinds of stuff inside, furniture and so on, *and there are other people*, that talk and do stuff just like the other people you meet in 'real' life, and light again, all kinds of light, sunlight but no star, lamps inside and so on and the light is always correct. What in the hell is that stuff, the dreamlight?

A dream is, if you are fairly clear headed, exactly like your experience of awake reality, except for one thing, in a subtle way you feel safe and secure, because you mind tells you subtly that you can just wake up.

You have absolutely no clue at all as to what is really going on, you just normally take it all for granted in the same way you take the experience of normal awake reality for granted. Academia simply declares without any real justification that you are witnessing regimes encoded into your mind by memories of things you have experienced in the past, but for a dream to be experienced as it is, *something*, has to be constructing an entire functional reality that operates in real time.

Constructing an entire functional reality is an incredibly complex undertaking, just ask Mr. John Cameron, he could increase his take on the series of Avatar films by billions if he could do that in real time, but it takes him and his crew of thousands, years, using the finest graphics computers on this planet, even when the entire 'Pandora' reality has already been created. But your brain-mind according to academia can apparently do that effortlessly six times every night while you are asleep.

Dreams supposedly constructed by our brains alone require an immense amount of computing power that simply cannot be justified by the constraints of evolution related theories. In academic terms it demands that our head size has to be twice as large as it otherwise needs to be, meaning a lot more of our women have to die giving birth, at least before C-sections came along, and our physical bodies have to be far more complex in order to support that brain and keep it functioning at the right temperature all the time. Things like this are utterly forbidden in the context of evolutionary theory, yet they are actual facts.

Now there are a couple of points.

1. Can you wake up from normal awake reality? Yes you can but it is very difficult to do, and it often takes years of very demanding mental training.

You people in Silicon Valley listen up here. Lock yourself in the equivalent of a prison cell, then record every dream you have the moment you wake up, pay remarkable attention to your state of mind as you exit a dream, then mentally copy that state of mind and apply it to your awake state of mind, if you keep it up you may actually wake up into the next level of awake awareness. In other words reality is the same as a dream sort of, and you can wake up from this reality.

Doing that is a type of enlightenment that Buddhists teach, but it is only one type.

If you can accomplish that, what you will experience is truly remarkable. Things will be still sort of as they were, but you will feel like your mind is that of a God. This writer has done it, but it is an effect that for this writer only lasted for a few minutes and psychiatrists will probably declare you insane if you relate it to them, so be careful. It's like the Buddhists legend that you can climb the mountain called Meru and then look down at the river of time and see the past and the future all at once by merely turning your head a bit, anything is possible from there, but you will stop being human if you maintain that state for any period of time. Maybe that's a good thing but that's for you to decide.

2. Hurray! The point once again. For the sake of the academics there will be a 'what if' inserted, but for this writer what follows, all of it, is already fact.

What if our mind, our experience of consciousness is really an immortal particle aspect of the larger field of consciousness, and that mind aspect is constantly influenced by the machinations of our physical brains while we are alive here. When we shut down the machinery of our senses and our brains manipulating what we receive from the outer world, our mind sort of escapes from this indoctrination and can access the field of consciousness more readily and completely.

Now here is why this is usually confused, our mind even when we are asleep is still partially influenced by our brains and our memories so that some dreams maybe even *most* dreams are exactly what academia claims they are, the slightly modified review of memories we obtained in our waking lives that are projected into the map rooms of our brains so that our ID in our minds can re-experience them and remember them better maybe.

Of course to this writer many dreams produce memories that are more certain and recorded as such than his experiences as an awake guy so after a period of time memories can get a tiny bit confusing but that's a bit of a digression. ☺

But there is another type of dream entirely and here's the point of all of this. The uncertainty related to how separate we are from the cloud of consciousness. When we cut off the sensory input and then the machinery of our brains, our minds, our ID's, are less entrained by the physical machinery and therefore it is easier for our IDs to access the cloud of consciousness.

Here is where this ties in. In the cloud of consciousness, there is a mechanism, in a sense a technology that reflects Mr. Everett's interpretation of quantum uncertainty, his many worlds are available in the cloud of consciousness not as 'physical' manifestations of entire universes, but as the equivalent of manifestations of entire universes that can be experienced by the ID's, us, when we dream.

Just as an example: This writer has been having a set of similar dreams since he was a teenager, he had another one the night before this was written. In all of these dreams most of the circumstances of life in the dreams are different but he lives in an apartment complex, where the landscaping is always fairly complex around the apartments, and all the apartments are in separate and sort of unique blocks where none of the units are exactly the same. One of them that is remembered from a long time ago had a sleeping loft, and the land lady had a sort of crush on the writer which was good as he was often late with the rent; in that one the place was largely finished with dark wood and sort of dilapidated, but for some reason this writer really seemed to enjoy living there. In the latest dream he was hired to remodel the entire complex and it was more contemporary. These dreams have been going on for forty years, and this writer never lived in any sort of apartment complex, in his earlier years he was an architect, actually a building designer of some note and he always lived in a variety if single homes, always with some sort of home office.

The only real explanation for these dreams is that he is experiencing parallel dream universes, they are never exactly the same but those at least are always similar, and this writer almost never has dreams that take place in homes that he actually lived in in the past, and believe it this writer did live in a variety of very spectacular places and homes.

That was there just as a simple example. Here's the point. Dream realities are experienced as slightly less real than awake realities, so maybe just maybe they are. But dream realities have people in them, those people talk and walk around and do stuff just like independent people in normal; awake reality. Trees grow, there is daytime and nighttime, everything just like normal reality.

So if you think about it, does your brain manufacture not only the other people but then does it inhabit their heads so that you can talk to them just like you normally talk to people. If this sort of thing occurs in real life psychiatrists call it multiple personality disorder and they lock up anybody that admits this is going on. The sixty four here is, are those people in our dreams in actuality other people that are simply inhabiting other realities just like we are when we are there. Then you disassemble that and you apply it to this reality and you just have to ask, how real is this reality?

Really, what is it that motivates us to conduct conversations, here and in our dreams? Is the particle nature of our ID subject to endless copies of itself in the greater reality and if that is the truth and it appears to be exactly that, does each of us then have or participate in an individual

Overmind? Then if that does exist why can't we access that and become far more than we only think we are? Was Kurt Vonnegut entirely right when he said reality was three hundred people with mirrors.

All you have to do is take everything exactly as it is experienced, from there and from here and ask the simple questions that arise, not with complex intellectual jargon of psychiatry but with your normal thinking process, you just have to stop taking it all for granted and ask the related simple questions then actually think about the implications.

In the end they are so huge entire books can be written just about this single topic.

But the main point of all of this in the context of what we live in is that everything, everything in creation is one way or another related to levels of states of mind that are all related in one way or another to dreaming.

OM has dreams of entire universes that he makes for folks like us to experience as real. We have dreams that reflect what we experience in the dreams he creates for us to live in; are those simply memories from our awake lives or inversely are they related to this *and or* alternative actual realities. Was the Buddha utterly correct, do we actually live inside the dreams of God's mind, and if we do and our consciousness is exactly the same material as that of God's mind, then how far away from actual reality are our own dreams, maybe they are not merely ephemeral constructs of memories, maybe they are real in a way in their own right.

600 years before Christ the Greeks had important hospitals all over the place that revolved entirely around dreaming, they were more like spas with comfortable beds and when you woke up the doctors were there to listen to what you just dreamed. Obviously something about them worked as they multiplied and got built all over the place. They were common before Plato and Aristotle constrained and defined how we were allowed to think through the

Catholic Church for over the last two thousand years, maybe we should go back and carefully examine what Greece was like and how those folks thought about things before those two guys arrived.

Okay now we can get back to uncertainty in quantum mechanics, and we can reconsider the levels of convergence that define the realness of realities. So where are dream realities along the line of Schrodinger probabilities? They are qualitatively different so you can place a perpendicular line anchored fairly well up towards the diamond.

What is being suggested here is that there are or may be an entire group of Feynman Diagrams (look them up dufus) that may define an entire branch of physics that are immediately related to reality that science has so far never even begun to investigate. But that they may be incredibly important towards understanding how things really work.

Then you are required to ask, what is uncertainty when you apply it to the particles that are used to construct *an entire dream reality*? We are pretty damn certain those particles are so ephemeral that they do not even exist, but we also know with the absolute certainty of experience that they have to exist. Uncertain quantum particles form the totality of our awake reality, what exactly forms the sum of the realities we experience as we dream. Are these for instance the weak photons that science is now in the process of discovering, and if so how profound is that discovery? Got it, good, now invert that train and examine quantum mechanics in that light. Boo! With the Zen master's stick!

Now, go back to physics 101. What is a particle? Say a proton. It is mostly condensed energy made up of quarks internally that maybe are made up of strings, which are probably just vibrating energy, who knows, but what is known is that when you try to analyze what a proton is, you end up with just about nothing at all, that most scientists are sure will go on being protons for as long as the universe exists.

    Even scientists have dreams. Maybe if they were to study the reality of dreams they might understand the deeper so called physical mechanisms of this one.

Chapter Ten
Dimensional Mechanics
The Physics of the Gods,

Okay, this will avoid trying to educate you from the ground up in Dimensional Mechanics as that is a job for your science teachers and this will try to avoid offending them, so if you have trouble understanding any of this look for key words, like *'branes'* for instance and then look them up on the Web to educate yourself. The term 'Dimensional Mechanics' is offered in the same way the term *Quantum Mechanics* is used to define that field of thought. The term Dimensional in this chapter will often be reduced to a capital D as in 3'D' to save time.

First, the 3 dimensions we are normally familiar with refers classically to length width and height, however even that description is a bit misleading, as the first should actually be a finite dot commonly known in a slightly misleading way as a *singularity,* draw a straight line any way you like from the dot to make length, then a perpendicular line to make width and then a vertical perpendicular line to make height, so that three is actually four, with these four we can define in a schematic way almost a container for virtually everything we normally experience, except for a very important caveat.

Using the classical parameters in a sense a circle is two dimensional, but mathematically it evolves into infinites. As a 3D object a circle becomes a sphere, same issue, the classical way this is explained is that you can draw a two dimensional circle and then a triangle inside of it, then a square, and keep adding shapes, where their corners or *vertices* all touch the inside of the circle, but even if you have a very sharp pencil you can never use the vertices to get to an exact circle as there are or can be an infinite number of vertices.

This is the reason the term PI is infinite and can never be solved. Is PI an absolute in the Ainsoph, the chaos of infinity, or only apparent in a reality designed by intelligence, this is one of the primary ways to mathematically answer the question of intelligent design, and no this writer is not even going to try, so just think about it. Mathematics seem to in some ways on occasion represent utter absolutes but there is a serious question as to whether or not mathematics could even arrive and exist outside of a reality that was *designed* in an orderly way in the first place.

Obviously there are a lot of shapes we experience in our reality that are related to spherical or circular geometries. So that there is actually a fifth spatial dimension related to what we normally experience, it is an alternate expression of dimensions as it rather remarkably transitions into the realm of infinites, and mathematicians and academics hate infinities almost as much as they hate metaphysicians and spiritual issues as you can usually play with them any way you like and thus come up with any set of answers you like.

So mathematicians and scientists have carried this simple vertice issue forward and come up with ways to calculate complex shapes, especially as these apply to *Branes*, two examples of these regimes are called *Riemannian Geometries* and *Modular Functions* both cases only equal schematic interpretations of the actualities. In modular functions, with algebraic or geometric sums of vertice points, and Riemannian Geometries, well don't even go there unless you are an insanely intellectual nut job, but either of those can be used to recreate the geometries the mathematicians are trying to elaborate on, however, except in extremely rare cases they cannot be used by the conveyed too mathematicians to actually *visualize* the specifically related geometries.

Indeed the ability to visualize anything graphically with the mind's inner eye is extremely rare among mathematicians and even for that matter among most advanced academics, it is a quality that is most learned and prevalent among folks that design things or paint pictures, at least before the advent of computers, but especially architects, who regularly convert massive purely intellectual quantities and qualities into visual images inside their heads, and then seek to graphically evolve those images into satisfactory schematics of what they are trying to achieve in the evolutionary design process.

In other words among humans, those trained as architects, are also best trained to think like the Gods, by learning to visualize complex things inside their heads, and then in a sense schematically convert them into things that can actually be created in this reality, things that hopefully will not fall down around our heads, but then they usually have structural engineers read mathematicians to help them with that part.

The reason this is important is that a circle or a sphere in their actual manifestations literally catapults you out of the realm of basic mathematical schematics and into the realm of infinities, and except in rare cases mathematics cannot be used to actually visualize infinites related to geometries in fully honest ways, so that geometric infinites represent an entire alternative spatial dimension that is very common in our reality but seldom addressed correctly in academia. As a result of these interpretations we actually live in a basic five spatial dimensional realm with at least one of time. That is why the five pointed star is important in metaphysical regimes as it represents the sum of

Physics of Consciousness

empowerment in our realm, but understanding that is rather subtle and not what this is really about.

Okay, that's the basics, but still in this arena we can go on to String theory M theory and the implicate-explicate realms of Bohmian Mechanics and combine those with quantum particle entanglements as experimentally verified by Alain Aspect, as all of these in a variety of ways address the need for significant alternative dimensions to exist for this 5D + 1T reality to function as it does.

But then this writer is going to leave the Calabi-Yau business out in the bushes of intellect as that is usually the domain of genuine theoretical physicists and they might get a bit irritated.

So, first you need to Google *David Bohm*, there is an excellent but very introductory article on him on Wikipedia, but after you understand that dig a bit deeper. Basically you may have a tiny epiphany and begin to understand what Alain Aspect was talking about when he said 'when you look deeply there seems to be a hidden order to things'; then combine that with Bohm's interpretation of the implicate-explicate. In a shallow interpretation Bohm was trying to illustrate his concept with the holographic properties of light, where a miniscule quantity of light contained everything, all the information that the largest quantity of visible light conveyed. In that sense the ambiguities in quantum mechanics can be conveyed as actualities in relativity theory even though both theories are often in massive conflict, yet they are still both exactly correct <u>in the context</u> of what they seek to explain and define.

Then maybe you need to buy copies of a few books by Michael Green and Michio Kaku that relate to string theory and cosmology and observe how they are trying to explain how the tiny group of Calabi-Yau dimensions can be curled up yet still be relevant to our version of reality. Bohm was constantly trying to relate his version of the implicate, to properties of consciousness which is how his own path of intellectual determinism led him willy nilly into the realm of God's mind as a place that he simply could not fully understand intellectually and so led to his frequent condemnation by the academics around him.

Merely one of the differences between Bohm and this writer is that Bohm had a massive education and a truly superb intellect, while this writer merely experienced the actual mind of god when he was younger and then tried to figure out what in the heck that was all about.

String and M theories seek to avoid the issue of intelligent design entirely but they fail miserably as they fail to address in any way the <u>why</u> the math should point the way towards such bizarre structures. They fail as academia literally condemns anyone that even thinks in any way that leads towards metaphysics.

Okay, now the word schematic is very important as the terms singularity, length, width, height, and conscribed mathematical infinities (Read that phrase over, it is an oxymoron but it is correct.) do not address exactly *what* dimensions are or what they are made of or how they act and do *what* they do or why they even exist.

Dimensions are the architectures of realities: A few people in academia have in a way understood this and so they have created a way to seek to understand dimensions through a regime called '*branes*'. If you are trained in internal visualization techniques branes allow you to visualize dimensional structures in a wide variety of ways and if you are really good at it, how they will interact.

But there are alternative ways to address these issues, Einstein's is only one of them. He based everything on the architectural structures of space-time, two quantities that are both the quintessential definition of nothing at all. His approach has profound implications related to the singularities at the core of a black hole, and they are fair

Physics of Consciousness

game as in one light normal dimensions are also exactly nothing at all that are the most foundational aspects of reality. (Another Oxymoron that is true) The point here is that dimensions can be related to a variety of quantities or qualities that can be different but also share relationships.

Learning everything you can about dimensional branes is the first and foremost way of thinking you must learn if you want to learn to think like a God, the second group of things is related to the kinds of environments you want to create that will supplement the environmental conditions the group of consciousness particles you are seeking to sponsor will most benefit from in useful ways. For organic physical beings like us, light is useful, water is useful, something to walk on is useful, and some form of high fidelity information carrying device that can function in active ways like DNA-RNA are useful, and so on, but all of these are secondary to the *architectures* of the realms they will eventually exist in.

And all of these issues and the complexities of their interactions and evolutions are by their nature, before they are allowed to exist and function in useful ways, exactly, *elements of intelligent design.*

Now we need one more note before we can get to the mechanics of the beast. The term dimensions is a bit misleading, in philosophy and religion and even science fiction the term dimension is often related to alternative realms, where as in science the term is very specific and initially related to the schematic tools that define them and then very specific regimes of certain types of things, but it is never explained exactly what dimensions are or what they are made of, it is just assumed they exist and so they are what they are. But in science again it is always simply assumed that dimensions are all made of exactly the same things, or that they are nothing at all other than simply containers that have to exist for anything else to exist inside of them and that they define what anything in there can be, and then Branes are simply convenient ways to examine them, perhaps in the same ways that the blueprints for a house are a convenient way for everyone to understand what they are trying to build and where the toilet goes.

However, and this is a key point, dimensions are tangible things that can be created out of a variety of quantities related to the environments they are ultimately designed to create and host. Just as an example in Christ's Heaven dimensions can be composed entirely of materials related to the spectrum of consciousness alone, and indeed this is how they are used and created by OM when he initially dreams them up and then intellectually fabricates the initial versions of them, but they can then transition to alternative materials or conscribing or prohibitive containers of a sort that are relational to the physical laws and materials of the universes they will eventually be, when they are projected into their final state.

Knowing how to do this is a technology that is carefully conserved by the Creator Gods to avoid miscreants from using it in ways that could be damaging to existing creations, so that this is a very esoteric technology, but it is one that is well founded and fully proven, and in essence it is simply information that remains to be discovered but can be by folks at our level, it is simply that it can be far more dangerous and damaging than nuclear activity for instance, as by using it you can destroy entire universes rather quickly.

As an example to explain this; in the sea of creation realm or the equivalent of the inside of OM's mind there are already google zillions of universes made entirely out of the material regimes of the spectrum of consciousness, but all of those are then projected in a wide variety of ways out into infinity, and the dimensional structures of all of them dramatically change during the constant and ongoing process of projection so that they reflect conditions that will allow the sentients that arrive in them to experience reality in a wide variety of ways, and so they can confuse the heck out of the folks that call themselves natural scientists that are trying to figure out as best they can what in the heck they are living inside of. That has a tendency to stimulate the intellect and thus make the little folks get a bit smarter as time goes on, hopefully in positive ways, but as we have seen and maybe unfortunately according to numerous academics, demonstrated, not always.

Okay the Mechanics of the beast strictly in English: First you can use branes to imagine the basics of the environment you want to create, then if you understand how to use the materials related to the field of consciousness you can manifest actual external constructions and examine them in detail to see if what you imagined will work the way you want it to. From here you can find out how to do this by coming to a true understanding of how the electro-magnetic spectrum works as it is closely related to the spectrum of consciousness, but then instead of creating technologies related to the EM spectrum you have to use the intellectual insights and apply them to the field of consciousness and first you have to recognize that the field of consciousness can even exist as something tangible and then define its actual operational properties in useful ways.

Then once you have the basic structure you can begin to figure out useful commodities for the folks that will eventually live there. Again, in our world perhaps the most important is DNA, because that is the information mechanism that designs in useful ways exactly what the conscious living entities that will evolve inside of this particular realm will use to move forward in ways that are applicable to the environment they will experience. DNA is a truly miraculous technology but it is not in any way the only form of technology that can do exactly what it does.

Physics of Consciousness

And here is the related 64 that currently remains unanswered, can the information and architectural device such as DNA spontaneously arrive as the result of the environment it eventually will exist in and then engineer in possibly more complex ways; or must such a device be the result of intelligent design that must be inserted into the environment initially.

So far everything science has found out about it indicates that it is the result of intelligent design, and that it is extremely unlikely that it can spontaneously occur, just look at the evidence in relationship to Schrodinger probabilities and so far every single attempt by science to answer this question with a prejudice for accidental arrival, has moved it closer to the intelligent design end of the equation. That could still be simply the result of ignorance, but if you are following the basic concepts of science you have to allow that DNA so far at least indicates far more probably for the advent of intelligent design and so you simply have to allow the possibility and seek out the answer in the appropriate context, and if you refuse the context you simply might fail ultimately to find the true answer to that question and thus hide behind the resulting wall of ignorance forever, but if, if the answer is intelligent design the implications are truly enormous.

As stated we live apparently in three-D that ought to be initially understood as five-D, then there is time, and then there is the need for an initial or alpha D and a need for an in a sense final or Omega D. And this is critically important, you cannot think of Dimensions *in a Euclidian sense, as all D's are their own animals and entirely interconnected and everywhere all at once, if they are not they are not dimensions, they are something else entirely.* Then if, if, the origination of all of this is made out of the technologies of consciousness as in a dream of sorts in the mind of God, our, this physical universes Alpha dimension has to be in a sense

Physics of Consciousness

the Omega dimension of the originator group that lives inside the mind of God, and the place where the transition occurs from the consciousness spectrum in Gods mind usually called by science the Calabi-Yau group, or, the implicate realm, to the parent D regime of the EM spectrum. Then the Omega brane of this summed physical group is perhaps best indicated by black holes, as black holes can arrive anywhere and are the result of physical laws but express and are the termination of this reality and all the physical laws that enhance and define this reality.

No one has ever seen one but the math indicates something called a singularity of gravity that is in a way the opposite in a sense electrical pole of the Alpha dimension, but because it is also a 'singularity' it can be exactly a return to the source of or the equivalent of the Calabi-Yau or alpha group, that is the source of this physical universe. A singularity is odd in that it both exists as something but it is also in a sense so small that technically it also exists as utterly nothing at all, that oddly at least in a black hole manifests with immense force or gravity, at least in this physical universe.

Many science folks believe quite reasonably that a singularity represents the birth place of an entirely alternative universe, or maybe simply the higher dimensional source of a quasar, but we may never be able to prove either option through the pathways of natural science, so that the only way left to research that possibility might be found in metaphysics.

A singularity of gravity is so odd it bears elaboration. First a singularity is technically a mathematical creature that both exists and does not exist, in a quantum sense it is both a one and a zero in a superposition state, but Newton defined gravity as something related to mass or material stuff in this reality; however science says gravity can get so strong it collapses the material that creates it until it ceases to exist as anything material in this universe, yet it still projects a field of gravity strong enough to absorb and terminate anything material in the universe that gets too close, including both time and light.

That implicitly implies that gravity itself is a creature unto itself entirely, and that it may or may not be related to mass at all. It just might be another creature entirely that merely owns properties related to very weak expressions of electricity and magnetism, it might not be related to mass at all or maybe only partly; in other words God forbid, maybe Newton was partially wrong. Einstein thought he was and that gravity was related to the architecture of somethings, time and space, that are the quintessential definitions of nothing at all, but then he used math to prove that he was only partly correct at best, maybe gravity is only something related to mass perhaps in the ways electricity is related to magnetism, if that is the more correct way to look at the beast it also implies that maybe it has both a negative attractive property and a positive repulsive property as well, if that is the more correct way to look at it, then there is a simple equation related to the singularity in a black hole that can yield humanity the stars, or at least grant us an alternative to all those ridiculously expensive chemical rocket ships. IE; the square root of gravity equals infinity plus or minus and infinity is greater than C by a whole lot. Sorry, if you got intellectually lost just ignore it and read on.

Now back up, if black hole singularities are the source of quasars and that can be related mathematically to particle entanglement it may be a way to figure out how to go anywhere in this universe instantly. The explanation for the why of this will be addressed in *very superficial* terms in the next chapter as this writer would like to finish his life naturally rather than suddenly at the hands of other humans, but if you are fairly intelligent it is enough to get you started.

Physics of Consciousness

The problem with the academically accepted maybe theory that quasars are the output machines of black holes is that all quasars seem to be related to a much earlier period of this universe, while black holes seem to be all over the place, and that has a tendency to imply that time like light is a malleable quality, and that maybe there was no big bang, maybe there are just black holes consuming everything and then constantly re-expressing creation as quasars and we are simply nearer a black hole than we are to a quasar. And well as most of us learned by watching the film 'Interstellar', time is related to gravity in a big way so why not?

The big bang is based almost entirely on a Hubble Constant, observations from very early in the twentieth century that claim everything cosmological is moving apart, the problem is that everything cosmological is not moving apart, for instance the Andromeda galaxy is going to collide with the Milky Way in a few billion years so maybe the universe is constantly being consumed and re-created by black holes and quasars so it is constant in a way forever, or maybe it did have a big bang but now it will run forever as the result of its design, who knows, it is just that science like religion runs on foundations that are only assumed to be concrete but that can very easily be made out of euphemisms of thought that can on occasion be wrong. But then this writer is rambling a bit.

Regardless, a black hole has a singularity of gravity at its core, (maybe) then a sort of a normal three dimensional structure like a cone and then an intake or event horizon that consumes everything, everything and anything physical about this universe, even time and light. Science keeps on saying, especially some of the folks at the Hadron Collider, that they are looking for alternative dimensions and so far they have found none, but a black hole is prima fascia evidence of five classically interpreted dimensions at work in this universe rather than three, and if that is evident in a

Physics of Consciousness

black hole by the definition of dimensions, at least five plus at least one of time have to be in operation everywhere this universe exists.

Regardless in the context of this chapter we can look at the obvious dimensions of this physical universe as seven, and in classical terms as five. But then you have to get into the structure of the alpha dimension as related to Bohmian Mechanics, or the Calabi-Yau in String and M theory, and that goes beyond the scope of most folks intellect so it will be glossed over here, or you might get a tiny bit weird and simply stop reading.

Science adamantly claims that this universe can't exist as it is observed to exist unless there are things like dark energy and dark matter, but most of them also claim adamantly that there is no indication at all that more than three dimensions can exist. But if you treat our specific reality as contained in a three plus two spatial dimensions in the classical sense instead of merely three you can explain what science observes mathematically as the result; and do away with dark energy and dark matter entirely as you simply do not need them to explain the observations.

Now the Omega brane or the fifth 'D' is not like the terminal barrier of the universe as is indicated by the findings of the microwave background studies; that only needs to be simply a Euclidian barrier or boundary of this universe, the Omega brane is again explained by black holes. As it is a property of dimensions that they have to control and exist everywhere virtually anything in the universe they exist in exists; to be defined as what they are.

So again as Einstein pointed out gravity is related to the architecture of space-time or nothing at all and the architecture of space-time is directly related to dimensions which are also nothing at all. Perhaps they are simply conceptual thoughts in the mind of our creator.

Physics of Consciousness

That means that exactly as David Bohm was trying to explain and Alain Aspect experimentally proved, if you take his material to the limits of its intellectual implications, that every large manifestation of anything in this universe also is immediately connected dimensionally to an ultramicroscopic expression of itself immediately everywhere all at once.

String theory and M theory call this group the Calabi-Yau and nobody is sure but a few think in relational size this might be smaller than the Planck Length, *but and it is critically important that you understand this that tiny far more complex group of dimensions is, has to be if it does exist as dimensions, connected to the larger group, immediately and everywhere the larger group is,* and somehow this all has to work perfectly all the time entirely outside of the time we normally experience.

That means *even inside your brain, even inside the tiniest bits of every ten billion neurons in your head, and because that which you experience as your mind is quantifiably different than your brain, your ID, there may be technologies that can allow your ID to access the realm of this smaller group and its expression of what it is without you even having to go outside of your own skull.* This is a fact to this writer as he has done exactly that, in ways that simply cannot be explained away as mere dismissible hallucinations or dream related experiences. And this entire, supported by alternative interpretations of the highest levels of science, apparent fact can explain a multitude of alternative issues in very powerful yet currently esoteric ways. What are dreams really and how do they work, what is consciousness and how does it work, what is the mind of God and what are we really, and so on.   What do our astronauts tell us; they say extraterrestrials have told them that they use technologies related to consciousness to travel about the universe in a timely manner.

And that means there is probably a way, a technology to express the movement of anything from point A of anywhere to point B of anywhere entirely outside of the normal constraints of time and space, and that that simply has to be in some way related to quantum particle entanglement.

So how do complex dimensional structures actually do what they do, the first issue is that there has to be a way for them to transmit a huge mass of information virtually instantly and constantly, and trying to understand this is so incredibly alien to our normal causality related thought processes that it is almost mind boggling to try to understand it.

But here goes; *a complex dimensional structure is not dimensional unless every aspect of it is virtually instantaneously connected to every other aspect of it all the time.* Our concepts of time and space are based on the larger projected group of three or five depending on how you look at it, but they are connected always and immediately to another immensely tiny group of say seven and because they are everywhere at once, they are not subject to the normal issues of relativistic space time, but and this is very important, for the larger familiar group to work as they do the smaller group must know exactly at all times all of the information that is relevant to the larger group, and as has been indicated there is a way to circumvent the technologically debilitating issues of the larger group through technologies related to consciousness, by accessing the smaller group.

This writer has had this capability demonstrated to him graphically. Our mind is not a hallucination generated by our brains; it is a quantum particle that is not constrained by its size. Our mind, in particular the ID aspect of that mind particle, can still be entirely functional when it is smaller than the Planck Length and someplace else entirely.

Part of the issue of understanding this is that one aspect of that information has to do with the equivalent of a map dimension that is related to the dynamics of dimensional design, the schematics beneath the actualities that have to be incredibly exacting in order for all of it to work exactly as it all works. (We'll get to that in the next chapter)

This is exactly what David Bohm and Alain Aspect were talking about but neither of them explained it in any way anyone else could understand, possibly because they both only suspected the truth but refused to fully contemplate the implications.

The universe is not *contained in* a grain of sand the universe *is* a grain of sand in the mind of God, and there is a level of uncertainty as to how individualizing or disconnected we are from the mind of God because on one level we are all the same thing. So as what you are, how long does it take to get from point A to point B on a grain of sand? Can that be done, of course it can; you just have to understand the full nature of dimensional mechanics to do it, and you simply will never understand that if you forbid anyone intelligent from thinking about it.

It also means that there has to be a way to go from here to the full on experience of the sea of creation domain that comprises the dominion of Gods mind, simply because what we are as our minds is an in a sense ephemeral particle expression of consciousness and we all exist in a complex dimensional structure as indicated by the mathematics of String and M theory and of course Bohmian Mechanics as well. This writer has done that and the entire process was demonstrated to him graphically as it occurred, so it is a fact that there is a way and it is remarkably simple to accomplish it!

Really! After you finish with this book, read and *try to understand* what David Bohm was trying to say in the context of what Alain Aspect experimentally proved, then come back and really try to think about this stuff.

These issues generate serious questions that can be addressed by the institutions of science using the entirely objective tools of science, but only if science is willing to admit that they just might be legitimate questions and then seeks to answer them. This writer has shown everyone already exactly how to follow the paths that might, just might, lead towards those answers in empirical ways, if, science will simply allow the related questions to be addressed with an open and objective mind.

This has been said it in other places in this book but it will be said again. Massive amounts of information are held in and conveyed by properties related to light, understanding how this works is a relatively inexpensive way to begin to understand and realize insights into the full nature of dimensional information communication. It is not just about printing seven hundred million bits and no bits on a plastic disk to convey movies to everyone in the human race, as this writer has already done, this is far deeper, it is technology related to the minds of the Gods, and understanding this technology will allow human beings to think as the Gods do, and eventually maybe just maybe to become legitimate adults ourselves. It would be a real shame if we blew ourselves up for incredibly stupid reasons, just as we were beginning to understand maybe what we really are or at least can be.

When this chapter started out it was going to get deeply into dimensional mechanics, but at this point folks that are reading this would maybe get bored to tears and start claiming this writer was just trying to brag about how smart he was by talking about stuff few people would understand, so if you are reading this and you are reasonably intelligent and versed in basic physics send an email and maybe he will work on a proper academically formatted paper that seeks to describe what he is talking about here.

Chapter Eleven
The Holographic Universe & The Map Dimension

The term holographic universe is a bit misleading but it is used as the term is currently rather popular in academic circles and related bizarre theories, a few of them related to quantum mechanics.

Technically a hologram is made by fixing the field patterns that arrive with a photon that is reflected off an object into a medium such as clear plastic resin or gelatin. These patterns comprise circular field groups usually called interference patterns and lasers normally have to be used because the patterns have or can exhibit very regular and intense coherent characteristics that importantly can almost exactly be replicated.

They are or were considered important because the medium can be three dimensional like a cube, and thus in theory can store massive amounts of information compared to a DVD for instance, which is two dimensional; but to date there have been a variety of problems with fidelity issues mostly due to imperfect recording mediums, that did not arise with the DVD. They can also be used to trap and then display true 3 dimensional images.

The term holographic in the context of the universe applies mainly to the property that a holographic medium can be written in a cube that is say one sq. foot on each surface and then the medium can be chopped up until you have a bit the size of a grain of sand and if you then illuminate that bit with a laser properly you can still get the entire image slightly degraded that can be enhanced in various ways to restore the fidelity of the original image. If you think about this carefully you may be able to find a determination that explains a few of the exquisite properties of light in general.

In other words the smallest bit contains all the information of the larger bit, and now there are a variety of theories that say the entire universe is holographic and everywhere the smallest bit of it can be re-inflated with all the energy and stuff of the universe and then others that say this is constantly going on every couple of trillionths of a second.

To say it another way; if you carry that idea forward to a related field, quantum mechanics has a variety of theories related to the structure of the universe that tend to say that at every point in space time all the way down to the Plank Length, maybe even smaller than that, there is sufficient information and energy to reconstruct the entire universe from scratch. Thus, it is, only in a sense, a dimensional property. Meaning as Alain Aspect was apparently fond of saying 'if you look closely there seems to be a hidden sense of order in things'.

While some other people say this is the justification for the zero point energy and that consequently UFO's use this to get around and energy ought to be free for everyone anywhere anybody needs it.

Alternatively in string theory, M theory and related theories, the math keeps on saying pretty much adamantly that the three dimensional and one time universe we enjoy has to be an illusion, and the thing just won't work at least mathematically unless there are at least ten spatial

Physics of Consciousness

dimensions; and various interpretations indicate one to three dimensions of time, where usually the other seven spatial dimensions are all curled up into a tiny realm smaller than the Planck length, or roughly just for the sake of conversation, a trillion-trillion times smaller than an atom, so that rather conveniently the theorists can never hope to be able to actually measure or investigate the other seven except with numbers on a piece of paper, and... it is a fact that math is simply a rather complex type of language that anyone sufficiently skilled in that medium can use to say pretty much anything they want to say. Sort of just like this writer does using simple English that other normal people can hopefully understand; the difference being that this writer always tries to tell the truth in his non-fiction because he does not need to obtain funding from this work, and he is doing it out of gratitude to the god's that wasted their time on this writer and rest of us humans, so that ethical conduct is mandatory.

A variety of very smart and usually gifted people like to make complex graphic computer models of what they imagine and or the math says these tiny complex dimensional realms, usually called Calabi-Yaus would look like to people that can only see in two or three dimensions. They all look like rather convoluted interwoven balls of a sort, but trying to experience exactly what experiencing life inside of one of these multi-dimensional realms is something pretty much nobody has tried to illustrate, as... well to us it would just seem to be utterly insane.

Then there is another fairly recent theory that says the universe is only two dimensions of information sort of like a DVD, and we are all sort of just looking over the horizon at an illusion that seems to be 3 dimensional. That does sound very bizarre, so you can think about this sort of like a T3D TV and a pair of T3D polarized glasses, the image you are looking at is entirely two dimensional on that DVD; but you

Physics of Consciousness

put on those glasses and suddenly because of parallax you are for all intents and purposes a blue skinned Avatar on the lush planet of Pandora fighting off alien coyotes with a flaming stick!

The point here is the same one that was made with the quantum computers, the important thing about theories is that only those that lead to technologies that yield things that actually impact our lives in useful or legitimate ways, or, honest anecdotes that relate actual awake real experiences are the qualities that led to *convergence* in our lives in ways that might actually turn out to be true in useful ways.

Okay, this writer went around and around this issue trying to figure out how he was going to deal with it here, the foundational background of the salient experience is fully detailed in 'The Promontory' and then in this book in a non-comprehensive way, so if you are really curious go and read the Promontory', but the salient points here are as follows.

Perhaps surprisingly this writer is almost fully in agreement with the math in string theory and David Bohm's related theories, not because of the math, but because he actually went to the implicate realm in his soul body and mind and directly experienced it in a fully awake state of mind.

The issues that are relevant here are...

1. The experience of that realm was not like one might imagine of an insane multidimensional ball, but only in a sense like a perfectly normal three dimensional realm, except that even though the experience of light there was exactly as it is here, it was as light is experienced here in outer space.

In other words if you go outside in the daylight on the Earth on a clear day the sky seems to be filled with pale blue light everywhere you look because the light from the sun is reflected off of the atoms in the atmosphere and so it seems to be everywhere, but in space everywhere you look the sky

Physics of Consciousness

is black unless you are looking at the sun which is incredibly bright, however even though the light is in a sense invisible it reflects off of everything and thus illuminates everything perfectly.

So that it is a fact that the sky above the Sea of Creation that is comprised of all the universes OM has created has no atmosphere. This is fine as obviously when you are entirely in your soul you don't need to breathe, and in a way this adds a form of legitimacy to the experience.

2. Again it was experienced in a sense just like a three dimensional realm is experienced. There was a sense of gravity on the 'asteroid' that comprises the Promontory, but no sense of gravity as the black blob out in space near the virtual reality exhibit of what OM was as a young God, but then there is a sense of gravity of sorts and a sense of down when you are pushed off the Promontory by the Curator and then flying 'above' the sea of creation.

So that all in all there is a normal sense of gravity where it seems appropriate and three dimensions of space and one of time, except that you go through several sort of realms that can only be described as dimensions of time to get there, and one of those dimensions of time is at least potentially terrifying as you are at the mercy entirely of some sort of more comprehensive being that clearly has the power to delegate your existence into a featureless place literally forever.

3. In the miraculous event that an academic physicist is actually reading this, even though this writer did not actually go there, it was very apparent that in the Sea of Creation there is the tiny version of this universe and inside of that is the tiny version of the earth, but that that version can be experienced almost exactly as it is here, sans the people the human technologies and artifacts and most of the animals. In other words Joni Mitchel could go there and discover that paradise has yet to be paved.

There are three spatial dimensions that affect the experience of existence there just as there are here, but in order for that reality to exist in the obviously tiny expression there, there must be a variety of alternative spatial dimensions that are sort of in a way containers for that expression of reality to exist as it does exist, and that set of container spatial dimensions must exist in a fully co-operating way where at least one or more of them is in a sense larger than the three we experience when here or there.

This needs to be interjected here in a digressive way so it will be in your head so you can understand a point that comes later. Physics believes and that is all it is that no type of communication is required in spatial dimensional structures as the lessor dimensions are enclosed by the larger and so things just have to be as they are, but in String theory and M theory there is an expectation of sorts that somehow information travels down to the tiny versions of reality and then travels back up so that everything in a sense is copasetic; they often say something like 'Our reality is entirely filtered through the Calabi-Yau; and, this reality constructing information is required to traverse that structure 'instantly' or utterly outside of and beyond the time dimensions that are related to the spatial dimensions operations. Now we can go on for the time being.

Sorry this may be a bit difficult to visualize mentally but it helps if you look up the science of dimensional brane structures on the web and study that extensively until your brain begins to grasp the nature of what is being described here. You also need to understand that a tesseract is a four dimensional cube that can be described perfectly with fairly simple mathematics but that when you go to a tesserractic *sphere* you are immediately mathematically catapulted into *infinities* and you can then only achieve true mathematical *approximations* through Riemannian geometries and modular functions, so that you are forced to leave

Physics of Consciousness

mathematics behind if you really want to understand the truth, and go entirely into visualizing replete topologies.

The impression this writer got from thinking fairly deeply about all of this in the ways an architect thinks about and visualizes things, recall what you just read in the last chapter, is that our universe is in a larger sense the three spatial dimensions but that there is a fourth larger or containing boundary of a sort that can be thought of as an Omega brane and a fifth that can be thought of as the Alpha or origins brane.

Because the Omega brane is dimensional in nature, cosmic black holes are an example because like black holes the Omega brane can be anywhere but they comprise *dimensional* expressions where the idea and reality of three spatial dimensions and time break down entirely and the structural integrity of the normal three dimensions fail internally, so that you *cannot* think of the Omega Brane simply as a container sort of sphere for the universe.

(While the physics of the film 'interstellar' was in an academic sense rather silly, it did make one very important point somewhat subtly, it did assume consciousness was the dominant factor of all physical laws and regimes.)

Then the Alpha brane is in a sense the beginning but it is also everywhere, and this is incredibly important as it is the transitional brane from here in a sense only inwardly or down to the implicate version of our reality, and because it is everywhere it explains what dark energy is and why this universe apparently continues to expand.

To understand the why of this, recall that OM created his mental version of our universe in the realm where he lives; out of the same material sort of that our souls are made of, and then he sort of blew it up rather like blowing up a balloon but in several dimensions and that process is still ongoing. This issue will be addressed in greater detail shortly but for now you just need that in the back of your mind.

Thus this Alpha brane or the apparent in a sense only tiny source brane for our *physical* larger universe is also the Omega brane for the *implicate* three spatial dimensions.

Then you are required to have at least one truly containing brane, sort of an Omega-Omega brane that contains all of this universal creation, this can be interpreted as the Euclidian skin of the bubble, the skin of a balloon that insulates us from what is *out there*. However there is no actual need for this membrane of sorts to be dimensional in nature. This brane or non-dimensional membrane is currently being observed by academics studying the microwave background radiation of the universe, and they can see things that can currently only be explained as the results of other universes bumping into this one exactly as they would if they were all in a great sea of universes.

So that this writer's opinion and that is all that this is; is 4+(1 divided by 2, but as one constant, not one half)+3 initially or seven or eight spatial dimensions sort of like the academics and their mathematics claim, are required to explain everything that this writer has directly observed and intellectually derived from the observations, but that there certainly could be more of them. And, that there are at least three, but more likely at least five dimensions of *time* related to OM's creation or this particular universe that are directly related to the physics of our existence; but then, that there are essentially an immeasurable number of dimensions of time many of them related to local fabrications of light allowed and in use across the multiverse.

Now what follows immediately is mere speculation sort of. To understand that you need to understand that clairvoyance at least for this writer is not like channelors often claim, some voice talking with words in English into a blank mind and then the channellor mindlessly repeating what is said. To this writer it is simply knowledge that arrives in his mind that is not in any way explicable as the result of his histories of in effect intellectual consumption of regular external knowledge. The following is based on knowledge that came to him in the breeze that he experienced in Sophia's presence that was then verified in curious ways by knowledge that was delivered via the Web. It is related to the material that arrived in that way concerning the Solipsi Rai among other things.

This has to do 'finally' with the map dimension outside of time and how this is related to instantaneous dimensional communications, it's short form is here quickly, but will be elaborated on near the end of this chapter.

This is based only in part on numerous video's on the Web that show UFO's in effect going instantly through portals as such in the sky and completely disappearing. Obviously some of these are faked, but not all of them, and then there is the fact that numerous UFO's of widely differing types show up all over the place and again obviously most of these are not machines that people live on for the thousands and thousands of years that would be required for them to travel slower than the speed of light. Then there is this issue and it is a very big issue; space *is* as we have discovered fairly empty, but when you are approaching the speed of light even hydrogen atoms can become lethal projectiles to just about any kind of metal hull that can be imagined, and it is also a fact that radiation becomes lethal to organic beings at these speeds and it is even an almost insurmountable problem for humans just trying to get to Mars the slow way, these issues combined with the sort of knowing inside this writer's head made him try to understand what is really going on. That then lead towards the requirement for dimensional communications and the probability that an alternative dimension of sorts is required to let everything know exactly where it is supposed to be.

Physics of Consciousness

This is sort of cheating as this writer was originally trained as an architect. These days you just can't make a complex structure all by yourself, so at a minimum you need a schematic of the final structure, one that can be read by the builders and even the dufus folks at the Building Department. Did this writer actually say that? ☺

Maybe just maybe the universe, which is a tiny bit more complicated than this writer's current single wide, needs a schematic as well.

This can be thought of as a map dimension, it's a sort of schematic for creation that allows it to work in a consistent and well timely manner. It's sort of like a floor plan hanging on the wall of the single wide that helps you to remember exactly where the bathroom is. ☺

It was stimulated in this writers mind by a video on the Web made by a guy who claims he was often contacted by extraterrestrials when he wasn't drinking whisky, in effect telepathically, and when he asked them how they got about they told him they got about the slow way the first time, or they knew others that did that and when they got someplace interesting they took a sort of complex picture of the surroundings that included the very nature of the particles, then they just re-projected that picture out from the hull of their ships and arrived pretty much instantly where the picture was, anywhere in this universe that their computers had already taken a picture of. Apologies are in order but this writer simply cannot remember who this guy was only the mental impact of what he was saying. Of course recently this was then also verified by my friend Singre of the Solipsi Rai. Just kidding sort of again, but I couldn't remember how to make those emoticons, and well they were getting a bit repetitive anyway.

This is then based on the physics that says there are wormholes all over the place that connect particles together outside of time, and it has in effect been proven to be true by

Mr. Aspect once again, however he and all the other wormhole aficionados, well except maybe for Mr. Guth, do not seem to have any clue as to the why and how these wormholes work or what they actually implicitly imply, but most of them seem to be more or less secretly inclined to think maybe this has something to do with dimensional architectures, or well folded pieces of paper as in the film 'Intersteller'. It's a pretty good theory until you bother to ask what happens to all the folks and stars when the paper, read space-time, in the neighborhood, is folded over to make the wormholes?

Okay; now a tree for instance drops a seed it gets blown by the wind and the tree grows, that is simply physical laws at work.

While all the theories related to string theory and Mr. Bohm demand some sort of dimensional architecture that involves a tiny realm that everything in the larger realm is, to use their words, filtered through.

Apologies are in order as this is going to more than likely exercise your brain in ways that are entirely outside the box, sorry it just is what it is so a bit of foundation is in order once again.

1. Physics is the science of the study of nature and if you boil that down it is effectively the study of physical laws, and related issues that follow those laws into this reality.

For instance salient to this topic physics has more or less proven that everything that is experienced as being solid is actually 99% nothing at all, and that what actually is there is simply a few expressions of condensed energy, and that even those particle expressions are always well, uncertain, or rather just like the material of thoughts, sort of ephemeral, they can be one thing or another thing and we already expressed the why of that.

Physics of Consciousness

One of the things that physicists seldom address is the why and the what of the thing. For instance almost nobody is ever allowed to ask, *why* does energy exist, or *what* exactly is energy? The reasons for this have to do with the fact that if you think about these issues that way it almost invariably leads to the issue of a designer, and thus the verboten and dastardly issue of God crepes in. Mostly physicists are only allowed to entertain and try to figure out the how things work end of things.

This writer has read a whole lot of serious books and an endless supply of academic papers now on the Web, but nowhere was there a single attempt to explain exactly what energy is, likewise nobody has made any attempt at all to explain exactly where physical laws come from, or even how they really work, only that they exist and then what they do in this reality.

2. When physicists discuss spatial dimensions especially branes and related issues they usually make an assumption that everybody understands that all spatial dimensions are in effect part of the same quality or thing, without bothering to define exactly what spatial dimensions really are. A few science fiction writers have tried to deal with related issues but most of the time they are dealing with entire alternative realms rather than the technologies of dimensions. You might understand the why this is here shortly.

3. This writer does not understand why he is still physically alive as when he went to The Promontory he was about as far out of his normal body along with his mind and the physical soul's bits of his physical body as anybody can be for well over two hours of time here. This needs to be in your mind to understand what is coming.

4. Say you send an astronaut to Mars and he dies, does that astronaut's soul then have to wait for a few years for an angel to get there and take his soul onto Heaven. This

255

is here to stimulate your mind to understand that spatial dimensions do not have to be made from the same 'material' and that the 'small' version of our universe is actually made from material that is in some way related to the material of our souls.

5. This point is counter intuitive as you have to think in terms of the Gods as they exist in the context of infinities. When we think of stuff getting smaller we think in terms of stuff usually getting sort of compressed and as a result denser; this is exactly *not* the way it really works. In what follows we are in a realm that exists everywhere dimensionally in almost full agreement with the salient issues in string theory, in other words at least a trillion trillion times smaller than an atom.

To grant you approximate clarity, this means that there is dimensionally something everywhere in existence including inside your own head, that in relative terms is the size of or at least fully as complex as this entire physical universe but compared to what we normally experience is way smaller than a single atom, and that thing can be experienced by the mind and body of your soul as entirely tangible and in a sense normal, and precisely because it is dimensional in nature it is literally everywhere that anything in this universe can be. Like that poet said, 'the universe in a grain of sand'. But that grain of sand is *everywhere the universe is.*

The point sort of! The realm of the alpha dimension mentioned above is directly related to the same material your soul is made out of, and the material of your soul can access it perfectly. God, just about none of the Gods, do not live in this physical world and drastically importantly that which is commonly called the Calabi-Yau is not made of physical material that is the same type of material that this physical realm and its dimensional structures are made out of. Again; let it sink in; the material the Calabi-Yau is made out of is

Physics of Consciousness

the material that is related to the same material that your soul is made out of, it is fabricated from 'material' aspects of the spectrum of consciousness and billions and billions of people and God's live there, not other versions of you or your soul, but entirely *other* folks, living out what to them are entirely normal lives.

What this means is that there is a *transition* of some sort that occurs in the brane fabric of dimensions, where that which was constructed entirely of material that was fabricated inside the intellectual authority of God's mind as a complex entire structure equivalent to our entire universe translates and is blown up in a way only to become the physical out there world we 'enjoy', and that physicists study and try to understand.

What is being said here is that in this writer's opinion David Bohm was entirely right in his interpretation of the implicate realm, he just had to figure it out quite remarkably with only his intellect, whereas this writer actually and quite unexpectedly went through the process of going there and experiencing it firsthand. David Bohm was universally respected as a great mind but ostracized by the intellectual and academic community for what he figured out and this writer is simply declared a flaming nutcase. The problem is that this writer has to figure out what he experienced directly and the implicate explicate realm theory is the only thing that comes even close, and David Bohm's physical interpretation was found by this writer long after he directly experienced this truth.

Okay again so it can sink in another analogy of sorts. As this writer sits here tapping keys on a keyboard, there is a massive amount of stuff that is entirely hidden that has to go on to translate what he is trying to convey to you by turning that input into sort of reasonably acceptable letters on a screen. That hidden stuff involves pages and pages, hundreds even thousands of pages of code in 1 and zeros, that make

Physics of Consciousness

the computer operate in very complex ways to do that and then remember sort of perfectly everything this writer is typing. All of that is utterly invisible to the writer and to you but it is there. In a way you can think of this as another dimension and it is in a way equivalent to a mapping dimension that all of us are usually blissfully unaware of, just as we hopefully are when typing on the computer..

Because of the various factors related to the more complex dimensional structure required to make this universe work, it is extremely likely there is another dimension of sorts in the background of reality that is the equivalent of this computer that constitutes a map of sorts so that everything everywhere can know exactly where it is and what it is supposed to be. And the functions of that zone as it were have to function outside of the time that allows experience to proceed in a normal manner in the ultimate expressions of the reality realms.

So in terms of the computer to keep it simple imagine you convert what you are to 1s and zeros and you flow into the computer and then pop back out again instantly back into your head. Then apply that to a technology inside a UFO, that in effect allows you to go into the mapping realm and then come out in exactly the place that somebody else has been before instantly because the computer in your UFO has a snapshot of exactly where you want to be, and that snapshot is perfect but it only exists in a single specific location in all of creation, so you just project that snapshot perfectly all around your UFO and you are there outside of time instantly.

Now recall that Alain Aspect actually proved quantum entanglement, and that that entanglement and the information that must be there for it to happen must not only happen far faster than the speed of light, *but that it must happen with <u>incredible precision</u> across vast amounts of space* to get to its partner particle and tell it that its original partner has changed its nature. That simply demands that every particle in creation has to have a place and certain properties that something, *something*, knows about very precisely and utterly absolutely or particle entanglement simply cannot work, but it is a *fact* that it does indeed work.

Indeed the Chinese have now proven categorically that it works perfectly with a satellite that allows them to communicate to anyone else in China instantly in a code that cannot be broken using particle entanglement as a technology. If the theoretical material here is correct the Chinese might be the first human folks to figure out how to travel anywhere in this universe instantly. Maybe the folks at the skunk works in the U.S. should listen up.

If two particles halfway across the universe can know exactly what their partners want them to know instantly, why can't a machine that takes a photograph of those same particles and then projects that photograph out around itself, be in exactly that same spot instantly?

And if it can, if, there simply must be some sort of schematic sort of dimension that allows this to happen perfectly, as it must if it is going to work for the particles, and then by the related technology.

Now recall that reality in this writers experience is only half physical and that the original 'half' is in a sense made out of 'material' aspects of the field of consciousness. That means that in a way it is ultimately consciousness that rules everything and that OM may have decided that the best way you insure this, was to create a way for his consciousness and as a result the same bits of consciousness's that everybody that is sentient owns, can find ways to overcome all the physical laws that OM designed into his outer creations and actually arrive anywhere instantly so that he and by derivation all of us can overcome any and all physical laws if any of us need that capacity.

The implications of that realization go far beyond map dimensions and overcoming the constraints of any physical laws; we are in a way talking about how the ten billion year old Gnomopo get anyplace in creation instantly with no spaceships at all using merely their bodies and minds; but for now we need to remain salient to the point, except to say that this is the secret to becoming a sorcerer and even a God, or the equivalent of a God, and to getting out of the matrix as such, if that is what you really want to do.

Okay physical laws were incorporated into the version of this universe inside the implicate realm before it was expanded in, as science calls it 'the inflation event', and there is an earth just like this one here with the same literal physical laws there. There may be people there, or there might not be people there, there are no roads there, cars various technologies and so on but the structure and material reality of what we experience here is there and again the physical laws are there and then here precisely because God generated them in his head and put them there. But when you are there in the implicate realm you are taught in a way literally that each and every universe in the sea of creation and there are literally gazillions of those universes now, each have differing properties and laws, and in a wide variety of them the people that evolved in the outer blown up version similar to ours have discovered what they really are and they have decided to move to the tiny version of their realms entirely to live entirely as immortal beings in the soul version of what they really are.

It is a fact because this writer has done it that you can literally fly over billions of entire universes in the sea of creation in a very timely manner, so that if you can do that there it is very likely there is a way to get about inside this universe alone more or less instantly as well. You do not have to just take this writer's word for it, in the Promontory it has been thoroughly explained how you can go and do that as well, at least well flying over the sea of creation, defeating the physical laws of this universe may be slightly more complex.

Why, partly because in *that* world, in OM's mind, even though the physical laws we all evolved in are still there in our version of this universe there; there is a sort of versatility available that is related to the intellectual ability to adjust things in ways that allow you do and be things you could not possibly be when you are absolutely constrained by those same physical laws when you are here.

As an example; initially when entering the Lightweavers universe there is no gravity, and no air is required and light is like it is in most places like it is in outer space, but when several Lightweaver minds get together they can create entire new 'physical' realms and universes on their own. They began by building palaces of solid light just out there floating in black space that were fully lit up internally by their own material. But all the Lightweavers had the bodies that they had originally evolved inside of as these were appealing to each other naturally. Admittedly they were sort of terrifying for a while to this writer when he first met them but they can pretty much instantly make that feeling of fear go away telepathically.

And the world they built by going inside this writers head to find out what humans like, was a lot like this planet Earth, but there is slightly less gravity than here and the atmosphere is a bit denser, so you can fly and physically experience that as if you were doing that here, forests, wind, warm sunlight and so on but it is mostly oceans entirely dotted with smaller continents and islands of all sorts of familiar geologies and climates and floras and faunas, just so far at least when this writer was there, there are no people. And the thing is when you are there you are entirely in your soul body but you don't feel any different than you do here, you feel entirely physical and awake, except you never feel cold or hot or hungry unless you want too and if you want to feast you can cook all kinds of meat that never had any idea that it existed, in other words nobody ever has to kill anything, and, you can have a body and have sex there just like you do here, but only when and if you really want it, and you can live there without any sort of judgement of any kind by anybody literally forever without ageing, it basically is a place that is the equivalent of a perfect place for humans, and most importantly it is accessible from here as it is exactly inside your own head!

Sorry got carried away in that digression. The real point here is about the map dimension.

If the implicate realm exists, and it is a fact to this writer that it does, in a way that is similar to this in a sense only larger physical universe, there has to be a type of communication of information that is in some way related to dimensional communication. Dimensional communication is instantaneous, or occurs outside the passage of normal time and space.

This is in a way related to the current academic theories related to wormholes. Typically in the academically accepted explanation of how these work you have to think of space as a sort of membrane like a sheet of paper, you have point A at one end and point B at another and if you are say a worm it takes you quite a while to crawl across the sheet from A to B, but if you just fold the sheet in half so that A and B are on either side of the sheet, the distance and therefore the time required to make the journey is sort of nil, or almost instantaneous, all you need is a few teeth to eat though the paper, in physics massive amounts of energy are the equivalent of the teeth.

However the new related theories say that something else has to be going on that no longer requires folded paper or space, because as Alain Aspect pointed out and proved, if you have two photons made at the same time one can travel across the entire universe, while the other stays right here and you can change the spin of your resident photon and the spin of the traveling photon no matter how far away it is will also change instantly.

The only answer academics have so far seriously discussed is that there must be some sort of wormholes that we can't see that are causing this to happen outside of time, because the information that one of the particles have changed has to be transmitted to the other one far away.

However there is another alternative; various spatial dimensions have to transmit the information that they exist to other things and spatial dimensions instantly and the nature of this information transfer is so counterintuitive it almost seems to be impossible, yet it is also so utterly mundane that we never even think about it.

But, if all the particles that make up the bones and structures of this reality are also expressed in the tiny version of this reality then there simply has to be some form of the transfer of information between all of them that has to happen in the context of an outside of time instantaneous way.

You simply cannot dismiss this as impossible, by for instance saying that the same particle that has to exist here as an already microscopic little bugger, has to also exist in an entire equivalent realm that is in its entirety a trillion trillion times smaller than an atom, it just seems impossible that anything that small could even exist. But then you have to remember that we are talking about the properties of dimensions as a technology residing in a context where infinites both up and down in scale are the normal container.

In this context our entire reality could very well be unfolding in that tiny realm and there would be no way you could prove it isn't. Voyager the spacecraft could all of a sudden pop through the local membrane of the neuron we live inside of and pop out into spaces between the cells in what might amount to God's brain. Just making a point with a pun on what was in the 1800's a popular philosophy that explored the possible reality that we all lived in God's big toe. ☺

We don't of course, but we do live inside of what amounts to a dream occurring inside God's mind that we only think is real.

Now apply this way of thinking about the issue to the fact that your mind, not your brain but your mind, is a quantum particle and quantum uncertainty is there so that God or something akin to God can make us experience reality the way he, it wants it to be experienced.

Another way to look at this has to do with what an architect does once again. There is an immense amount of time and thinking and drafting involved to make a set of plans for a house and then more time, reams of it involved to build it, but now a computer can take those plans and almost instantly create an actual true 3D model with all the inner spaces instantly and you can see it all with a glance without even building the thing. As was explained earlier it is likely that quantum uncertainty in a way does the same thing with all of this reality that we experience as we experience it. If that is going on in any form it is very likely it is going on in other forms as well. When you glance at a three d picture of a home the floor plans are not gone they are still there you just are not looking at them, so maybe just maybe the floor plans for the universe are still there as well, you just have to find out where you filed them and take a look.

The problem here is that there are half a dozen ways at least to look at what spatial dimensions are exactly and if or if not they have to transfer information between the various elements concerned in order to function as they do.

The normal academic argument is that no existential information is transferred because all lessor dimensions exist in containers that both allow and demand whatever is occurring in the lesser dimension to occur, so that at each successive layer of complexity things just have to happen as they do.

But try to understand it really try, consciousness is a qualitatively different thing than the physical realms and rules that it exists inside of. Consciousness is the equivalent of an entirely other dimensional quality. Does this book even exist if nobody wrote it and nobody reads it?

It's really simple, if you are reading this on a computer or a Kindle for instance, this entire book and all the software related to it are still there when you are not reading it, but it is residing quiescently in another dimension you are not aware of, and then you bring up the book. What exactly is it that is doing the reading? Your mind reaches out and grabs the words on the screen and this writers mind is speaking directly to yours across time, across a whole set of 'dimensional' boundaries, instantly. Yes you can take this as absurdly unimportant but there is something hidden here that is remarkably difficult to convey with words that is vastly important and that may be intentionally obfuscated so that we have an incredible difficulty in coming to understand exactly what the nature of consciousness really is.

Consciousness is something else entirely than physical issues, than what science normally examines, but it is absolutely and utterly real and by any measure certainly just as important as all the other stuff science seeks to examine. Consciousness is simply *not a hallucination* caused by the operation of our physical brains, it is something else, utterly as real as everything else physical, just different. So why, really why, does science so adamantly refuse to investigate and seek to understand exactly what consciousness really is? Why is no one trying to understand that there is a physics of consciousness and that that field of inquiry is by far the most important thing to investigate and that it is by far the most powerful thing in all of creation?

If string theory and the related higher dimensional structures are correct in any way the complexity of the occurrences and structures in the various dimensions becomes so complex that some form of information transfer becomes required. For instance, say a star explodes here; this is an immensely complex process that has to occur simultaneously in the implicate realm as well, and a lot of that has nothing to do in any way with dimensional structures, so that information has to be transferred instantly, the normal intuitive thinking almost demands that this proves the implicate realm cannot exist.

This writer's problem is that he is certain it does exist because he has been there, and to get there you have to pass through what amounts to several alternative for lack of a better term physical structures to get there.

And again, the material of the implicate realm is not the same sort of material as this realm, so that some form of complex information has to be transferring between the two realms instantly all the time.

Again, as it is anti-intuitive. Two consciousnesses' are talking to each other, the writer is speaking and you are listening across technical dimensions of up in scale and down in scale, and both are entirely different than the technology that allows it to happen. A star explodes, the question is; is reality designed or is immediate reality all there is to the beast, if; if reality is designed what is the point if the designer cannot know what is occurring in reality, and if it can know, then on numerous levels consciousness has to have *very powerful tools* related to the information that is being generated by reality as it unfolds. If, if this is all the result of intelligent design then these information related tools are without question the most important technologies in creation, yet no one, no one in the host if intellectual pursuits is even allowed to ask these related questions, much less investigate the implications.

Okay here's another way to look at this issue. A photon, or at least the information that will be expressed eventually by the photon when it is actually created at the end of its life, is created by a quasar thirteen billion years ago and travels across almost this entire universe, then hits an astronomers telescope on this planet and a variety of properties contained in or related to that photon tells the astronomer that it traveled across almost the entire universe, that it was born in a quasar and exactly where that quasar was at the time it was born. During its journey it had to cross the paths of gazillions of other photons from other stars and quasars along the way, and all photons are never entirely segregated from the original field of light that permeates the universe and that that photon shares with all the others, and now it is a fact that if a photon was created at the same time as our candidate photon interacts in any way that causes the other photon to change its character, it will communicate that to all its brothers and sisters, but still somehow the photon that hit the telescope remembered *exactly* and individually what happened to it during its life.

That seems to implicitly imply that somehow someway inside the greater cloud of light that all the photons arrive out of there is a memory or a map, more or less similar to the map the wave form interference patterns creates, that is or are made in a resin medium by a holographic laser, that indicates exactly where everything is and exactly when whatever that thing was, that gave birth to the photon was where it was.

Sorry went a bit fast there; certain mediums use interference patterns that arrive with laser photons and can be used to resurrect the exact patterns again, it is thus extremely likely that one of the properties of the fabric of space time, or the field of light itself is the equivalent of a

Physics of Consciousness

holographic medium, and as a result once again, (it may be important to recall that actual light is entirely invisible, especially in the vacuum of space, until it converts into photons and gets recorded by something) if you had a vehicle that could project perfectly the appropriate image entirely around itself, that vehicle might very well sort of fool the dimensional information cloud and arrive instantly at the only place in all of creation where exactly the same picture existed. Then it could simply turn off its projector and become a part of that new reality.

Sorry again this is about a property that is rather subtle and difficult to understand, but if you spend a few days studying light and thinking about it you might have a rather subtle little epiphany and come to an understanding of this issue, but only maybe. It's very difficult to convey with mere words, and like the fine structure constant there are a lot of complex factors involved to get to the prime number of understanding with clarity.

The thing is that this has to do with properties of light that can be studied here on the earth. There are literally trillions of photons that you can see in action by simply glancing about as you are driving down the road, they ought to be interfering with each other and causing a massive blur of stuff before what you see gets to your eyes, so that it seems probable and that is all it is that there is some sort of other dimension of sorts behind or in the light that in effect maps out everything that the photons reflect off of and that the photons can access instantly. If science can figure out how that occurs, if it occurs, it means it has to exist all across the universe, and if that is the case you get really close to verifying the technology that the guy who was told how UFO's work was saying.

A lot of so called primitive folks used to believe that if you gave someone a picture of yourself or you let them take your picture you granted them an immense amount of

Physics of Consciousness

power over what you are. Maybe, just maybe they were correct.

Now academically you can say that photons are really small and there are a lot of them and space is really empty so it just works, but remember every photon is accompanied by essentially an almost infinite set of interference waves, and it is those waves that generate an image in a holographic medium, but that requires a very exclusive sort of set of conditions to imprint properly, while out in nature the conditions are immensely complex and the interference patterns ought to yield a mush of conflicting information so that the photons almost have to be able to access a sort of map of reality that they can access instantly as they impact our retinas, or our telescope mirrors, if that is not the case then you are almost forced to interpret reality as something that is created almost entirely inside our minds, perhaps by the resonance that comes back down the tube from God's technical brain and thus the alternative to the map dimension is in effect a proof of God running our experience of reality constantly, either proof is sufficient to win a Nobel.

Now obviously there may be all kinds of purely secular alternative answers to how photons really work as perfectly as they do. But as said before this writer has tried to find legitimate answers to these issues and all he was able to find was an anecdotal story about one academic that invested years of his life trying to figure it out and as a result nearly went insane and almost utterly damaged his career. There is a whole lot of stuff about how light actually works that science has either refused to address or simply has failed to understand, and that deeper understanding can almost certainly lead towards technologies of profound consequence.

Now the problem with the UFO that moves by photographic capture and projection, is that all the particles it had in its computer drastically change over time and no one could predict what would happen to those particles over time, so you would almost always arrive in the past of the photograph's reality. Extraterrestrials have addressed this issue, specifically that group known as the Pleiadians, and this writers friends the Solipsi, (just messing with your head a bit) they have all said that they own time, so that they get to where they are going and then adjust their location in time appropriately, and it is a fact that there are literally thousands of accounts of abductees that have said over and over again that they experienced inexplicable losses of time when on or even just near a UFO, that includes the salient first-hand experience of this writer. Obviously many of these accounts simply reflect the failure of consciousness, a black out, but often there seems to be something else going on that actually has to do with the passage of time itself. This writer does not know how you or any extraterrestrial can own time; just that it seems to be extremely likely that it can be done.

Actually one of my Solipsi friends, a pilot said they just pop into an alternative universe with an alternative time engine related to the speed of light, as the equivalent of virtual particles, and they are very careful not to interfere with any local operations when they are there; then when they catch up with the appropriate time here they just pop back into this one, but I was writing a fiction when he told me that so who knows.

It is a fact to this writer that if anything seems likely to be possible eventually with enough intellectual effort consciousness will figure out how to make that issue real.

Now if this writer keeps on with this train of thought a whole lot of readers are going to be bored to tears and well quit reading, so this will end with this request of any true academic that want's to tackle a serious problem in a serious way that has the potential, if you can solve it, to yield a

Nobel Prize. You cannot prove it as a negative, but you may be able to prove it is required.

Please seriously explore the issue of dimensional communications, not the structure of dimensions, but the probable necessity that dimensions can or even must communicate information to their various parts in order to exist as they do exist. To this writer it is already a fact that if this is required or is even possible that communication must occur outside of any normal passage of time. Maybe study Alain Aspects stuff to get you started. Then while you are doing that try to find out how it is that light works as perfectly as it does all the time, there is a secret hiding under the table there that can only be described as utterly profound, so profound that it makes understanding gravity and its counterforce seem trivial, even though it is not.

Chapter Twelve
How To Be *Decent* In The Arriving Future Here

Before we begin this you have to adopt a mindset; read it as if you were born into a race of truly ethical folks that have existed in a civilization of ten billion fully telepathic souls that is two billion years old and supremely positive and successful by any and all philosophical measures. These folks are known as the Solipsi Rai, they live on planets located in the constellation known from here as Cygnus, and they are well known by both the Russian and American 'intelligence' agencies on this planet. The Solipsi can and will give humanity virtually everything we need for all of us to live comfortable and constructive lives; and heal our planet as well, and, they will even give us the technologies that will grant us access to the stars in a timely manner; but they will not do those things until we fix the destructive cultural attitudes that have plagued us since we existed as humans on this planet.

Indeed as this is written about twenty very curious mummies or preserved cadavers were found by a grave robber in Peru, who was mystified so he turned them in to a group of non-government authorities. A few folks have tested their DNA and said it is all human, but obviously they are not human at all, of course chimpanzees are 98% human DNA as well and the DNA of an eighteen hundred year old body might not still be in perfect condition.

This writer has seen films of folks out on a backpacking excursion on the earth that look exactly like living versions of these Peruvian folks found near Nazca that came from exactly the same period of time the Nazca lines were created. This writer knows the Solipsi are real and important to our history as that was explained to him by Sophia our Creator when he met her previous to finding alternative evidence of the Solipsi.

What happened is that a spaceship with about six adult Solipsi crashed in Peru and their technology was destroyed but they survived, then eventually they made friends with the locals and the locals came to revere them. Then since their ability to communicate was also destroyed they had the locals create the Nazca lines so that any other Solipsi that flew over the area would see them from the air and investigate and save them. Unfortunately it did not work in a timely manner so eventually they all died.

One of the bodies found was almost as big as a normal human and their DNA is very similar to our own so it is obvious that at least one of them had sex with a human and produced a few offspring that were hybrid, the Solipsi are real people, that has now been proven, and if you are curious about them read my pretend fictional trilogy about them where I will address this issue in greater detail towards the end of the last book.

So read this in the context of *why* the Solipsi will not help us and try to understand the implications of exactly what will happen in a positive way if we truly learn how to act like socially civilized people and we stop acting like an entire planetary culture of incredibly selfish mentally challenged and suicidally warlike individuals that have dementia.

If you think this is hyperbole just turn on your TV and a major news channel; then examine their take on the lunatic corruption that is driving the American political machinery these days, dementia describes it all perfectly.

This needs to be said up front and it needs to be said with absolute clarity. Speaking against a small group of humans that think they deserve to rule this planet and all of humanity as the utterly selfish and deceitful abominations they are, that call themselves Zionists, is not the same by any measure as being what is often called anti-Semitic. This is not an attitude of racism made up by this writer; it is instead very politely paraphrased from a quote written by Benjamin Franklin, one of the primary founding fathers of America, he called them vampires; that survive by drinking the life blood of society.

This writer has known many Jews in his life, made love to a woman of their kind and in a way loved her and her people; and in business known and dealt with many of them and ethically they were about the same as for instance plain old English or American people, but there is a small group of that population that has subscribed to what is known as Zionism mostly so that they could get rich through fraud and deceit of the highest orders in ways that are very similar to those of, just as an example, the Masons, an organization that may have indirectly evolved out of Zionism.

It has become more than evident if you are even moderately intelligent, partly as the result of the Internet, that a very small group of folks that subscribe to Zionism by using a variety of wrongly powerful Americans as their soldiers and puppets, have through fraud and deceit basically taken over the so called Western social structures of this planet, and they, along with the American based military industrial complex and the neocons are even as this is written driving the human experience irrationally towards the end of all of our experience on this planet.

What they are all doing and what they are is simply and entirely wrong and one way or another, if we value what we are as humans living in a *civilized* society, those groups of individuals need to be carefully and fully identified, indicted, tried for their crimes and punished, or at the very least removed from their positions of power in our political structures, and our media, not just the Zionists, but their puppets as well. America and England are no longer governments that represent the people; they are governments that represent the specialized groups of lobbyists that pay corruptly elected officials under the table money to do what they are told to do by those same lobbyists. This does not by any means justify being racist against all Jews, or anyone else for that matter, the Jews are in many cases the most intelligent and constructive, even wise, people of our species, and they often make very entertaining movies.

But if the human race is going to succeed across the immediately arriving future the misguided and corrupt people in power need to be stopped, period.

People, regular humans included, exist that are devoid of ethics or empathy, and people that are obsessed with money and power over others are particularly an expression of these deficiencies, and because of the various ways humanity has evolved socially, these types of people, usually known as sociopaths and psychopaths are by far the dominant group that has almost always risen to power over others on this planet; precisely because they are unencumbered by the necessity to feel what other normal humans feel. Those positive feelings are usually related to something called empathy, and thus the selfish folks do not feel obligated to do what is best for everyone, so they just do what is best for themselves and their very small group of friends, associates, and family, yet in most cases they are the people that are running many of our nations.

It's very simple and it is exactly the reason AI can be dangerous. Selfishness is inherently evident in all expressions of consciousness; and even in schematic pretend versions of consciousness called AI systems, *it is related to our need to eat to survive*, whereas empathy and selflessness are qualities that must be learned over time. Empathy and selflessness ultimately yield by far the highest order of personal security for everyone including the monstrously selfish, and they are by far the ascendant positive ways to be, but again they have to be learned and carefully installed in the psyche, whereas selfishness is the inherent natural quality that must be defeated.

In social terms selfishness is the engine that drives capitalism, in the Western form it is simply spread out and designed to make everyone selfish, whereas in all totalitarian regimes it is focused on one head of state and the few folks in power around them. In very rare cases these types of leaders can be wise and benevolent, as is the case in Russia and China currently, but that is rare, at least historically. That is not to say Russia and China are currently totalitarian, their leaders are now democratically elected and representative of their peoples more justly than anyone in the western world currently is.

All social structures that operate in the most secure manner for everyone involved are based on the understanding that everybody in your society is your equal by any and all measures, and so they are all to be treated in exactly the same way *you* want to be treated by everybody else. In cultural philosophy this is called Egalitarianism and in theology it is called the Golden Rule, and it is supremely important for a host of very important reasons.

No one lives alone, an individual becomes a family, a family a neighborhood, a neighborhood a city, a city a state, a state becomes a nation, and a nation becomes a planet. Initially it is almost always an island planet by itself, but eventually if it is positively successful it is adopted in a positive way by the galactic family and the planet can join in an entire universe of positive folks.

None of us truly succeed by being selfish monsters; ultimately we all succeed through co-operation with the folks around us. This is exactly the philosophy that Russia and China have adopted and it is the right way to be, called right thinking. And if you have to deal with a selfish monster you do not try to kill them, you simply try as best you can to walk away peacefully, and you seek positive co-operation with alternate others around you to your mutual benefit.

Our condition here is massively exacerbated by a planetary culture based strictly on capitalism, as capitalism teaches everyone from birth that they will *not* be successful unless their mindset in life is based entirely on selfishness, and, that empathy for others is a liability in that context. Then we try to use laws to keep things under control, but that then fails when the law makers figure out they are not subject to those laws that they create and then something that could have been almost grand falls apart from the top down as is happening in America and the rest of the western world as this is written. *Laws are not laws unless they apply equally to everyone.* When they do not they become simply tools that defend totalitarian corruption.

This is blatantly apparent in just about everyone in charge of the western nations of this planet, in part because those nations represent the sum of what capitalism on this planet teaches and is based on, something called dark Sumerian money magic.

Ivy League colleges teach that Machiavelli was a great guy as he knew exactly how to manipulate everyone else, so that he could grow richer and more powerful at their expense. This is simply wrong, but because of this and things like this, this is what almost all our western national leaders become, the imperators of Machiavellian philosophy.

One of the other tools the dark ones use to keep themselves in power is to limit the knowledge that their underlings are allowed to learn, and this has been going on, on this planet since humanity existed as various cultures. Among many other things this is why we do not know as fact that *this* universe is massively populated by an endless variety of very intelligent races both benevolent and evil, that all focus their intellect primarily on understanding metaphysical issues.

So one thing that almost all of the extraterrestrial races have in common is, comparatively speaking, a far deeper understanding of the metaphysics of creation, than humanity, as a general rule, is allowed to understand. We positive folks are incredibly lucky as the primary metaphysical creators among us are the ultimate power; they are The Holy Spirit, the Mother, The Father, and now for us here on the Earth, Christ, and they are very alive and with us even now.

So this is going to start with how the academic system has been corrupted; as in our society. That system designs the mentality of pretty much everyone that assumes a leading role of any sort in our western societies. However oddly perhaps that is also rather insidiously supplemented by religions and then massively supported across life by the social structures that have evolved on this planet.

First, all of the issues in our reality, and the complexities of their interactions and evolutions are by their nature, before they are allowed to exist and function in useful ways, exactly, *elements of intelligent design.* The issue of intelligent design is verboten in academia, but it is with certainty to this writer, the reason we exist.

This is an inverse philosophical argument related to the philosophical arguments that all natural science has followed and evolved under since the related academic institutions have existed, but it is an entirely valid approach that under the strict interpretations of the absolutes of philosophy simply cannot be argued against satisfactorily by any branch of academia.

The very exacting and constraining philosophical rules of science and academia were created by a few rich naturalists in the seventeen hundreds, based on intellectual interpretations of philosophical concepts that were originated on this planet probably by Plato and Aristotle, and while a few of them are very useful, they are not all entirely correct.

Actually it is quite ironic but if sciences arch enemy the Catholic Church had not conserved the knowledge and trains of thought Plato and Aristotle tried to grant us science and academia probably would not be as it is today.

Since Darwin, actually way prior to Darwin, again all the way back to Aristotle and Plato, natural science or science in general has looked at nature and tried to determine the best and most exacting ways to determine and explain exactly what we live in and the nature of what that is, so that it can generate technologies that will work in the context of this reality, and that approach is unconditionally glorious, as it usually works until it is corrupted for reasons related to capitalism. But science never asks the single most important question of all, *why*, are all these things the way they are?

The problem is that as the philosophical concepts and underpinnings of science and the related fields of academia were being born, religions were far more powerful socially; and religions were based entirely on effectively legendary foundations that apparently had little or no basis in real fact, or at the very least were usually not capable of being empirically demonstrated as facts, and, those foundations had been seriously manipulated by selfish men that had used the power of what the original voices of the various religions had sought to explain to empower themselves, while avoiding entirely actually learning what the original founding voices had tried to teach. If you want to understand this deeply simply learn and follow the evolutions of the Catholic Church across the two millennia of its existence with an open mind, then go back and seek to understand exactly what Christ was trying to teach us when he was here.

The net result of all of that was that the founding voices of science were in many cases exiled into oblivion or burned at the stake. However as society evolved the truths that science had found and tried to explain were proven to be in most cases correct, and so the institutions of academia evolved and in a variety of ways became the dominant social institutions of the truth.

However and it remains a huge issue even now, at last count often quite inexplicably 95% of the populations of this planet still believe adamantly in some form of divinity, or of divine intervention in our reality, which is academically interpreted as *intelligent design*, and the way science seeks to explain this is that in terms of the absolutes of philosophical arguments, represents exactly the same ways that religion sought to explain away science as it was going through its intellectual birthing pains. Science claims as is best exemplified verbally by Professor Stephen Hawking; this is paraphrased for context; 'that religion and metaphysics are fairytales for those afraid of the dark'.

And like all statements that are valid Professor Hawking's is absolutely correct, but he is also wrong, because the now leading institutions of power, academia and science have closed their minds to the seeking of the actual full truth in an attempt to insure the continuation of their economic and social power, while in often subtle ways everyone else that has not been indoctrinated by science has had some sort of very strong personal experience that told them that divinity was a powerful reality in various ways. Yet science is still adamantly ignoring this reality and is now constantly making statements and acting in ways designed to insure its continuation of power and wealth based on a closed mind attitude which is exactly the same as religions sought to do when they were in positions of unconstrained power.

Here is why this is incredibly important: Questions related to intelligent design are by far the most important questions that humanity has still failed to answer, not because they cannot be answered but because science has failed to seek out those answers, in part because of the antipathy of science and religion that occurred as science was being born, and because science will simply not allow the imperfections of religious thought to infect their foundational attitudes of thought, they refuse to investigate or even allow the existence of the issues related to religious regimes.

You scientists simply take a look at the photo of the Venerable Maria of Jesus Agreda on the web. She died in the sixteen hundreds, but she is laying there in her decorated bed obviously content and she looks just like a really good looking lady that is simply fast asleep. Then you folks in academia try to explain to this writer or anyone else why there is nothing worthwhile at all in any theological regimes.

The huge problem for academia is that despite what they are taught in schools, just about everyone still seems to believe that there is at least something related to divinity that must have something to do with the experience of being a conscious being. And now God forbid a few scientists of the highest order are beginning to try to explain things by treading in realms that are very close to the metaphysical, so that the pillars of the society of science that are currently in control of the financing, are acting in ways that can only be interpreted as being slightly paranoid and anti-socially radical.

One huge social problem that results from this is that religions are or were almost universally the real teachers of ethics, while academia dismisses or minimizes ethics. Religions are often very hypocritical in this arena, teaching that they only apply to their adherents but then ignoring them as they apply to the institutions internally, but science simply ignores them entirely, by assuming that the legalities of governance will take care of the related issues. But then lawyers and lawmakers are all taught that laws only apply to everybody else, and then how exactly they can negate the values of all the laws that do exist.

Now, early in the evolution of science a man came along named Darwin, he said in essence as he was interpreted by folks in the fields of academia that no God or ascended being was required to explain us and what we live in, and, that evolution was merely the result of survival of the fittest. This is severely edited just to make a point. Then Francis Crick and James Watson came along and discovered DNA and this solidified the foundations of what Darwin was saying into a kind of curious fact.

And again, Darwin Crick and Watson were and remain exactly correct, but like Bohm tried to explain, Quantum Mechanics and Relativity are also exactly correct but only in the *context* of what they are trying to explain, and so far no one in science has even come close to determining exactly where DNA came from, they simply continue towards proving, much to their dismay, that the idea that DNA arrived by chance on the earth alone is, to be kind, not very likely at all.

However in the sterilized philosophy of Darwinism, a few extremely rich and powerful individuals in America determined that the best possible path related to Darwinism and science was called Eugenics. It was also by an odd coincidence useful to them as the best way they could insure their own power base and the continuation of their wealth. Eugenics basically says if you are not the physical and mental definition of a perfect human being you are an expression of social malfeasance that needs to be terminated with extreme prejudice. But the founders of that philosophy must have failed to look in a mirror as most of them were a bit odd physically and mentally, again, to be kind.

Then Hitler came across the Eugenics movement in America and took its philosophies to the extreme, until his expressions of power were fortunately terminated. However the wealth and power and yes partial anonymity of the first eugenicists in America kept them in positions of extreme social wealth and power across several generations, often discretely but often not, and some of those folks still have a hand discretely in determining who gets research grants and tenure in the institutions of academia, so that the issues of intelligent design simply cannot be addressed with an open mind in any effective way in academia.

Quite oddly this writer agrees utterly with the philosophical precepts of natural science but with the caveat that they must be used with an entirely open mind at least in the initial stages of hypothetical inducement.

In other words, a huge amount of religious doctrine is as science declares, absolute crap, that massive amounts of people believe without any question, as concrete in their heads, but and it is a huge but, a real badooka, a vast amount of science is also the equivalent of crap as well. Nuclear Bombs and nuclear electricity is crap that is there just to make obscene people rich. Eugenics is crap as it is impossible to determine exactly what a perfect human being is and it is utterly wrong to base that determination on purely physical characteristics as the most important aspects of being human are ephemeral in the terms of the measurable quantities of science, so it is just used by already wealthy people to insure they remain wealthy and powerful without any shred of empathy. Most of the science and technologies related to vaccines pharmaceuticals and chemistries as they relate to the welfare of humanity are false or at best seriously constrained science as well and simply there to enrich their progenitors.

Virtually the only moral or ethical guidelines that honestly control the results of science have to do with how much money and power over others the resulting technologies can generate so that the ways science is propagated in the modern world can be interpreted in only one way, as the tools of the worship of money and power over others.

That is how evil works in this world, by using things that can be interpreted as good, like using the Catholic Church to commit and justify wrongly, genocide against the Cathar's and the Muslims and by using science to generate nuclear technologies that can and very well may cause the end of the human experience.

Sorry you can argue that evil is an imaginary construct, and ethics moralities and empathies are transitory philosophical abominations that are entirely intellectually dismissible quantities when held against the importance of money and power related regimes, but socially the positive venues are the most important things in existence, and unless science is held to the constraints of positive philosophical laws we will as a race of beings utterly cease to exist, simply because we held to the laws generated entirely by money and power over others, laws and philosophies that condemn anyone that fails to believe exactly as you the scientist does, or whoever you are in places of power and wealth, that believes wealth and power are the ultimate expressions of existence

And there are the huge questions related to this reality and the experience of consciousness and being human that simply cannot be answered in the absence of any sort of investigation into the metaphysical or spiritual side of existence.

It is also a fact that the issues and technologies related to metaphysical questions yield the highest levels of science and technologies, how to travel across the universe outside of time, how to own time, how to experience the very mind of God and thus know the truth and nature of divinity, how to know the true nature of what we are and then our actual immortality and so on. So read it again if you need too.

    The initial point here is the Solipsi are very real and they can offer us everything we need to inherit the stars and solve virtually every problem we face in our future, if, if, we only recognize what we have become and why we have become as we are. So you politicians, manufacturers of weapons, heads of capitalist corporations, bogus *leaders* of the real terrorist nations, professors that teach the ways to be successful in this world by ignoring ethical conduct, just take a moment after you read this and simply look in a mirror, is the person you see there somebody you want to spend your life dealing with, is that person the best you can be, and if not why not?

    Now... what follows here is not about becoming a god directly on a singular this world human level, that is probably impossible, but if we manage to survive what is coming and do what is suggested here it may very well be a cultural miracle of epic proportions. But it will require an utterly *fundamental revision* concerning personal selfishness as opposed to empathy and decency, across the entire human race; that probably will not happen in any easy way, but at least somebody needs to start talking about it, right now!

    Keep in mind as you read this that this writer has followed the news carefully since he was able to read, and not a single supreme capitalist, or a mere handful of politicians could be classified as truly decent human beings, and none of them, not a single one was happy as a result of their money and power, during their retirement.

    Fairly often the rich folks do create philanthropic organizations but more often than not these are created to minimize tax losses and further their twisted semi-political and extended money making programs, or to squander money on bizarre programs like silly but very expensive modern art, just as an example; while institutions like banks, again just an example, that are bailed out of their own bizarre failures with taxpayer monies then turn around and commit outrageous and unbelievable fraud against their own customers simply to enhance their corporate and personal director's cash flows.

This writer is not even going to get into the obscene flows of monies to weapons manufacturers that all our politicians and apparently even our so-called neutral major media newscasters hold sacred, as this will begin to resemble a rant of unhindered proportions. The leaders of government in charge of the big check book justify their military perversions by claiming military Keynesianism is good for everybody, but the truth is, it is in sum the result of unfettered corruption pure and simple

The point you need to keep in mind is that unconstrained capitalism is not the only economic cultural foundation that works, and it is a fact that unconstrained capitalism breeds and encourages sociopathy and murderous psychopathy, and the worst venue in this category is weapons manufacturers and the banks that make trillions financing their wars. Sorry now to the point.

The arriving future here is almost exactly the same as this writer's friends the Solipsi Rai experienced and successfully dealt with *two billion years ago.*

We are in the process of building *machines* that in effect exhibit what seems to be *intelligent behavior*; complex machines that can function as humans do without the need for souls.

On the Earth we are now creating cars and even trucks that drive themselves, and probably trains and ships shortly; tractors that do everything required to produce food, now they can even pick strawberries and tomatoes. Machines that cook and sell hamburgers in China and Japan, and can even call the police if someone attempts to get away without paying, they can now; or soon will manufacture virtually everything we need, they even will soon manufacture endlessly evolving versions of themselves.

While the internet in effect makes all forms of service industries and what were intelligently based industries that we thought would always require humans, *obsolete*.

In roughly fifty years, virtually everything developed society needs to survive and prosper will be created by mindless machines, in a hundred years if we manage to survive our own idiocy, this reality will dominate this entire planet.

There will be no *necessary* jobs for humans as a result! No jobs, means no income for anyone! Except for the people that own the machines... depending on how this reality evolves, that will be a select group of a few hundred or a few thousand people or maybe even a few tens of thousands of people, out of ten BILLION souls, but those few people will be incredibly wealthy, while everyone else will be *redundant*; or as Mr. Rockefeller is reported to have once said, 'worthless mouths that must be fed', in other words, what he failed to say but certainly implied, 'worthless mouths that must be killed'.

This is not something that will happen in the distant and nebulous future, it is going on right now. Why do you think there are currently less people employed in the *productive* work force in America than there were during the last 'Great' Depression?

Why do you think the American federal public debt is now exceeding Twenty Trillion dollars? You could simply stack up hundred dollar bills that represent that much money and completely do away with NASA, just attach a ladder to that stack and we could climb all the way to Mars and colonize a new planet. Just making a point sort of.

Why do you think that Federal Government jobs mostly designed to hinder the enjoyment of our lives are now two and a half times more prevalent than productive manufacturing jobs in America? You think the NSA is about national security, no, it is about employing thousands of insidious people that would otherwise be unemployed

Why do you think hundreds of thousands of people are right now being put out of work even in China, Europe and the Middle East?

Why do you think politicians that preach war, and the remarkably wealthy secretive leaders of the military industrial complexes around this planet are so incredibly successful, and why is there an endless supply of young men and women voluntarily making themselves available to fight those constant lunatic wars and be crippled or even die?

Do you honestly think ISIS is about Islam, it is about money from Western Saudi and American-Israeli politicians and establishing a violent caliphate, an obscenely evil dictatorship of humans that has absolutely nothing to do with God and everything to do with pure evil; so that there will be wars upon wars to enrich the weapons manufacturers; the murderers of innocent souls that do what they do, just to make frigging pieces of paper with numbers printed on them. It is all going on partly because being a soldier and getting paid is the last option just about everyone has for their own temporary money based survival, and that includes simply protecting the contents of your refrigerator as a freaking bummed out survivalist.

Maybe this is news maybe not, but even those that are willing to give up their lives for a few pieces of paper are currently in the process of becoming redundant as the military industrial folks are now making semi-intelligent robots with guns; to fight their wars with no humans involved at all, except well all the folks on the other side of their killing machines that thankfully for the weapons manufacturers, don't believe exactly as their own politicians and generals believe, or well maybe they do, but the weapons manufacturers can still make money by killing them, all that is required is a little bit of fraud, usually called false flags, and a paid off mass media.

Except when that endless supply of wars escalates to the nuclear or engineered virus level and then all of us die as a result of this endlessly obscene form of greed.

Just as one example of what is now going on. Russia is now trying to become at least a semi-benevolent western style democratic republic with a western style economy. The U.S and especially the rest of Europe should be following the lead of France and Germany and encouraging that reality, while at the same time China has become like Russia, and in China they have done that so successfully that America would not even exist economically if it was not for this evolution in China and now China is using their wealth to massively construct modern and useful infrastructure across the entire continent of Africa and thus massively improving the lives of literally billions of people.

Maybe the people in the American Congress and the Executive Branch should stand up and ask the simple question. Apparently the entire world outside the U.S. for some miraculous reason just wants to be friends and co-operate with each other for the welfare of all humans, oh my God; maybe just maybe we should try to encourage that, instead of trying to create false justifications for wars to protect the incomes of a few monstrous capitalists that make weapons of mass destruction for the decaying western world.

America exists now just to *sell death* and yes murder, and their major media constantly propagandizes this to a level of almost sacred expectations, and every politician running for every office holds this military madness to be the highest possible parameter to identify with. It is insanity of the highest and most dangerous level and it will not stop until humanity recognizes it for what it is.

The leaders of the BRIC nations and especially Mr. Vladimir Putin, Mr. Medvedev and Mr. Ji Jinping have seen the fallacy of this western progression and taken steps towards seeking co-operation among the nations they rule, and for and with as many others that can see the basic sanity they represent. They are simply trying as best they can to peacefully walk away from major corruption and do the best they can for the people and the nations they are tasked to direct.

Just as a personal aside, this writer honestly appreciates Mr. Medvedev, he owns a truly intelligent decent and benevolent mind that is probably hampered as a great leader by a good heart and his significant internal empathy for his own people. It is a thing, a continuing hidden sadness you can see in his eyes without words from a mere photograph.

Our western leaders try to call him evil and corrupt because he bought a nice house in warmer Europe, big frigging deal, you think our congress people and senators don't work the limits of their six million a year *expense* accounts they voted themselves constitutionally illegally just because they figured we are all stupid and so they could get away with it.

But Mr. Putin is a greater leader in a worldly context than Mr. Medvedev because Mr. Putin was trained to think strategically as a young man, but it is a fact that as long as Mr. Medvedev remains a true and gifted friend of Mr. Putin that both of them together will represent the highest and best hope for all the peoples of this planet.

They along with President Ji Jinping are trying to build a world where nations can be nations that represent the interests of the people that live in them as individual nations, in exactly the same ways the founding fathers of America tried to do when they wrote the Constitution and brought the American states together. But now the states are entire nations that simply *co-operate* with each other in a peaceful and constructive manner with respect for the benefit of everyone involved. They are building massive banking systems that are involved entirely in creating infrastructure for impoverished nations that need it desperately. They are plagued by a great 'liability' in this international world designed to reflect the current hegemony of the United States, it is called simply 'right thinking'.

This is in part the result of learning from the federally sponsored mistakes of their own pasts, not simply their own predecessors domestic mistakes, but the federally based mistakes of other nations that tried to psychopathically invade their domestic peace of mind; while the actual leaders of the western world have so far never known the results of the mistakes of their own pasts and the various forms of corruption that can infect government and cause endless amounts of suffering for the innocent peoples of a nation. The leaders of the western world think empathy is a liability, while collecting pieces of paper with numbers on them is the most important priority of their experience of experience here.

The leaders of those BRIC nations have to take steps to defend themselves from this obscene corruption that has infected this planet as the result of the American so-called Hegemony, or they will be replaced by ex-wall street gangsters as the democratically elected leader of Brazil recently was, or the leader of Syria is constantly trying to avoid, or worse.

While since the end of WW2 the leaders of the western world have learned only one thing, obscene corruption will grant you mountains of paper dollars with absolute impunity so that you can join the movie stars and buy a grand house with a swimming pool on the beach in

Malibu or Florida when you retire. And you don't even have to worry about the so-called law any more as you can simply pay off the judges and the media.

Of course your wife or husband will probably be a money obsessed utterly shallow minded bitch or bastard, that will torture you endlessly in your retirement, but what the heck you can just go to church and Christ will forgive you for all your sins when you die, and you can avoid your spouse entirely by simply joining a pedophilia club?

This writer has news for all the obscene banksters the politicians and the weapons makers of the western world, along with the business men lawyers judges and doctors that support policies of making a big unearned living by stealing the lives of all those that actually tried to decently earn a living around you.

Once again so that this is utterly clear: *You do own a soul*, almost all of us so-called humans do, it will go on experiencing and living after your body dies here, and for you negative selfish folks this should be the most terrifying thing you can possibly imagine. Why, because there are none of you monstrous humans in Heaven, not a single one of you, and Hell is not the wonderful place with endless obscene and perverted forms of sex, and even the sacrificial murder of innocent children with impunity that you have been led to believe is so much fun.

This writer is not saying this because he is afraid of the dark or he believes in fairy tales, he is saying this as he has been on the other side entirely in his soul's body over and over and over again in ways that simply cannot be denied and lived to tell about it, maybe for reasons that just might have some value.

And no, you will not be able to survive here as obscenely decrepit old men on an endless supply of new livers and hearts from Israeli and maybe even Chinese doctors that took the lives of innocents and the already underprivileged in South America and elsewhere in the developing world, so they could collect ten million a pop in cash from you.

Purgatory is not as the Catholics sometimes claim a nebulous place where the angels can decide if they should send you to Heaven or Hell, *this place, this planet, is the exact equivalent of Purgatory*!

Sorry an occasional rant is what writers always once upon a time only wanted to do, but now that editors have been replaced by instant publication it is entirely allowed, at least until the writers are shot for speaking out loud the truth as they understand it, in a nation where free speech was once protected by the Constitution. A document that one recent president that arrived from nearly the largest organized crime family in the history of this planet, called simply; "just a fucking piece of paper!"

Again, sorry, the salient point here is that our world is in the process of changing in ways that are without question *utterly fundamental.*

A great mind published a book when this writer was still only a child, his name was C. Northcote Parkinson, and his book was called 'East and West'. Basically in that book he argued that this planet was set up in such a way that the preeminence of society would evolve from East to West and West to East over time. Apparently most of the time people that make predictions are wrong, but this guy was entirely right.

But where he was wrong was that he could not have foreseen the evolution of technology. *In a hundred years on this planet there will be no jobs; and no earned income period; none at all, not in the west and not in the east.*

Except for the need of a few personal slaves to cater to the needs of the automation machine *owners*, who will be *incredibly* wealthy!

Those few incredibly selfish sociopathic and even psychopathic humans will have both the power and a massive incentive to <u>reduce</u> the population of the worthless mouths that must be fed across this entire planet, and they will most likely seek to accomplish that with deadly engineered viruses, as they will be able to protect themselves and their pretend loved ones with vaccines that will be one hundred percent effective and no one else that is sick and dying will be able to figure out who to blame, and the environment those nasties will inherit as a result will still be effectively perfect. That is so long as you don't have to live near one of their furnaces.

That is the path this planet is headed towards now, if we manage to avoid the nuclear holocaust that the imbeciles actually running our governments at the moment are trying to foment.

<u>There is an alternative!</u> It was already addressed successfully by the Solipsi Rai, our close neighbors in this galaxy over two billion years ago. It's very simple and it has been proven utterly across the last two billion years. You simply have to give up worshiping pieces of paper over everything else and learn how to act like decent responsible adults, and then realize that everyone else is just like you, that you are not better than everybody else just because you believe that you are, just because you can't get inside *their* heads you can only get inside *your own head*.

When the Solipsi figured out that in the near future everything, everything they needed or even desired would be provided by mindless machines, and that as a result there would be no jobs, at first they gave up on the Sumerian money magic called debt, but their government kept on printing money and just handed it out to everyone for free, but after a while they realized that was just silly, so they quit doing that and just gave everyone everything they needed or wanted for free.

Physics of Consciousness

    This writer has written and published another book that details a few evolutionary ways we can approach this reality, and tries in the beginning to remind people what the great minds that founded The United States of America were trying to do, it is called 'Egalitarianism'. This writers work is not by any means a set of perfect solutions but it may be useful in the future we are walking into.

    There is one thing that makes this all incredibly easy if you can pull it off. You have to entirely get rid of the Sumerian money magic psychological implant called *ownership*. Machines can't make food for free if the farmers still own the farms, you don't solve this dilemma by taking the farms away from the farmers, you solve it by giving the farmers everything they desire for free if they just quit working their farms, so that they can simply spend all of their time enjoying their lives.

    And you don't solve the problem by granting individuals and imaginary legal entities called corporations ownership of all the automation, and the farms and all the real estate, you simply create an entity like the United Nations that is owned by all human beings and then you give that entity ownership of *all* the automation. You just have to be careful that power hungry sociopaths don't end up running that new institution.

    It was a tiny bit easier for the Solipsi than it will be for us because they were born completely telepathic and they learned as fact a very long time ago that they could reincarnate as Solipsi over and over again, and as a result they usually valued each other as much as they value themselves. In other words true empathy is merely the normal way they are. It just means we will have to try a tiny bit harder, but they were right and they have proved it utterly over the last two *billion* years.

    The incredibly fundamental change that they introduced into their culture, was one that was fundamental in America before the white man showed up here. The Native Americans just never had to deal with the *idea of personal and corporate ownership, from the very beginning of their cultures.*

Except that everyone was allowed one good home to live in for their entire lives more or less for free and if they wanted to live someplace else they simply traded that home with somebody else for free, or they just walked away, exactly as the Solipsi have done for two billion years.

Their societies were both based entirely on exactly the same cultural ethic that *all* of humanity enjoyed by living in commutarian, not communist but *commutarian*, villages before the Annunaki and their slaves the Sumerians infected our reality here with that damned Sumerian money magic and debt and turned the entire human race into a species of slaves.

The difference for the Solipsi is as it soon will be for us; machines made virtually everything they needed, and in a hundred years, just a single generation, they will do that for us. The choice we have to make is simple; is that utopian vision going to exist for a select few of the most selfish and evil human beings, or is it going to exist for *all of us*, and if it is going to exist for all of us we simply must rearrange our cultural foundation that is based on absolute ownership of *stuff,* everything we can possibly amass simply because our egos tell us that makes us in some very strange way better than everybody else around us. This western business ethic called keeping up with the Joneses is utterly absurd by any interpretation.

This writer can say these words with some authority, as he once owned a massive architectural masterpiece that he designed and built himself on a private lake and a year round stream, he wrote the papers that were directly responsible for the DVD and T3D media, all of that and a great deal more was utterly stolen using a crooked small town attorney and his partner an obscenely evil judge in a satanic manner. The primary perpetrator of that theft even tried to kill this writer when he tried to respond to the court he was required to go into, with the truth of what was going on, and again the court refused to even acknowledge this writer even existed, except to kick him out on the street and even denied him; an utterly innocent man not guilty of any crime at all, the right to go back and collect his few important personal possessions.

Yes it did take this writer a while to adjust to the loss, but now he owns absolutely nothing, so he does not have to spend three days doing the domestic housework before somebody shows up to visit, but in truth he is no less happy in his day to day life than he was then.

But then like his friends the Solipsi, this writer knows with absolute certainty that he is immortal, and that for him what happens in a single dream of a life is easy to overcome; and for what it is worth Hell is a very real place and everyone involved in that personal travesty will come to understand that intimately in the very near future. Sorry it does help to write down stuff like this.

Obviously we cannot give up everything instantly, and rearrange society entirely in a moment, but we simply must commence that psychological evolution one way or another now. We simply have to recognize the truth of what is coming and take steps to take advantage of that now or we will most certainly pay the consequences.

The most intelligent and wealthy nations across this planet, Switzerland and especially currently Finland are prime examples as they are in the process right now of contemplating this evolution and taking tentative steps to implement it, they are offering to hand out a basic comfortable income to every citizen of their nation simply for being born there. Switzerland is the nation that has been known as the banking capital of the world for hundreds of years, if they are doing that there; maybe the rest of us should take a good look at that and consider exactly what it means.

You may find this to be a fictional interlude but it is not, although this writer simply does not have the means to prove it right now, but it is a fact to this writer at least, that if we simply give up being an insane suicidally warlike race of idiots and we seek out constructive co-operation with everybody else on our planet, and then over a fairly short period of time we succeed in proving that is what we want to become by actually doing it, the Solipsi will show up here publically and assist us with our transition, and in the process of doing that they will grant us the technologies that will allow us to inherit the stars, and even show us all kinds of alternative places that are perfect for us to move to; to help with our overpopulation issues here, and even in the process grant us the tools to heal this planet from the constant abuses we have heaped upon it as the result of our own adolescence as a race.

What happened after the Solipsi gave up on working for silly money? After a while they all began to become bored, then after a while they realized that learning skills and doing useful constructive stuff for other folks was the most satisfying alternative. Now except for metallurgy where they are surpassed only by their friends the Tingre Tingre, the Solipsi are the finest craftsmen in this galaxy and when they are finished creating something of great artistic value they simply give it away to their friends, and as a society they have become known as, the greatest most helpful friends anyone that's decent can know in this galaxy.

They spend their time trying to help others by giving others the technologies they have developed and trying to make everyone decent and happy in the process. Finally it is a fact to this writer, Sophia, the true creator of everyone in this multiverse has become their true friend, she loves them and they worship her in a very simple way with all their telepathic hearts. The choice is entirely up to us. But as Mr. Trump is constantly saying, "what in the heck do we really have to lose?"

A caution has to be added to these words. Saying that the Solipsi will come and help us does not in any way imply that we should welcome all extraterrestrials with open arms. This *universal* reality is a lot like this planet there are truly decent folks with decent souls here, and there are total assholes here as well, all mixed up and all over the place. Out there not very far away at all there are even entire societies that own no souls at all. If any of those negative folks do show up here in force *our only real hope* will exist in generating a true alliance with the Solipsi Rai. And you cannot use this logic to falsely empower the weapons makers again, as to any extraterrestrials that can actually make it here, we will be exactly as capable of our own defense as the southern Amerindians were when Columbus showed up.

But you also have to address these related issues with an open mind and so far the best person and group that has a good grasp of how to deal with this is Dr. Steven Greer and his Sirius Disclosure group. They make a lot of very good informed and logical arguments, for instance if the extraterrestrials were all bad we would have ceased to exist a very long time ago, simply because their technologies are so incredibly advanced compared to our own, and that if any extraterrestrials actually do seem to be invading it will probably be the Satanic fools running our own governments rather than true aliens, as they can use that as yet one more powerful way to further justify the insanity called the Military Industrial Complex and the selfish politicians that support that madness.

So again, this is in sum incredibly important reasons that we should try to make ourselves worthy of the Solipsi, because the Solipsi are an ancient race with ancient technologies and if anyone is stupid enough to antagonize them too far, the Solipsi can and will simply annihilate that aggressive race. They have been *forced* to do that many times before, they do not enjoy being forced into anything, especially things that can be interpreted inversely as evil, but sometimes being forced to do something is simply unavoidable, so that what they are and what they are capable of has migrated across the galaxy, so no one that is not totally insane will even consider antagonizing them in any way any longer. Having them as great friends and close allies is the greatest security anyone in this galaxy can find, but you simply but thoroughly have to earn that status in their eyes.

The Solipsi are a lot like the Russians, they are incredibly patient and they will take a fist in the face over and over again before they will actually fight back, they are not really turning the cheek, they are simply incredibly patient, but when they fight back they always win, at least eventually!

This writer was simply born and raised in America, but given the evolution of America towards intransigent corruption and banal stupidity in American governance during his lifetime and the evolution towards common sense and decency in Russia and China during the writer's lifetime, simply in this writer's humble opinion being a close ally of Russia is currently preferable to being a subject of America's inherently intrusive and corrupt federal government.

And again it is simply a humble opinion, but since there has been for the last eight years a serious question as to whether or not the recent president was actually born on American soil, and because the current electoral process is by any definition beyond bizarre and can only be explained if there is indeed a massive organized crime syndicate running this nation behind the scenes, it makes a massive amount of sense to run Vladimir Putin to be the next president of the United States, and if that actually occurred there is a very good possibility he would win and then the entire world would have virtually no reason to have any more wars at all and virtually all the negative issues on this planet would be resolved in a very positive manner. ☺

That may have been a sort of tongue in cheek passage, and this writer is not offering to be a traitor in any way shape or form, although inherently national interests that currently define what a traitor is, seem to be left over from antiquity and rather silly to any decent and moderately intelligent mind, that simply wants to live on a planet of wise human beings, but it does make a large amount of sense in this writer's opinion only, to make Mr. Putin the President of this nation. And again, no this writer is not offering to commit treason or even sedition of any sort, this writer is and always has been the ultimate expression of a pacifist, he was simply cursed with a moderately high degree of intelligence and simultaneously cursed with a sense of absolute ethics both mental and metaphysical from almost the day he was born as a man, so it is just what it is.

The real point here is that like it or not technology is even now in the process of offering humanity either the greatest gift or the greatest curse it has ever received since it has existed, paradise for either a select few evil money mongering shallow souls *or paradise for all of us*, and it is entirely up to all of us right now to decide how we want this almost certainly arriving reality to play out.

And it is a fact to this writer at least, that if we choose the correct path, the Solipsi Rai will come and assist us in the transition and in the process they will grant us the stars and even more, they will prove to us in unequivocal ways the truth about spiritual and religious matters, and most of the contents of this book, while granting to all of the decent among us, true immortality, and show us our concrete path towards becoming Gods, if that is what we want.

The Solipsi have been quietly watching us from a distance since we even existed here, maybe it is time we simply tried to be worthy of their interest and maybe just maybe for the decent among us it's simply time we tried to say hi.

Chapter Thirteen
The Other Side

Nothing in the pages that follow should be construed as some kind of justification for allowing you to commit suicide. It's simply an undeniable fact to this writer that experience continues after the death of our physical experience here, and that the reality on that side is far more complex in its full nature than the reality we experience when here.

How in the world can anyone call life after death a fact? Complex astral projection events can be considered after they occur in intelligent ways, and some of the issues related to them cannot be explained in any way as dismissible hallucinatory dream related events, they are real events that have nothing at all to do with your physical body or brain. When you are in the midst of a true astral projection event you leave your physical body and brain far behind and you exist entirely as what you are, as an independent living creature in and as your soul.

Either that or our mundane physical brain is capable of creating entire realms, universes of fully awake experience, that are entirely beyond and utterly different from anything it has experienced during its existence in one lifetime.

When you are in a true astral projection event, you simply know as a fact that you are not anywhere close to being in your physical body, as you can be a mere cloud of being flying very fast over a roadway you are familiar with, and then take a turn off of that road and instantly be someplace else entirely, someplace you simply know you have never been, and when you are that cloud you can examine what you are. There are no physical eyes, yet even though in regular physical life your eyes are almost legally blind you can see *perfectly* obviously without your contacts, and you can hear the wind whistling by as you are flying, then for some inexplicable reason you land and instantly realize you are in your regular body, but that it is oddly different, more perfected in a way, and even though you are still in a familiar universal realm it is oddly different and in that place things that can only be described as miraculous can occur, and you experience them *as if you are fully awake,* because you are exactly that, wide awake!.

If, if our brains alone can do this, then that interpretation is almost as miraculous as what it actually seems to be, and it happens not because you took some kind of drug, but because the deity you will shortly meet obviously wanted it to happen and made it happen utterly spontaneously without any mental preparation at all. It's not like psychedelics where there are all kinds of odd mental confusions, everything about the experience is utterly real and in a way normal, but it is not that in any way.

If you simply take the experience at face value for what it is, it becomes a fact that there is something inside of all of us that is fundamentally different than science tells us is the sum of what we are, and whatever that thing really is, we tend to call it our soul and it is by far the most important aspect of what we are, it is not by any interpretation once you have experienced it any sort of hallucination, it is utterly and absolutely as real as our day to day experience of life.

Then if you are incredibly fortunate you will meet other people over there, some of them might even be ascended folks and even deities like this writer met, and having those sorts of experiences will completely but subjectively prove absolutely that the experiences and the folks you meet are absolutely and utterly real, and this implicitly implies that what you are now and what you will be after your body dies is not entirely your physical body and brain, it is something else, and that something else is in effect immortal. You just cannot prove this empirically or academically to anyone else, you can simply tell the truth as best you can.

If you read what follows, you might think something like 'wow that sounds cool, certainly-maybe better than my life here'; so you might decide to go over in a rather dramatic way. Suicide is not what you have been taught by all kinds of silly religious paradigms. Suicide is simply a way of saying 'you *do not* appreciate the experience of experience', which is the greatest gift anyone can receive, in whatever form it arrives, and it may affect the angelic attitude towards your soul in negative ways, something you definitely do not want to facilitate.

You also need to consider this. There are no distilleries over there, so you can't have a drink in the evening to deaden the pain of being alive and help you go to sleep. Planting grapes to make wine was the very first thing Noah did when he found dry land, so this is far more important than you might think, and no you can't even smoke a joint, it just will not work over there, you also can't have sex the way you can here. The other side is very different in a variety of ways, and some of those ways are not really desirable even in the vast variety of heavens. That in part explains why so many of us eventually get bored and decide to get reincarnated back here or elsewhere.

This writers' take on death is as follows. Experiences in this life have remarkably proven to this writer that he has a soul that will go on experiencing after he dies. He ascribes a 90% + probability to that proof and he has lived his life accordingly. If, if everything that occurred to this writer was as psychologists academics and scientists constantly yet un-effectively try to prove, that there is nothing at all after death and our brains are all there is to the game then he will simply cease to exist and there is not much you can change about that after it happens.

This writer did not conduct his life in an utterly ethical manner because he wanted to earn a glorious future after he died. It was odd but he was a bit precocious and determined this was the best way to be while still a child, just before puberty so he ascribes that to a function of his soul's mentality, it just is what it is.

The important point here is that this writer is over 90% certain that there is life after death, and that what you experience there and how you experience it is directly related to what you do here and how you conduct your life, and fundamentally there is nothing at all that is special or remarkable about this writer that is different from you, beyond the remarkable nature of his personal experiences outside of his body. So that there is a very distinct possibility that your soul will go on after your body and brain dies in this world, and, what follows immediately is incredibly important for everyone that is part of humanity to understand.

By far the majority of the human race does not conduct itself in ways that are considered by the folks that are ascended and empowered as in effect judges on the other side; in a positive manner. Apologies are offered but by far the majority of the human race will not be happy to learn that there is indeed an afterlife, most especially all those so called Christians and Muslims that believe they can do whatever they like in this world and they will be forgiven by their imagined saviors on the other side. *There are certain principles and conditions that transcend all levels of the hierarchy,* almost first among these is true immutable justice for the soul, in the souls' time, and the performance of that justice can be experienced as utterly brutal. It is entirely up to you as to what you want to earn but nobody, *nobody,* gets a free ride.

It's also a fact that you just cannot tell with certainty what will happen to your soul. By far most of the time you will just enter Anu's reincarnation tunnel and 44 days later you will be back here to do a do over, and it probably will be in circumstances that are far worse than the ones you just enjoyed; or you may simply wake up in the for lack of a better term the astral world next door. If that happens try not to make noise and quietly pray for the assistance of an angel, because you are not by any means safe and if you make noise it's a good bet one of Satan's employees will hear you and collect your soul, something you desperately do not want to happen.

This writer already knows as fact that angels will show up and collect his soul and take it back to Christs' Heaven, but this is in a sense a how too book for you. The angels will immediately know the quality of your soul and the individuals you may meet in the astral realm tend to be a bit more generous, than the ones that hold the keys to the gates of Heaven, so there is a slight bit of hope unless you are total human monster, in that case basically your fate is already determined.

From here Christ or Gabriel really are the best bet. Recently a few Buddhists, folks that probably lead entirely decent lives had near death experiences and ended up in the equivalent of Buddhist Hells, but were then saved by Christ or actually his angels and sent back here to relate what happened to them, and as a result thousands of Buddhists are currently converting to Christianity. The truth is that Buddhism is a lot like Christianity was originally, in its deeper expressions, it is a truly Gnostic religion that focuses on developing higher quality souls; so for Buddhists conversion is a fairly simple very familiar thing to do.

This writer is not trying to be a proselytizer here just relating what he is aware of, and he really has no idea what will happen to Muslims, except that he did meet and talk to the Arch angel Gabriel who said in no uncertain terms The Gardens of Allah are real and in some ways like Heaven, he also said that those Muslims that practice Jihad and murder for the sake of pieces of paper, or rape and thus destroy the lives of innocent women just because they are horny, or murder innocent men just because their greedy power hungry Imam told them too, will most certainly go to Hell.

Your soul, when your physical body and brain ceases to exist, manifests to your experience and the folks you may meet as almost exactly what you owned when you were physical, simply because your physical bodies soul cells are used to being what they were and that is what you are comfortable being, except that you will not worry about being too hot or cold or hungry, your physical deformities will no longer exist and you will no longer worry about dismemberment or indeed much of anything at all. If you want an example of this you can look up Kirlian photography on the Web, or learn to astral project.

But after you get used to being what you are over there eventually you may learn that what you are can now be just about anything you can imagine, but that is a sort of skill that you simply have to learn to do when you can do it. It is just that sex and what you are sexually is a very different thing on the other side.

If you want an excellent but rather excessively conveyed example simply find an old film starring Robin Williams called 'What Dreams May Come', then set back and enjoy it. This writer knows quite a few folks that have been on the other side and that film impacted all of us in deeply emotional ways, as all of us experienced the film after we had been over there. It is not by any means like a documentary, but it is moderately close to the truth we all experienced, or at least potentially so.

The caveat here is that what you will experience on the other side is not experienced as dreams at all, it is experienced far more brilliantly that your normal awake lives are when you are awake here in this life.

The point here is that if you do make it to Christ's Heaven or the Gardens of Allah you can relax and hang out perfectly safe for as long as you like, but then if you do get bored you can in very sane and positive ways move on to a wide variety of alternative life experiences, and no one there will stop you. If you have a lot of friends they may try to tell you that you are an insane idiot, as they did to this writer when he decided to come back here, but they will not stop you.

But if you are a male Muslim you don't have to worry about wearing out your pecker trying desperately to keep 37 virgins happy, that's just pure silliness. Again, this writer met Gabriel and asked him that question as politely as he could, it was an odd embarrassment that was kind of scary at the time, but Gabriel told this writer that directly; those virgins just do not exist period. But the Gardens of Allah most certainly do. You just have to earn your passage in the eyes of the angels that hold those keys.

The issue is not about your endless suffering here during this lifetime. What you need to understand absolutely is that if you own a decent soul that shows any kind of potential, whether you are a bible thumping Christian or a genuine Muslim or Buddhist or Hindu for that matter, you can and may live forever, and one life here even though it seems like it might go on forever, is in the context of immortal existence, merely a singular dream that will pass, and then from your point of view on the other side it will seem to be merely a momentary bad dream, an odd memory you can certainly forget about. But it was an important way to teach your soul things you might not have learned otherwise, so the best course is to accept your life with grace, earn it by being a responsible adult, and then let it unfold as it will entirely, and expect to die hopefully with grace when the time naturally arrives.

If you are astute you can say what about that Buddhist that went to Hell and became a Christian? The Buddhist Hell he went too is a bit different than Satan's Hell and it is likely that eventually he would have figured out how to go someplace else better, if he was decent; but he was right to act as he did as the venues Christ has set up for us if we are decent believers in him are by far the most secure and positive for all of us shortly after the death experience.

The Buddhists actually have this all figured out. 'All experience in this place, on the Earth, is suffering, one way or another for everyone, accept that, learn from it with grace, and the quality of your soul will grow'.

Okay this needs to be repeated sort of so that it will be utterly clear. This writer has been out of his body entirely and in his soul body entirely many times and except for a few times that were simple float up to the ceiling and look down on his 'sleeping' body all of them were the result of people from the other-side inviting the writer to visit or engineering the event to teach the writer something; so hopefully he could then maybe figure out how to share it with you.

On occasion these events occurred from inside brilliant dreams, but some of the times they occurred in ways that when analyzed are not defined in any way by what the psychologists and academics claim are the mechanisms that our physical brain uses to fool us into thinking we are outside our bodies, so that from a purely intellectual analysis this writer simply cannot agree that his experiences were fake or psychologically trivial, but that they were or they reflected utterly real things and events.

Physics of Consciousness

What is being said here is that this writer knows as fact that he owns a soul body capable of experiencing without eyes ears nerve endings and so on and that that soul has a host of properties and capabilities that are by any definition categorically miraculous, and that other than the events most of which have already been related in this series of books, there is nothing particularly special about this writer, which again means there is a very high probability that you have a similar soul as well.

The caveat here is that most of the time the realm(s) you are experiencing when in the related alternative states of being are not exactly like the normal awake realm you normally experience; the other realms have differences, sometimes subtle, but still differences, although he has met people that have had similar experiences and stayed entirely in this reality.

When you go out on extended journeys in your soul or for the sake of the metaphysical types out there, your astral body, one of the things you learn absolutely is that your astral body is not in any way reliant on your physical body or brain to exist, and that your mind and your ID remains the same exactly as it is when you are in your body and brain. The strangeness of the events that you experience in that condition all come from the massive alternative types of experience you are capable of experiencing and the alternative ways that you can and do experience them, exactly because you are in what amounts to a variety of alternative universal realms.

But and this is incredibly important, those experiences are experienced with the same validity as experiences you have when you are wide awake and here in this physical world. Except for one thing most of the time, again, you no longer have to worry about your physical body being dismembered or getting sick and becoming a burden, you just don't worry about anything at all. What is being said here is that *you do not die when you die, you go on as a different type of creature,* and that there are millions of heavens and millions of hells over there and gazillions of alternative universal realms over there, and if you do not enjoy life in your soul body there are uncountable realms other than this one where you can have yourself reincarnated into once again as a 'physical' being. The only problem with that most of the time is that you will be stuck in that new place for an entire life experience, so be careful what you ask for, as it is pretty certain you will get it. This writer has clear memories of his friends in Heaven telling him he was crazy just before he came back here, and they were all absolutely right.

This is not bullshit or fantasies you have been *told to imagine* because you were afraid of the dark, by the various religions all your lives, this is the utter and absolute reality of what we all exist inside of. This material may be less than perfect in all its details but it is pretty damned close. And you do not control what happens to your soul, or you do not have free will at the time that you die, for a while after that happens it is a fact that other more comprehensive beings control what you will experience and where you will go after that event happens to you.

If you are an asshole selfish human during your previous life here this should be the most terrifying bit of news you can imagine, but if you are a decent person it is the most glorious news you can possibly imagine as it means you have earned one more chance to evolve towards becoming a God. Then, this can be said as well, you don't have to utterly believe all this stuff or you will be condemned to Hell, all these words are just about one guy trying to figure out his own personal undeniable truths that are the result of unimpeachable events, except for one that is really important, try to find out and understand what it means and then try to be a *responsible adult* and *respect* all the other folks around you, and really try not to be a liar and a thief; just do that and you will have learned something that will be incredibly valuable towards your future existence.

This needs to be said again as part of the reason for this book and what this writer experienced was to try to improve the sum of the human condition. If you are a selfish stealing person, you will not die when you die, there will be no glorious blackness of non being, you will go on experiencing reality in ways that are greater in intensity than you are experiencing reality now, but you will not like it one bit at all. There are no distilleries over there to help you muddy up your experience and try to avoid its effects, no opium either; you are unavoidably what you are over there period. Your mind will be exactly the same as the mind you own now, your senses and the world around you will simply be enhanced, and for a long while your mind will be programmed to experience only torment of extreme proportions. Then if you are lucky and your prayers are answered your soul and your experience of existence will be terminated with extreme prejudice, forever. So people if you suspect you have earned this terrifying future, clean up your frigging act while you still have the chance to do it.

Sorry if this seems a bit preachy and repetitive but it is that way as it is important. This writer has met a lot of people in his business career and his life and unfortunately truly ethical people were extremely rare, so this is being said over and over not for the decent as they will already be rewarded, this is for the wealthy and *un*-ethical folks and it is being offered out of a sense of pity for them. Christ and nobody else on the other side will forgive you for all your sins, sorry it just is what it is.

This writer was trained in rather an odd way, in the scientific process, and in the validity of logic and he has tried over and over again to discount what he has experienced as invalid hallucinations and misleading sort of dream related pointless excursions of useless psychology, but every time doubt creeps in and he analyses the events he experienced, he has always found aspects of the events that deny the critical negative analysis and enhance their incredible validity.

This writer has studied an entire library of books on psychology and psychiatry and it's a fact most of them are academic bullshit that have little to do with solutions to the salient problems, so that now most of what those mediums teach academically is how to prescribe an endless variety of pharmaceuticals to make the pill makers and practitioners wealthy, while they seek to insure that the patients will never actually recover from anything, they simply attempt to treat the symptoms. Or you can simply watch the TV series 'Hannibal' to understand some of the darker pitfalls of psychiatry.

Even the classic perpetrator of the entire field, Sigmund Freud was utterly obsessed with sex and tried to prove that all dreams had everything to do with that alone. This writer has been celibate for over ten years now, after having made love extensively to twenty seven women in his younger years, he was sort of a good catch once upon a time; he still has constantly brilliant dreams, and dreams that are just about sex are still extremely even remarkably 'unfortunately' rare. Freud was a serious nutcase, Carl Jung was the only one that came close to figuring even a tiny bit out, but he was ostracized from his professional community for thinking out of the box and trying to understand the things he had personally observed.

So-called scientists are obsessed with proving that astral projection events are merely bizarre anomalies of our physical brains, but the truth is that true astral projection events have very little to do with just floating up to the ceiling and looking down at your body or reading some message in this world on some kind of bogus clock above your hospital bed. In true astral projection events you are basically entirely *in your soul*, you can analyze the experiences intellectually only if you have experienced them, and there simply is no alternative explanation to that truth.

When you have a Near Death experience and or a true astral projection event you are in an entirely different universe, a universe with entirely different physical laws; there are all kinds of similarities initially, but you just can't put a message clock above the bed and expect the pilgrim to read it, as it just is not there where the pilgrim is. But the pilgrim can on occasion see his or her body on the operating table because there are different rules that apply there, distinct overlaps that are very difficult to quantify by scientists from here, in a way it is almost as bizarre as quantum mechanics. That is entirely intentional by the designer so that we will never be utterly certain regarding exactly what we are and what we live in, so that we will experience *this* reality as being as real as it can possibly be.

The true astral projection event utterly implicitly implies that you do own a soul that will go on living after your physical body and brain dies here, but time and space as we experience them here are an odd sort of illusion; over there you can travel immense distances across familiar territory and then on to other places entirely, utterly alien places, that oddly, as you are experiencing them seem perfectly normal, and things happen, things that simply cannot be explained as bizarre dream events because they are experienced as being utterly real with a fully awake mind.

The problem is and it is potentially a huge one, all such events are by their very nature entirely subjective, meaning they simply cannot be related in any kind of empirical way unless other people take an interest in the related methodologies and actually repeat the experiences enough times to validate them in an empirical way.

Many of those methodologies that applied to this writer were related in "The Promontory" but a few of them may be potentially dangerous, that does not make this writer brave by any measure, he had no idea most of the time that the events were going to happen; so here this writer is simply being honest for your sake. The best that can be offered here is that you can believe what is being said here or you can take it as a fiction, or as some kind of personal philosophy that the writer likes to write about, it really does not matter, this guy can survive just fine with no income from these books, and as a young man he was sort of famous for a while and it was not in any way something he enjoyed or desires now; and this is most certainly not about ego. With these books he is simply expressing his gratitude to those he met on the other side; by writing all this down over and over again as best he can.

One note that may be important as this is supposedly a how too book. This writer never learned how to willfully induce an astral projection event; just about all of the events he did experience were apparently induced by the people and Gods that he subsequently met while out on one of those events. This writer did try to learn how to induce them on his own but failed utterly and so he just gave up... as once you learn things of these types from deities you have apparently learned what is important and out of respect to the folks on the other side it just seemed more right to not push the matter, for what amounts in a way to selfish reasons.

Numerous people on the other side for some entirely unknown reason decided that this writer would be a good candidate to be their student, so they invited the pilgrim over to the other side to learn important things many times. This writer has absolutely no idea why they all invested their magnificent energy in this plain old dufus human. But then on one of those excursions this writer did meet an old man named Enoch; that apparently both Christ and Gabriel valued immensely, personally he did not seem to be that big a deal but for some reason, or well who knows, maybe genuine humility is a bigger deal than any of us suppose? But what follows is what this writer has learned unequivocally about the other side.

It's very simple, if you lived a decent life here and as a result you avoid being collected when you die and getting sent off to any of the millions of hellish domains that exist on the other side, you will either be reincarnated or go on to some form of the millions of heavens, from here usually the angels will show up if you are decent and have genuine faith and take you on to either Christ's Heaven or The Gardens of Allah.

And this is very important to understand, if you are lucky or simply decent and you do get into any form of Heaven, you will not be stuck there forever. You will not be any sort of prisoner in Heaven. This writer has clear memories of being in Christ's Heaven just before he came back here, once again, all his friends there told him he was insane to come back here but this writer thought he could get reincarnated into a family here that would grant him the means to do useful things in this life for the folks that were forced to live here in ignorance. That was not the case and this writer was simply very foolish. But there is a small non-descript archway in a drab room sort of under Heaven, it's in a sort of cave and you go down some steps to get there, then you simply walk through a non-descript stone archway and your soul mind is wiped clean of your memories or, well most of them usually, and your ID, your mind particle and soul stuff is sent on down here to be reincarnated, then you are stuck here in this lunatic farm once again and forced to endure for another entire life, it really is pure lunacy.

One curious oddity about being a decent soul among humans is that even though this writer met Satan as a young man and like Christ defeated him and what he was offering, in a very odd way this writer ended up spending a major part of his life in a way working for Satan, as by being an honestly decent and ethical sort of fellow he became the constant victim of an ongoing host of human monsters, both male and female; just about all of them will be going to hell to become fodder for Satan as a result.

If you think that makes this writer some sort of monster, consider how many people went to hell instead of simply being reincarnated back here because Christ came here and offered his alternatives to us. How many Catholics are in Hell for what they did to the Cather's, how many Crusaders for what they did to the peaceful Muslims, how many Muslims for what they did to the Christians, how many Christian preachers drive around in Limos and fly private jets while their parishioners starve and stink in the streets? Think about it, things changed when Christ came here but in general terms a monstrous human soul remained just as it always was, it just found other ways to pretend to justify what it was and that is still going on in very big ways, just because humans for the most part worship pieces of paper and what they can steal from other humans that actually earned their lives, over the worship of God, ethics and decency.

When in any heaven you can get comfortable with your then current reality and then move on if you want too, to any other place on the other side that will let you in; and there are literally millions upon millions of other realms on the other side and the various forms and physical realms on this side as well.

The other side is without question the dominant reality of multiversal creation, it is in its greater nature the realm of the Gods, and, evolving new gods is the primary purpose of creation, the first thing those new gods do to prove what they have become, is usually to create a new realm of their own, so that the number of new Gods and new realms at this point is virtually uncountable, and the process will in all probability go on literally forever.

That is the incredible gift that OM and Sophia have granted all of us, it is the *complex* expression of the Holy Spirit's gift of creating positive order in the midst of infinity, and it is very real.

If you are successful in transiting to the other side, these are the things you will notice almost immediately. Aside from the very real angels that will hopefully show up at your death bed, sex is very different, it is not compulsive, it is simply an expression of friendship and yes love. Sex, if you can call it that, is accomplished by actually blending the bodies of your souls for a little while, and indeed gender is not even an issue.

That does not mean you should immediately go out and become gay or some form of half and half, but it does explain in a way why that is going on, and if you are decent it is a way, a justification, that allows you to treat such people decently, but the truth is you are what you are and love between a man and a women is simply slightly more right than the alternatives. 'Slightly' is important there.

You will never again as long as you stay on the other side feel too hot or too cold, you will never be hungry or thirsty in any debilitating way, you will never have to worry about dismemberment, but only on odd occasions you may risk the cessation of existence, but oddly it will not be terrifying in the ways it is here, simply a fact of reality as the sum of a judgement by beings that are more comprehensive than you are, and usually if you are a decent soul you will always pass by those momentary worries as if they were non-events, and if you are not you will simply cease to be instantly, in other words you will have absolutely no chance to think about it and contemplate what might have been, you will simply cease to exist.

There is an oddity here in that the only way to truly kill a soul is to cast it into the Lake of Fire, but there are numerous beings over there far more comprehensive that we are that can in effect wipe your ID clean of memories and your sense of identity instantly, they can then send you on to be utterly destroyed or use you in ways that might change you in positive or negative ways, or they can put you into featureless rooms outside of time forever, so it's just a thought but if you are warned about or by these folks before you meet them it may be a good idea to try and avoid them. One of them holds the gate before you are allowed to enter the realm above OM's sea of creation, so be *very* certain your soul is worth saving before you try to enter that dominion. There are no attorneys over there to argue your case with endless lies, there is just you and the Archon and the record of everything that you have been and done in your Akashic record so be aware of what you are.

As a result of this you will on a variety of occasions lose your sense of free will entirely to others, but usually that will be to your benefit, it is simply a way that those more comprehensive beings including mere angels, insure that you are not a threat before they invite you to enjoy being taught something by them, or a way to protect what they are protecting from the damage you might inflict on their realm, and it is also a way that they use to collect your soul when they invite you to their own dominions, places you would usually have no idea at all about how to access unless they decided to in effect show you the way.

Yet again, the other side is not a fiction, it is by far the dominant side of the reality of this multiverse and it is experienced as exactly that then you are there. That which we experience when we are here is massively conscribed, by a huge set of physical laws that were emplaced into this reality by OM when he was creating it.

In his mind the entire purpose of this reality was to sort out the decent souls from the indecent souls in ways that were-are entirely outside of question, so that he could eventually deliver the truly decent souls to his Creator, Sophia, and those souls that he delivered to her would own an innate reason in their souls to go on living and eventually enhance the multiversal creation that they both began together endless trillions of experience years ago. Remember their argument detailed in the beginning of this book. OM did what he did with his realms of his separate creations to defeat the boredom of perfection that was killing off entire races of their early creations.

It was also in his mind simply one more way to enhance the varieties of the experience of experience, simply one of many ongoing experiments. Our universe and us are simply one the many things he enjoys creating, in that sense we are merely an entertainment for God, but we are also his children, and if we grow up as responsible adults he values what we are, while Sophia cherishes us, as all mothers almost always cherish their children.

Understand this utterly, everyone in creation exists because they own a single individualizing particle expression of the field of consciousness. *Everyone*, Gods and humans alike, and Solipsi's and all other extraterrestrials as well, *everyone*. None of those ID particles are identical by any means, those Gods mentioned just above have evolved at this point to be incomprehensible in their full nature to us, but we all have certain similarities. We are all the children of the true Gods, the Holy Spirit, OM and Sophia, but they are like our parents here, just earlier versions of what we are, we just have to grow up responsibly and express our worth and our gratitude to them for what they gave to us.

The Other Side is not like The Game of Thrones where all the kings and queens spend all their time trying to figure out ways to kill torture and use everyone else; that is simply entertainment for lunatic humans. And this writer is not the lord of the seven gods trying to figure out obscure ways punish everyone that reads this. This writer is simply trying to warn you that it is better to at least try to be a decent ethical person in intelligent ways, and to respect everyone around you in real ways, at least until you are certain they are not worth your time, and in that case for your own welfare it is best to simply walk away.

No one anywhere in academia any more is teaching ethics 101, so for your own sake again look ethics up and learn it all and adopt them as the driving guidelines of your lives and please try to do the best you can with what you have learned as there is no lying attorney that will help you in the end, and virtually all of those professional money obsessed liars here will be going to hell, that is a certainty.

Consciousness rules the other side entirely and we as individuals are simply expressions of consciousness unseparate from the many realities that surround us when we are there; so that we experience them with an immediacy that is utterly uncanny in its brilliance of experience. We are simply unseparate aspects of the various realities there, except that we *experience* them as separate individualizing elements, just as a photon is an individual element of light that is never truly separate from the field of light it expressed itself as an individualizing element out of.

Okay this writer had absolutely no previous knowledge that he was aware of, that it was possible to go to the realm where the Sea of Creation is located, until in this physical life he was taken there entirely by surprise as the result of what still seems like a silly soundbite called Steambubbles that he manipulated in a way related to the descriptions of Monroe Institute based Hemi-synch technology.

It is reasonable to assume that Christ knows about it and knows how to get there, the Mahayana Buddhists certainly did, but this writer met Christ in person long before the mentioned event occurred and he has no memory of Christ suggesting that you could go there, it is very odd to say the least, but this can be said again, the various Heavens related to humanity are related to humanity, it is unlikely that you will meet very many Solipsi Rai in those realms and a certainty that you will not meet any Zeta- Reticulans, the after death realms that humans normally go to when they die are designed or located by Christ and Gabriel to be places for humans, but you *will* meet all kinds of angels.

    Angels are odd in that they can manifest in this physical reality but seldom do as it requires a massive amount of their energy to do that, but they can see and hear what is going on here and they can on occasion affect things here from the other side in a variety of seemingly subtle ways.

    So again, everybody, everybody on this side and the other is primarily in their soul's mind an individualizing singular mind, and most of the time they cannot be bothered to waste their time or listen to whiny humans praying for help. If you are any sort of God listening to common help me prayers, it is like having ten billion babies crying all the time, so the gods that maybe could help you, usually just tune you out, but angels are odd in that most of them exist entirely to assist others in a very wide variety of ways, so if you need help pray for the help of an angel and there is a far greater likely hood that they will hear you and do something useful to help out with your predicament.

    However don't even bother if you are sitting in front of slot machine or filling out a Lotto card and you want them to help you win, it will not work, period, trust this writer he has tried that many times.

    Sorry about the digression. There were at least eight heavens that were well known before Christ showed up here, *that he was intimately aware of,* and then after he left us behind he went and built one just for us, he can tell you how to get to one of them from his heaven for certain as that is the place he said he could show people how to get to when he was here, and it is a certainty that there are literally gazillions of alternative realms out there that you can get to from the other side. But many of them require that you be reincarnated in a variety of ways to get to them, and once you do that you will be there if you are successful for an entire lifetime so please try to be careful. The reason that is here is because all Heavens have the same problem precisely because they are Heavens, the word literally translates as 'perfect place' and all perfect places since the beginning of this multiverse have the same problem, eventually they tend to create a sense of boredom, that is something to enjoy as much as you can but it is not something you can deal with across the entire time of your immortality.

The point of existence is to grow your soul towards being worthy of being a God, or simply an adult soul, and male or female it simply does not matter, you have to *earn that*, period. Earning that has little to do with serving others, it has to do with respecting others with good reason and acting responsibly as best you can towards everyone else.

Again, sex is not a sin, it is natural, so long as you act responsibly towards your partners and everybody else, none of us would even exist here if it was not for sex. What is a sin is taking stuff including the enjoyment of life from those around you without earning it or giving something back in return.

Okay, this writer is only going to relate exactly what he has learned directly from being over there, and what that implies about what other people have said about that stuff.

First there are two 'local' heavens for the Christians and the Muslims, those places are real, but here is an issue, the Jews do have souls even if they refuse to believe they do, and they say they refuse to believe in Heavens of any sort, so either they are all going to Hell, which is pretty certain judging for many of the ones this writer has done business with, or there are one hell of a lot of Jewish ghosts walking around this planet. Just being a bit sardonic sort of, but actually since Christ decided to save the Jewish souls first it is a very good idea for Jews to explore what Christ tried to tell them and maybe adopt Christ in the process, as what he is offering them as well as the rest of us will certainly have greater value than those stupid pieces of paper the Jews are so obsessed with, at least in the long run.

Now the eastern religions particularly the various forms of Buddhism and Hinduism are aware of collectively literally millions of heavens and hells, those could all be related to the many universes this writer experienced in the sea of creation or they could be entirely other places. This writer has no specific memories of any of them if they are in the other category, but he certainly can say it is probable that the people that experienced them and came back here to report what they had experienced most of the time at least were being honest.

But here is the kicker. If you can convince someone on the other side to let you go there or you figure out the Steam-bubble key and survive Anubis so you can go there when you are alive here. There is in the realm that is inside the mind of OM, a literal sea of entire universal realms, and there are so many being created new every day by people that have evolved out of the older ones and are now expressing their power and craft of being Gods, that even if you live literally forever you will never come close to experiencing all of them.

Just as a single example; when this writer was the manta ray creature made of solid light flying over the sea of creation he had experiential fingers dipping into millions of them, but he did find one that for some reason he was drawn down into, it was the Lightweavers realm, and the

Lightweavers are engaged in a process that has been going on for eons creating their own entirely separate multiverse, and that multiverse alone is now so immense in its complexity of expressions that simply trying to experience all of them would pretty much fill up any definition of eternity you might enjoy. This writer cannot claim it as personal fact but there is a very high probability based on what he has learned that there are literally millions of races doing exactly what the Lightweavers are doing out there in infinity, so that the full import of what OM and Sophia have created is utterly majestic by any possible definition and one way or another it will most certainly go on existing quite certainly forever and forever again.

So yes if the Buddhist tell you there are millions of heavens and millions of hells that are all accessible to your soul, they are entirely correct, but they are just being humble with their terminology.

It is also a fact to this writer because he has been there, that for some unknown and unasked for reason the Lightweavers went inside this writers head and decided to make an entire planetary realm that is in essence perfect for humans, and it is experienced when you are there almost exactly like physical life is here, but with a significant variety of enhancements. The reason this is being said here is that it means if you go out of Christ's heaven for instance and travel around a bit you will probably find somebody out there that likes you and they may decide to build you an entire realm that they think will be utterly perfect for you alone, and once that place is built it will exist forever.

It is not like this universe where eventually this star and planet will crash into another or die out. What you can find there will really last forever, even if you decide over time that you want to be someplace else, you can just walk away, but it will still be there. Infinity and eternity are both very big places, and everybody in these parts, this multiverse, is just engaged in trying to fill them up with orderly expressions of realities.

Everybody is busy trying to defeat the chaos of infinity with order, and most of them are trying to do that in pleasant and creative ways, they are doing exactly what the Holy Spirit began doing so many ages ago; they are just doing that in a very wide variety of ways.

If you are simply a decent person here, that is just a tiny taste of what you will get to look forward to when you arrive once again on the other side.

With Respect, Eljin Yeats, IAORANA...

Author's Afterward
Is This All About Starting a New Religion; Or God Forbid; a Cult?

First, I wanted to say this before I closed this dialogue. The bucks were all gone someplace else this fall. The mothers of all the fawns had worry in their eyes; I went out in the backyard to feed the deer and while I was doing that I apologized to them; "I'm sorry, for my species, our fathers train their children to go out and be proud of the fact that they killed a buck deer with their bows, and our governments are full of people that justify killing other humans in the name of political power and the worship of pieces of paper with numbers on them." I did what I was supposed to do as a young man; killed a couple of deer, a silver back bear that was eating our child cows before the winter arrived, and a few dozen chickens as a young man in Idaho, it was wrong; but it was what it was when I was here as a human; and I still eat steak but now as an odd renegade Buddhist I let others do the killing for me and I simply cannot understand what is right about all of this, being an animal earthling is a very odd and seriously wrong thing, but as what we are there seems to be little choice, and I still can hear all the folks out there going arrgggh! This guy tricked me, I just read all this stuff and I don't understand half of it, maybe I'm just too dumb or maybe this frigging guy is crazy in a vaguely smart but lunatic sort of way, but I wanted to learn how to become a God overnight? And this frigging turkey didn't tell me how to do that!

I never said it would be quick and easy and overnight. Remember OM the father of us all never gives any- thing away for free, that's a feminine trait, well at least it used to be, in America at least, and Sophia has recused herself from acting on OM's creations in any significant individualizing way.

Perhaps the best example of how it works around here is Christ. He had already lived through numerous incarnations until he was the beloved in effect benevolent king of an entire planet full of fine folks not too far away in this galaxy.

Christ wanted to give what he had already given to his own people to a distressed planet of people, us, that had been historically abused by the Annunaki and then a few Roman monsters in our own culture, and the best way he could figure out how to do that was to circumvent the reincarnation system installed here on us by those frigging Annunaki; so he probably used the acoustical homage to Sophia, the bubbles in the sea of creation, to go and see OM.

The ancient Egyptians knew exactly how to do that; it is what the Well of Souls was really all about, and Egypt was right next door to Israel; the Essenes knew about it as well they based their society architecturally around holy spas in the center of their villages and Christ was raised a child in an Essene village. And; well Christ wasn't exactly too much in love with the Hebrew bankers either. So Christ one way or another asked OM, the father of us all, for the right and the means to offer us the ways to get to a then existing Heaven and maybe just maybe the right and the knowledge required to build a Heaven just for us, and well maybe even provide us with the wherewithal to improve the lives of humans while they were still on the earth as well. I'm sort of paraphrasing here a bit, as a great Zen master once told me in a subtle sort of way to lighten up a bit.

OM said 'that sounds fine but you have to earn it first, did you see the crosses on the dark-light sphere before you came in here?" (The cover of this book and a few others) Christ said rather hesitantly;

"Yes."

"Well those are there for a reason, they are a symbol that indicates universal creation rather esoterically... anyway, the people in power down there right now are regularly, killing folks slowly by nailing them up on one of those cross thingy's made out of wood and stuck in a pile of rocks and then letting them starve and bleed to death slowly... often totally innocent God fearing folks that they just don't like very much.

I don't like the folks that are doing that stuff very much, so get incarnated there and teach the folks to be a little bit better maybe, and then have yourself nailed to one of those thingies to prove you want to earn what you're asking for, and I'll give you what you want. It seems a rather appropriate way to get sort of even, inversely create a few ripples in the social structures there, and in a way deal with the evil that's going on around those parts."

"Oh, ummm, hmmm, will it hurt?"

"Yep, but if you do it I will give you what you asked for right away, and it will only hurt for a day or two, what the heck is that in terms of your immortality?"

So Christ agreed, but then when it happened it hurt a whole lot more than he expected and he asked for help from OM, but OM offered him no help at all until it was almost over. But then he made Christ into a genuine novice God overnight, and gave him back the full experience of life as well.

"Good job dude, come on back here and I will give you the keys to my library and you can learn how to do exactly what you asked me for. Oh, and by the way welcome to this very exclusive club."

No I am not intentionally belittling Christ or OM here just trying to make an alternative point in a way that it might have a tiny impact, and despite the fact that I have met both of them in person I have no real idea what exactly went on between them, if anything, but I do know with certainty that neither one of them gives a hoot about what us little people say about them, that attitude comes from human religions that want to falsely empower themselves.

Anyway; if you want to become a God, first study the life of Christ until you understand precisely what he taught objectively, throw away all your anthropomorphic tendencies, in other words stop imagining that being human is a good as it can possibly get, along with your ego entirely, then go see OM. I've shown you how to do exactly that in the Promontory, then come back here when you're done with that and then be prepared to earn what you asked for.

Then maybe read this book over again and learn to be a decent and patient person, as knowledge is all that you get to take with you; so when you die you can remember it all precisely and so make it useful in your endeavor and if you do get crazy and get reincarnated like me, you will remember it subtly in the mind of your soul, and it will give you an inclination towards relearning and discovering the related issues all over again and maybe just maybe it will make you a more decent person in your next life; thus you will have started out on the road that leads towards the ladder of the hierarchy towards being a positive God. It will take a while for certain but, like I said that's nothing because you will also eventually become certain that you are an immortal being.

And good luck in your endeavor, there you happy now?

Second: I want to say that in the original thinking for this book I intended to end it with a description of the realm, the planet the Lightweavers made for me, but then I decided this is a non-fiction and virtually no one, other than the three people that are reading this one, would believe I was telling the truth, so I decided to use that realm in the end of my 'fictional' romance adventure trilogy about the Solipsi Rai, so if you are a pretend adult, you might try reading that series; if you are interested. Okay onward.

Third: I read a question someone recently posted on a web site asking 'what is the point, or; what are the reasons for seeking enlightenment?' I thought maybe as a person that has experienced just about every possible variety of that condition available to humans I should try to answer that question.

The term 'enlightenment' can be literally translated as 'losing your innocence', thought I was going to say filled with light? Nope that's just a description of the effect, but when it happens you will eventually lose your innocence entirely. If all you want out of life here is to be a successful human being, don't waste your time seeking enlightenment, as it will hand you a huge pile of liabilities while you are here. (I was being civilized with that sentence.) Foremost among these is that, as time progresses you will be literally forced to be a truly and intrinsically ethical person living in a society that is composed almost entirely of intrinsically unethical people.

In America at least anyone that is 'good' is universally defined as someone that is good at taking as much as possible from the other guy while giving as little as possible back, that is the true definition of a successful capitalist. In the context of all the positive more comprehensive people out there in the cloud of consciousness that is an inherently _wrong_ attitude.

The other issue that relates to this, is that I was remiss in the Chapter related to 'The Ladder You Must

Climb'. Enlightenment, if you are a mere primitive human, in its various forms constitutes the first rungs of the ladder towards becoming a God, and there are all kinds of positive folks on the other side that will recognize that these types of things have happened to you and they will assist you in all kinds of ways you probably will *not* appreciate while you are here; but ways designed to insure that you are becoming in fact a truly ethical and decent person.

So if all you want is to become a 'successful' human being in this world, don't waste your time seeking out enlightenment, it will not make you rich, it will not make people love you more, it will not free you from disease or even bad emotions, most people here will not believe you and many of them will even decide you are a liar or you are worse, at least partially insane and at best dismiss you as inconsequential, or many of them will decide you are simply an easy mark to rip-off, just trust me I know this for a fact.

Again if you are a typical human and all you want is typical human rewards, and you believe that your soul is simply a fairy tale for people afraid of the dark, do not bother.

But, and it is a very big alternative, if you believe that you are more than you have been led to believe you are, or even just potentially so, then pursuit of enlightenment is aside from understanding the importance of ethical conduct, the single most important thing you can seek in your experience of life, if you achieve it in any of its various forms, your soul will be changed and you will have climbed the first rung of the ladder towards becoming a positive God, and you will lose your innocence. And others from the other side more comprehensive than humans will begin to assist you in your efforts to climb that mountain. As I said often in ways that you will not appreciate *but also in ways that you will*.

What's important here is that you have to find an understanding, an assurance that in your soul you are immortal, and that your soul is by far the most important aspect of what you are, when you find those two things out, whatever happens to you afterwards in this life will become inconsequential, but you will never want to actually die because you will realize that in whatever form it arrives the experience of experience and the knowing of that experience is the most important thing, the greatest gift in all of creation, regardless of its form.

Fourth: I was inside a facility, a virtual exhibit of sorts of exactly OM's mind, as he was when younger. He likes to create universes, and then he likes to put-self recognizing experiential nodes of consciousness inside of them, we humans are simply one type of expression of those nodes, that he can access whenever he likes so that he can experience in theory every possible form of experience so that eventually he can know everything there is to know. In order for those universes to work in the ways he needs them to work to serve his purposes, they simply have to be non-interference realms that unfold spontaneously.

That does not mean that beings like Christ cannot arrive out of or in those realms, that feel pity for the helpless subjects and do things for them, but it does mean you cannot expect to get anything resembling help from the 'father' period. So if you are seeking help through prayer focus on angels, or Christ or even Sophia or Mary, but do not waste your time on OM.

This is exactly why effigies of Mary often cry tears, they are expressed for the suffering that this expression of OM's experiment often creates here for us and it is our responsibility to generate conditions that alleviate that suffering; something that so far we have been incredibly feeble in trying to accomplish.

This does not in any way mean that OM the Father is evil, I have met a direct living avatar of him, he is a great guy, but he is a true Creator God, so he thinks in terms that may on occasion be difficult for us to understand, but he has made conditions that create the certainty that if *we earn it,* we will know full justice in the time of our souls, in positive ways.

Life here among humans, even at the highest levels of our current expressions of accomplishment, in academia, in politics, in culture, in how we are trained to act towards others, **is just plain silly**; and we will not evolve one iota until we realize that, and seek to address the truly important issues of what we are in ways that are legitimately important.

That is why you seek enlightenment. Just consider yourself warned, in this world the results will not all be experienced as positive.

"Recently I re-watched a legally legitimate copy of the film 'Contact', a fine film about the results of discovering extraterrestrial communications and the philosophical issues that resulted. In that film governments and private individuals built two copies of essentially an interstellar wormhole device for traveling across the universe at a cost of two thirds of a trillion dollars, and the results of that excursion were technically ephemeral to say it politely, rather like the results of all my own experiences, so that the film has a rather larger than normal personal impact on me.

I discovered effectively exactly the same technology almost by accident over ten years ago; an acoustical soundbite of bubbles rising in water, it can be copied and used by anyone effectively for free. But what I discovered not only allows anyone to travel across creation from the comfort of your easy chair, it also grants an intimate and very real knowledge of the very mind of our Creator.

The technology is simple to reproduce and a concise description of it has been publicly published now for over seven years in my book 'the Promontory', yet no one has commented or even discussed it, no one, except for one person related to Dr. Courtney Brown, an author who also owns questionable academic credentials related to what he is offering the human race. His unknown critic that read a small part of that book, simply called my work 'crap' when I sent a free copy to Dr. Brown for review because I mentioned him in it; but his critic offered no foundation or support for his comments whatsoever.

No one from NASA, an outfit I was professionally associated with briefly years ago, the CIA or the NSA, people that seemingly might be interested in unique ways to travel across the multiverse instantly have ever made even a peep, well I guess it might represent a potential threat to all their funding, who knows.

It is a tiny bit frustrating, that discovery, that simple soundbite, that key to creation, acoustical bubbles in water, an homage to Sophia and the Holy Spirit, that OM granted to every single sentient in creation and to me sort of first on this planet, has been utterly ignored. At this point I could not give a smaller degree of a hoot about money or fame or power over others, but it just seems a tiny bit odd that everyone in humanity that has actually read about it thinks it's absurd simply because it is so simple to reproduce and nobody can make any direct money out of it, so nobody has so far tried to reproduce what I discovered. It is a bit of a frustrating shame to say the least.

It is also a truth that I have never understood exactly how it is that ideas can cure into hardened concrete inside people's minds with little or no foundation, exactly as they tend to do with most religions and political regimes, but obviously they do, and the actuality of that liability has caused endless unearned forms of prosecution to the human condition.

Religions serve a variety of positive purposes, but when they become organizations, the necessity in this culture to find venues to absorb other people's money, by its nature attracts humans that are obsessed with finding power over others; and those organizations that were usually based on foundations left behind by great and benevolent souls become twisted and perverted until they reflect often only tiny glimpses of what their originators sought to teach us.

I won't get into all the tits and tats of religions and cults, that's pointless, but I will say please please please people try to keep an open mind about everything, and for God's sake do not kill other people or try to steal their possible enjoyments of their lives because they do not believe exactly as you do, or even worse they have stuff that you want to take away from them without bothering to earn it. Variations of experience, in other words variations of what we are, are in large part exactly what existence is all about, so honor and respect the lives and beliefs of others, please.

If you want a good example of how it is best to deal with others. Always seek first positive co-operation with others, but seek that co-operation with respect for the unique qualities and differences of cultures and peoples. Then be very patient in that process at least until all possible positives have been exhausted; then if co-operation becomes obviously impossible, try as best you can to simply walk away. Finally; only when every possible venue has been exhausted be ready to defend what you represent with absolute certainty as best you can. Then once again be patient and one way or another eventually right will become apparent to all the parties, and the potential suffering that might result from interaction will be defeated. Well, most of the time anyway.

The esoteric things I have tried to detail in these works are largely the result of fully awake personal experience. The currently accepted scientific regimes of this culture claim with an only occasionally twisted form of logic that personal (subjective) experience is the least valuable form of truth when those experiences are related by the experiencer to others, but on a slightly deeper level it is also ultimately the only form of truth there really is when it is conveyed directly to your personal experience of existence.

When I try, often when the doubts creep in, to analyze everything about what I learned, objectively, with logic and the so called academically accepted scientific process, I am forced in the context of the Schrodinger equation to grant it an 85%-90% probability of truth. In the same context even though I met the guy and know with certainty that he is the equivalent of a God now, I have too, using the same system of logic, assume that the probability that Christ actually died on the cross is somewhere around 75%; in part because I was not there to witness it and in part because I have to rely on the hearsay of others that say he actually did. When I did meet him as my soul being I was sort of in a state of awe and my questions, the few of them I did ask, were rather well stupid, as a result I failed to ask him that question and he is not much into bragging so the issue did not come up.

Sorry but I have to qualify what I just said. What I am talking about here is the actual experiences I had on the other side and the things those more comprehensive folks taught me directly, while the other stuff, the interpretations and well theoretical alternative explanations for scientific issues reflect simply my own intellectual efforts to understand what we live in, and I will be the first to admit that they could be entirely wrong, I've just been granted alternative ways to look at these things so maybe just maybe they might have some value.

And for the psychologists and especially the psychiatrists that will claim everything I experienced was or were some sort of trivial hallucinatory events that were the result of priming from say, the vast amount of stuff I had read previously, all I can say is that it is possible but extremely unlikely, as in almost every case I had absolutely no previous equivalent sort of input and also in almost every case I was forced to seek explanations for the events and found those usually only afterwards, and what I did find were often incredibly detailed accounts by others of the same sorts of events, with details that simply were too complex to have even remotely allowed that both or more of us were detailing events that they and or we only imagined.

The only person in psychology that even came close to understanding what I am saying here was Carl Jung, and he simply called them archetypal experiences that were legitimate to him because of the synchronicities they all contain; but he refused to explain or even hypothecate concerning what he thought they really had to represent.

Archetypal experiences are legitimate because we all are part of a cloud of consciousness first and those types of experiences are real, elsewhere in that cloud, but for humans accessing that cloud is a fairly rare experience, so that the accounts that arrive back into our experience are rare but most of the time the people that experienced them are compelled to relate them to our peers, and all we can do is hope that others will listen.

It is also a fact that every such account will be the result of mentalities with differing histories of experience and as a result every account will contain variations of the actual truth, this is also related to the quality of technical *uncertainty* of the particle we call our ID, our *mind*, so that rarely perhaps but usually the folks that relate such things will try to be honest as best they can, but by their nature the accounts will have conflicting factors and then synchronicities. One can seek to get closer to the actual truth by compiling the synchronicities and then seeking to understand them using the tools related to convergence.

God does this with the manifold 'quantum' probabilities of the various realities he creates through mechanisms related to *Convergence.*

We can do that as well in seeking to find the truth of what we are. That is the deeper reason that an open mind is so incredibly important and why religions and absolute belief in what other people arbitrarily tell you, including what I am trying to say, are massive potential liabilities.

There is an oddity that occurs in our experience of reality, as we are growing up and even as adults, things that are claimed to be the truth are absorbed by your brain and mind and often simply accepted as comfortable truths even though they are not, and these so-called truths combine into an often esoteric gestalt that shapes our reality in ways that make us usually accept them totally in comfortable ways.

Government and major media based propaganda are perhaps the most damaging of these, but just as alternative simple examples, the fact that we have to celebrate the birth of Christ by enriching the retailers by purchasing endless quantities of things that are usually totally inane because once upon a time a partially 'lunatic' old man in a red suit in Scandinavia or now maybe Turkey, went around giving away carrots and turnips to hungry people in the depths of winter, or that the speed of light in a vacuum is the ultimate constant in this universe so that we are trapped alone on this planet forever, or that we have to spend our entire lives worshiping pieces of paper with numbers on them and the usually unremarkable stuff we can purchase with them.

There are thousands and thousands of these that we learn in our lives and they create a psychology that is often comfortable but usually slightly twisted. The thing is the psychology that results dramatically alters the reality we are allowed to experience when we are here and it is not in any way the sum of the true potential of what the experience of experience can be; it is the box that defines our reality and if you want to defeat it simply try to learn to think in ways that are outside of it again with an open mind.

So to answer the original question here, am I trying to start a new religion or cult? Absolutely NOT! Unless that new way of thinking has to do with trying all your life if necessary to understand the deeper truth of what we really are and what we actually live in. And I will be the first to agree with you that my own efforts to do just that could very well be wrong, they just are what they are and I can only hope that they may have some slight value in enhancing your own life experience while you are here.

This represents probably my last efforts at writing books related to what the Gods have taught me, as at this point it seems to have been a significant waste of time and I feel like I have tried to say thank you to them enough times in this manner.

I have always believed that at this point I will be happy to die knowing that nobody on this planet will even remember that I existed here as who and what I really am, and at this point it looks pretty certain that that will be my fate.

I can only hope that what I accomplished when here will have some slight value to someone else, that maybe these words will have slightly more value than the little round pieces of plastic with movies on them that I also created with words, so I have been simply trying to do the best that I can, by walking as quietly as possible with a large walking stick called words…
IAORANA

Printed in Great Britain
by Amazon